MW00454624

THE OFFICIA

CHECK LIST
AND
RECORD BOOK
of United States and Canadian Coins

THE OFFICIAL RED BOOK®

CHECK LIST
AND
RECORD BOOK

THE OFFICIAL RED BOOK is a trademark of Whitman Publishing, LLC.
ISBN 0794849040

© 2021 Whitman Publishing, LLC
1974 Chandalar Drive • Suite D • Pelham, AL 35124

Printed in the United States of America

Visit us at www.whitman.com for a complete listing of numismatic reference books, supplies, and storage products.

Whitman®

HOW TO USE THIS BOOK

Use this book as a one-stop resource for keeping track of your United States or Canadian coin collection. It covers all popular modern U.S. coins from 1856 to date—from Flying Eagle cents to today's dollar coins, plus commemoratives (classic and modern), Proof sets and Uncirculated Mint sets, and more—as well as Canadian coins from 1870 to date. Popular minor varieties are included.

The images used throughout the *Check List and Record Book* are shown at actual size. Each listing gives the date and mintmark on the coin, as well as how many were minted (Proof mintages are in parentheses; italics indicate an estimated mintage). A series of columns in each chart represents the grades in which coins of that type and date range are commonly found. You can check off the grade for each coin in your collection and, in the Notes column, write down when and where you bought it, the price you paid, who sold it, and any other information you want to record.

Scattered throughout the pages, you will find blank charts where you can add details about auction records, purchases of unusual varieties not listed elsewhere, and other details important to your collection.

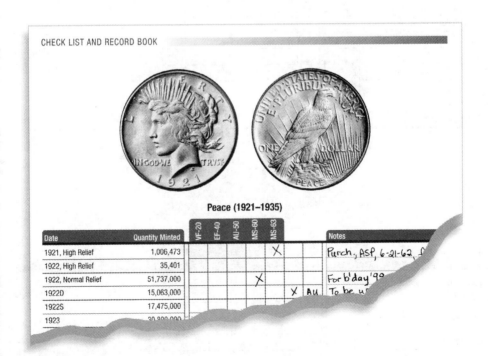

CHECK LIST AND RECORD BOOK

Peace (1921–1935)

Date	Quantity Minted	VF-20	EF-40	AU-50	MS-60	MS-63			Notes
1921, High Relief	1,006,473				X				Purch., ASP, 6-21-62, f
1922, High Relief	35,401								
1922, Normal Relief	51,737,000			X					For b'day '99
1922D	15,063,000						X	AU	To be u
1922S	17,475,000								
1923	30,800,000								

HALF CENTS

Liberty Cap, Head Facing Left (1793)

Date	Quantity Minted	G-4	VG-8	F-12	VF-20	EF-40	MS-60	Notes
1793	35,334							

Liberty Cap, Head Facing Right (1794–1797)

Date	Quantity Minted	G-4	VG-8	F-12	VF-20	EF-40	MS-60	Notes
1794, Normal Head	81,600							
1794, High-Relief Head								
1795, Lettered Edge, With Pole	139,690							
1795, Lettered Edge, Punctuated Date								
1795, Plain Edge, Punctuated Date								
1795, Plain Edge, No Pole								
1796, With Pole	5,090							
1796, No Pole	1,390							
1797, 1 Above 1, Plain Edge	127,840							
1797, Plain Edge, Low Head								
1797, Plain Edge								
1797, Lettered Edge								
1797, Gripped Edge								

Draped Bust (1800–1808)

Date	Quantity Minted	G-4	VG-8	F-12	VF-20	EF-40	MS-60	Notes
1800	202,908							
1802, 2 Over 0, Reverse of 1800	20,266							
1802, 2 Over 0, 2nd Reverse								
1803	92,000							
1803, Widely Spaced 3								

Date	Quantity Minted	G-4	VG-8	F-12	VF-20	EF-40	MS-60	Notes
1804, Plain 4, Stems to Wreath								
1804, Plain 4, Stemless Wreath								
1804, Crosslet 4, Stemless	1,055,312							
1804, Crosslet 4, Stems								
1804, "Spiked Chin"								
1805, Medium 5, Stemless								
1805, Small 5, Stems	814,464							
1805, Large 5, Stems								
1806, Small 6, Stems								
1806, Small 6, Stemless	356,000							
1806, Large 6, Stems								
1807	476,000							
1808, Normal Date	400,000							
1808, 8 Over 7								

Classic Head (1809–1836)

Date	Quantity Minted	G-4	VG-8	F-12	VF-20	EF-40	MS-60	Notes
1809, Normal Date								
1809, Small o Inside 0	1,154,572							
1809, 9 Over Inverted 9								
1810	215,000							
1811, Wide Date								
1811, Close Date	63,140							
1811, Reverse of 1802, Unofficial Restrike (extremely rare)								
1825	63,000							
1826	234,000							
1828, 13 Stars	606,000							
1828, 12 Stars								
1829	487,000							

Date	Quantity Minted	PF-40	PF-60	PF-63				Notes
1831, Original (beware of altered date)	2,200							
1831, Restrike, Large Berries (Reverse of 1836)								
1831, Restrike, Small Berries (Reverse of 1840–1857)								
1832	51,000							
1833	103,000							
1834	141,000							

Date	Quantity Minted	VG-8	F-12	VF-20	EF-40	MS-60	PF-63		Notes
1835	398,000								
1836, Original									
1836, Restrike (Reverse of 1840–1857)									
1837 Token *(not a coin)*									

Braided Hair (1840–1857)

Date	Quantity Minted	PF-63	PF-65						Notes
1840, Original									
1840, Restrike									
1841, Original									
1841, Restrike									
1842, Original									
1842, Restrike									
1843, Original									
1843, Restrike									
1844, Original									
1844, Restrike									
1845, Original									
1845, Restrike									
1846, Original									
1846, Restrike									
1847, Original									
1847, Restrike									
1848, Original									
1848, Restrike									
1849, Original, Small Date									
1849, Restrike, Small Date									

Date	Quantity Minted	VG-8	F-12	VF-20	EF-40	MS-60	PF-63		Notes
1849, Large Date	39,864								
1850	39,812								
1851	147,672								
1852, Original									
1852, Restrike									
1853	129,694								
1854	55,358								
1855	56,500								
1856	40,430								
1857	35,180								

LARGE CENTS

Flowing Hair, Chain Reverse (1793)

Date	Quantity Minted	G-4	VG-8	F-12	VF-20	EF-40	MS-60	Notes
1793, AMERI. in Legend								
1793, AMERICA, With Periods	36,103							
1793, AMERICA, Without Periods								

Flowing Hair, Wreath Reverse (1793)

Date	Quantity Minted	G-4	VG-8	F-12	VF-20	EF-40	MS-60	Notes
1793, Vine/Bars Edge								
1793, Lettered Edge	63,353							
1793, Strawberry Leaf *(4 known)*								

Liberty Cap (1793–1796)

Date	Quantity Minted	G-4	VG-8	F-12	VF-20	EF-40	MS-60	Notes
1793, Liberty Cap	11,056							
1794, Head of 1793								
1794, Head of 1794								
1794, Head in Low Relief								
1794, Exact Head of 1795	918,521							
1794, Starred Reverse								
1794, No Fraction Bar								

Date	Quantity Minted	G-4	VG-8	F-12	VF-20	EF-40	MS-60		Notes
1795, Lettered Edge	37,000								
1795, Plain Edge	501,500								
1795, Reeded Edge *(9 known)*									
1795, Jefferson Head *(not a regular Mint issue)*, Plain Edge									
1795, Jefferson Head, Lettered Edge *(3 known)*									
1796, Liberty Cap	109,825								

Draped Bust (1796–1807)

Date	Quantity Minted	G-4	VG-8	F-12	VF-20	EF-40	MS-60		Notes
1796, Reverse of 1794									
1796, Reverse of 1795									
1796, Reverse of 1797	363,375								
1796, LIHERTY Error									
1796, Stemless Reverse *(3 known)*									
1797, Gripped Edge, 1795-Style Reverse									
1797, Plain Edge, 1795-Style Reverse	897,510								
1797, 1797 Reverse, Stems									
1797, 1797 Reverse, Stemless									
1798, 8 Over 7									
1798, Reverse of 1796									
1798, Style 1 Hair	1,841,745								
1798, Style 2 Hair									
1799, 9 Over 8									
1799, Normal Date									
1800, 1800 Over 1798, Style 1 Hair									
1800, 80 Over 79, Style 2 Hair	2,822,175								
1800, Normal Date									
1801, Normal Reverse									
1801, 3 Errors: 1/000, One Stem, and IINITED	1,362,837								
1801, Fraction 1/000									
1801, 1/100 Over 1/000									

Date	Quantity Minted	G-4	VG-8	F-12	VF-20	EF-40	MS-60	Notes
1802, Normal Reverse								
1802, Fraction 1/000	3,435,100							
1802, Stemless Wreath								
1803, Small Date, Small Fraction								
1803, Small Date, Large Fraction								
1803, Large Date, Small Fraction								
1803, Large Date, Large Fraction	3,131,691							
1803, 1/100 Over 1/000								
1803, Stemless Wreath								
1804	96,500							
1804, Unofficial Restrike of 1860 (Uncirculated)								
1805	941,116							
1806	348,000							
1807, Small 1807, 7 Over 6, Blunt 1								
1807, Large 1807, 7 Over 6, Pointed 1	829,221							
1807, Small Fraction								
1807, Large Fraction								
1807, "Comet" Variety								

Classic Head (1808–1814)

Date	Quantity Minted	G-4	VG-8	F-12	VF-20	EF-40	MS-60	Notes
1808	1,007,000							
1809	222,867							
1810, 10 Over 09	1,458,500							
1810, Normal Date								
1811, Last 1 Over 0	218,025							
1811, Normal Date								
1812, Small Date	1,075,500							
1812, Large Date								
1813	418,000							
1814, Plain 4	357,830							
1814, Crosslet 4								

Liberty Head, Matron Head (1816–1835)

Date	Quantity Minted	G-4	VG-8	F-12	VF-20	EF-40	MS-60	Notes
1816	2,820,982							
1817, 13 Stars	3,948,400							
1817, 15 Stars								
1818	3,167,000							
1819, 9 Over 8	2,671,000							
1819, Large Date								
1819, Small Date								
1820, 20 Over 19	4,407,550							
1820, Large Date								
1820, Small Date								
1821	389,000							
1822	2,072,339							
1823, 3 Over 2	1,262,000							
1823, Normal Date								
1823, Unofficial Restrike, from broken obverse die								
1824, 4 Over 2								
1824, Normal Date								
1825	1,461,100							
1826, 6 Over 5	1,517,425							
1826, Normal Date								
1827	2,357,732							
1828, Large Narrow Date	2,260,624							
1828, Small Wide Date								
1829, Large Letters	1,414,500							
1829, Medium Letters								
1830, Large Letters	1,711,500							
1830, Medium Letters								
1831, Large Letters	3,359,260							
1831, Medium Letters								
1832, Large Letters	2,362,000							
1832, Medium Letters								
1833	2,739,000							

Date	Quantity Minted	G-4	VG-8	F-12	VF-20	EF-40	MS-60		Notes
1834, Large 8, Stars, and Reverse Letters									
1834, Large 8 and Stars, Medium Letters	1,855,100								
1834, Large 8, Small Stars, Medium Letters									
1834, Small 8, Large Stars, Medium Letters									
1835, Large 8 and Stars									
1835, Small 8 and Stars	3,878,400								
1835, Head of 1836									

Liberty Head, Matron Head Modified (1835–1839)

Date	Quantity Minted	G-4	VG-8	F-12	VF-20	EF-40	MS-60		Notes
1836	2,111,000								
1837, Plain Cord, Medium Letters									
1837, Plain Cord, Small Letters	5,558,300								
1837, Head of 1838									
1838	6,370,200								
1839, 1839 Over 1836, Plain Cords									
1839, Head of 1838, Beaded Cords									
1839, Silly Head	3,128,661								
1839, Booby Head									
1839									
1840, Large Date									
1840, Small Date	2,462,700								
1840, Small Date Over Large 18									
1841, Small Date	1,597,367								
1842, Small Date	2,383,390								
1842, Large Date									
1843, Petite, Small Letters									
1843, Petite, Large Letters	2,425,342								
1843, Mature, Large Letters									
1844, Normal Date	2,398,752								
1844, 44 Over 81									
1845	3,894,804								

Date	Quantity Minted	G-4	VG-8	F-12	VF-20	EF-40	MS-60		Notes
1846, Small Date									
1846, Medium Date	4,120,800								
1846, Tall Date									
1847									
1847, 7 Over "Small 7"	6,183,669								
1848	6,415,799								
1849	4,178,500								
1850	4,426,844								
1851, Normal Date									
1851, 51 Over 81	9,889,707								
1852	5,063,094								
1853	6,641,131								
1854	4,236,156								
1855, Upright 5's									
1855, Slanting 5's	1,574,829								
1855, Slanting 5's, Knob on Ear									
1856, Upright 5									
1856, Slanting 5	2,690,463								
1857, Large Date									
1857, Small Date	333,546								

SMALL CENTS

Flying Eagle (1856–1858)

Date	Quantity Minted	VG-8	F-12	VF-20	EF-40	MS-60	PF-63	Notes
1856	*(1,000–1,500)*							
1857	*(100)* 17,450,000							
1858, Large Letters	*(100)*							
1858, 8 Over 7	24,600,000							
1858, Small Letters	*(200)*							

Indian Head, Variety 1, Copper-Nickel, Laurel Wreath Reverse (1859)

Date	Quantity Minted	VG-8	F-12	VF-20	EF-40	MS-60	PF-63	Notes
1859	*(800)* 36,400,000							
1859, Oak Wreath Reverse, With Shield	1,000							

Indian Head, Variety 2, Copper-Nickel, Oak Wreath With Shield (1860–1864)

Date	Quantity Minted	VG-8	F-12	VF-20	EF-40	MS-60	PF-63	Notes
1860	*(1,000)* 20,566,000							
1860, Pointed Bust								
1861	*(1,000)* 10,100,000							
1862	*(550)* 28,075,000							
1863	*(460)* 49,840,000							
1864	*(370)* 13,740,000							

Indian Head, Variety 3, Bronze (1864–1909)

Date		Quantity Minted	VG-8	F-12	VF-20	EF-40	MS-60	PF-63	Notes
1864, No L	*(150+)*	39,233,714							
1864, With L	*(20+)*								
1865	*(500+)*	35,429,286							
1866	*(725+)*	9,826,500							
1867	*(625+)*	9,821,000							
1868	*(600+)*	10,266,500							
1869	*(600+)*	6,420,000							
1869, 9 Over 9									
1870, Shallow N	*(1,000+)*	5,275,000							
1870, Bold N									
1871, Shallow N	*(960+)*	3,929,500							
1871, Bold N									
1872, Shallow N	*(950+)*	4,042,000							
1872, Bold N									
1873, Close 3	*(1,100+)*	11,676,500							
1873, Doubled LIBERTY									
1873, Open 3									
1874	*(700)*	14,187,500							
1875	*(700)*	13,528,000							
1875, Dot Reverse									
1876	*(1,150)*	7,944,000							
1877	*(900)*	852,500							
1878	*(2,350)*	5,797,500							
1879	*(3,200)*	16,228,000							
1880	*(3,955)*	38,961,000							
1881	*(3,575)*	39,208,000							
1882	*(3,100)*	38,578,000							
1883	*(6,609)*	45,591,500							
1884	*(3,942)*	23,257,800							
1885	*(3,790)*	11,761,594							
1886, Variety 1	*(4,290)*	17,650,000							
1886, Variety 2									
1887	*(2,960)*	45,223,523							
1888	*(4,582)*	37,489,832							
1888, Last 8 Over 7									
1889	*(3,336)*	48,866,025							
1890	*(2,740)*	57,180,114							
1891	*(2,350)*	47,070,000							
1892	*(2,745)*	37,647,087							
1893	*(2,195)*	46,640,000							

Date	Quantity Minted		VG-8	F-12	VF-20	EF-40	MS-60	PF-63		Notes
1894	(2,632)	16,749,500								
1894, Doubled Date										
1895	(2,062)	38,341,574								
1896	(1,862)	39,055,431								
1897	(1,938)	50,464,392								
1898	(1,795)	49,821,284								
1899	(2,031)	53,598,000								
1900	(2,262)	66,831,502								
1901	(1,985)	79,609,158								
1902	(2,018)	87,374,704								
1903	(1,790)	85,092,703								
1904	(1,817)	61,326,198								
1905	(2,152)	80,717,011								
1906	(1,725)	96,020,530								
1907	(1,475)	108,137,143								
1908	(1,620)	32,326,367								
1908S		1,115,000								
1909	(2,175)	14,368,470								
1909S		309,000								

Lincoln, Wheat Ears Reverse, Variety 1, Bronze (1909–1942)

Date	Quantity Minted		VG-8	F-12	VF-20	EF-40	MS-60	PF-63		Notes
1909, V.D.B.	(1,194)	27,995,000								
1909S, V.D.B.		484,000								
1909	(2,618)	72,702,618								
1909S		1,825,000								
1909S, S Over Horizontal S										
1910	(4,118)	146,801,218								
1910S		6,045,000								
1911	(1,725)	101,177,787								
1911D		12,672,000								
1911S		4,026,000								
1912	(2,172)	68,153,060								
1912D		10,411,000								
1912S		4,431,000								
1913	(2,983)	76,532,352								
1913D		15,804,000								
1913S		6,101,000								
1914	(1,365)	75,238,432								
1914D		1,193,000								

Date	Quantity Minted	VG-8	F-12	VF-20	EF-40	MS-60	PF-63	Notes
1914S	4,137,000							
1915	(1,150) 29,092,120							
1915D	22,050,000							
1915S	4,833,000							
1916	(1,050) 131,833,677							
1916D	35,956,000							
1916S	22,510,000							

Date	Quantity Minted	G-4	VG-8	F-12	VF-20	EF-40	MS-60	Notes
1917	196,429,785							
1917, Doubled-Die Obverse								
1917D	55,120,000							
1917S	32,620,000							
1918	288,104,634							
1918D	47,830,000							
1918S	34,680,000							
1919	392,021,000							
1919D	57,154,000							
1919S	139,760,000							
1920	310,165,000							
1920D	49,280,000							
1920S	46,220,000							
1921	39,157,000							
1921S	15,274,000							
1922D	7,160,000							
1922, No D								
1922, Weak D								
1923	74,723,000							
1923S	8,700,000							
1924	75,178,000							
1924D	2,520,000							
1924S	11,696,000							
1925	139,949,000							
1925D	22,580,000							
1925S	26,380,000							
1926	157,088,000							
1926D	28,020,000							
1926S	4,550,000							
1927	144,440,000							
1927D	27,170,000							
1927S	14,276,000							
1928	134,116,000							
1928D	31,170,000							
1928S	17,266,000							
1929	185,262,000							

Date	Quantity Minted	G-4	VG-8	F-12	VF-20	EF-40	MS-60	Notes
1929D	41,730,000							
1929S	50,148,000							
1930	157,415,000							
1930D	40,100,000							
1930S	24,286,000							
1931	19,396,000							
1931D	4,480,000							
1931S	866,000							
1932	9,062,000							
1932D	10,500,000							
1933	14,360,000							
1933D	6,200,000							
1934	219,080,000							
1934D	28,446,000							
1935	245,388,000							
1935D	47,000,000							
1935S	38,702,000							

Date	Quantity Minted	VG-8	F-12	VF-20	EF-40	MS-60	PF-63	Notes
1936 (5,569) 1936, Doubled-Die Obverse	309,632,000							
1936D	40,620,000							
1936S	29,130,000							
1937 (9,320)	309,170,000							
1937D	50,430,000							
1937S	34,500,000							
1938 (14,734)	156,682,000							
1938D	20,010,000							
1938S	15,180,000							
1939 (13,520)	316,466,000							
1939D	15,160,000							
1939S	52,070,000							

Date	Quantity Minted	VG-8	F-12	VF-20	EF-40	MS-60	PF-65	Notes
1940 (15,872)	586,810,000							
1940D	81,390,000							
1940S	112,940,000							
1941 (21,100)	887,018,000							
1941D	128,700,000							
1941S	92,360,000							
1942 (32,600)	657,796,000							
1942D	206,698,000							
1942S	85,590,000							

Lincoln, Wheat Ears Reverse, Variety 2, Zinc-Coated Steel (1943)

Date	Quantity Minted	VG-8	F-12	VF-20	EF-40	MS-60	PF-65	Notes
1943	84,628,670							
1943D	217,660,000							
1943D, Boldly Doubled Mintmark								
1943S	191,550,000							

Lincoln, Wheat Ears Reverse, Variety 1 (Bronze) Resumed (1944–1958)

Date	Quantity Minted	VF-20	EF-40	AU-50	MS-60	MS-63	MS-65	Notes
1944	1,435,400,000							
1944D	430,578,000							
1944D, D Over S								
1944S	282,760,000							
1945	1,040,515,000							
1945D	266,268,000							
1945S	181,770,000							
1946	991,655,000							
1946D	315,690,000							
1946S	198,100,000							
1946S, S Over D								
1947	190,555,000							
1947D	194,750,000							
1947S	99,000,000							
1948	317,570,000							
1948D	172,637,500							
1948S	81,735,000							
1949	217,775,000							
1949D	153,132,500							
1949S	64,290,000							

Date		Quantity Minted	EF-40	AU-50	MS-60	MS-63	MS-65	PF-65	Notes
1950	(51,386)	272,635,000							
1950D		334,950,000							
1950S		118,505,000							
1951	(57,500)	284,576,000							
1951D		625,355,000							
1951S		136,010,000							
1952	(81,980)	186,775,000							
1952D		746,130,000							
1952S		137,800,004							
1953	(128,800)	256,755,000							
1953D		700,515,000							
1953S		181,835,000							
1954	(233,300)	71,640,050							
1954D		251,552,500							

Date		Quantity Minted	EF-40	AU-50	MS-60	MS-63	MS-65	PF-65	Notes
1954S		96,190,000							
1955	(378,200)	330,958,200							
1955, DblDie Obv									
1955D		563,257,500							
1955S		44,610,000							
1956	(669,384)	420,745,000							
1956D		1,098,201,100							
1956D, D Above Shadow D									
1957	(1,247,952)	282,540,000							
1957D		1,051,342,000							
1958	(875,652)	252,525,000							
1958, DblDie Obv (3 known)									
1958D		800,953,300							

Lincoln, Memorial Reverse, Copper Alloy (1959–1982)

Date		Quantity Minted	EF-40	AU-50	MS-60	MS-63	MS-65	PF-65	Notes
1959	(1,149,291)	609,715,000							
1959D		1,279,760,000							
1960, Large Date	(1,691,602)								
1960, Small Date									
1960, Large Date Over Small Date		586,405,000							
1960, Small Date Over Large Date									
1960D, Large Date									
1960D, Small Date		1,580,884,000							
1960D, D/D, Sm/Lg Dt									
1961	(3,028,244)	753,345,000							
1961D		1,753,266,700							
1962	(3,218,019)	606,045,000							
1962D		1,793,148,140							
1963	(3,075,645)	754,110,000							
1963D		1,774,020,400							
1964	(3,950,762)	2,648,575,000							
1964D		3,799,071,500							
1965		1,497,224,900							
1966		2,188,147,783							
1967		3,048,667,100							
1968		1,707,880,970							
1968D		2,886,269,600							
1968S	(3,041,506)	258,270,001							
1969		1,136,910,000							
1969D		4,002,832,200							

Date		Quantity Minted	EF-40	AU-50	MS-60	MS-63	MS-65	PF-65		Notes
1969S	(2,934,631)	544,375,000								
1969S, DblDie Obv										
1970		1,898,315,000								
1970D		2,891,438,900								
1970S, SmDt (Hi 7)	(2,632,810)	690,560,004								
1970S, LgDt (Lo 7)										
1970S, DbleDie Obv										
1971		1,919,490,000								
1971, DblDie Obv										
1971D		2,911,045,600								
1971S	(3,220,733)	525,133,459								
1971S, DblDie Obv										
1972		2,933,255,000								
1972, DblDie Obv										
1972D		2,665,071,400								
1972S	(3,260,996)	376,939,108								
1973		3,728,245,000								
1973D		3,549,576,588								
1973S	(2,760,339)	317,177,295								
1974		4,232,140,523								
1974D		4,235,098,000								
1974S	(2,612,568)	409,426,660								
1975		5,451,476,142								
1975D		4,505,275,300								
1975S	(2,845,450)									
1976		4,674,292,426								
1976D		4,221,592,455								
1976S	(4,149,730)									
1977		4,469,930,000								
1977D		4,194,062,300								
1977S	(3,251,152)									
1978		5,558,605,000								
1978D		4,280,233,400								
1978S	(3,127,781)									
1979		6,018,515,000								
1979D		4,139,357,254								
1979S, Type 1	(3,677,175)									
1979S, Type 2										
1980		7,414,705,000								
1980D		5,140,098,660								
1980S	(3,554,806)									
1981		7,491,750,000								
1981D		5,373,235,677								
1981S, Type 1	(4,063,083)									
1981S, Type 2										

Date	Quantity Minted	EF-40	AU-50	MS-60	MS-63	MS-65	PF-65		Notes
1982, Large Date*									
1982, Large Date**	10,712,525,000								
1982, Small Date*									
1982, Small Date**									
1982D*									
1982D, Large Dt**	6,012,979,368								
1982D, Small Dt**									
1982S* (3,857,479)									

* Copper alloy. ** Copper-plated zinc.

Lincoln, Memorial Reverse, Copper-Plated Zinc (1982–2008)

Date	Quantity Minted	MS-60	MS-63	MS-65	PF-65			Notes
1983	7,752,355,000							
1983, DblDie Rev								
1983D	6,467,199,428							
1983S (3,279,126)								
1984	8,151,079,000							
1984, Doubled Ear								
1984D	5,569,238,906							
1984S (3,065,110)								
1985	5,648,489,887							
1985D	5,287,339,926							
1985S (3,362,821)								
1986	4,491,395,493							
1986D	4,442,866,698							
1986S (3,010,497)								
1987	4,682,466,931							
1987D	4,879,389,514							
1987S (4,227,728)								
1988	6,092,810,000							
1988D	5,253,740,443							
1988S (3,262,948)								
1989	7,261,535,000							
1989D	5,345,467,111							
1989S (3,220,194)								
1990	6,851,765,000							
1990D	4,922,894,533							
1990S	(3,299,559)							
1990, Proof, No S								
1991	5,165,940,000							
1991D	4,158,446,076							
1991S (2,867,787)								
1992	4,648,905,000							
1992, Close AM								
1992D	4,448,673,300							
1992D, Close AM								

Date	Quantity Minted	MS-60	MS-63	MS-65	PF-65					Notes
1992S	(4,176,560)									
1993	5,684,705,000									
1993D	6,426,650,571									
1993S	(3,394,792)									
1994	6,500,850,000									
1994D	7,131,765,000									
1994S	(3,269,923)									
1995 / 1995, DblDie Obv	6,411,440,000									
1995D	7,128,560,000									
1995S	(2,797,481)									
1996 / 1996, Wide AM	6,612,465,000									
1996D	6,510,795,000									
1996S	(2,525,265)									
1997	4,622,800,000									
1997D	4,576,555,000									
1997S	(2,796,678)									
1998 / 1998, Wide AM	5,032,155,000									
1998D	5,225,353,500									
1998S / 1998S, Close AM	(2,086,507)									
1999 / 1999, Wide AM	5,237,600,000									
1999D	6,360,065,000									
1999S / 1999S, Close AM	(3,347,966)									
2000 / 2000, Wide AM	5,503,200,000									
2000D	8,774,220,000									
2000S	(4,047,993)									
2001	4,959,600,000									
2001D	5,374,990,000									
2001S	(3,184,606)									
2002	3,260,800,000									
2002D	4,028,055,000									
2002S	(3,211,995)									
2003	3,300,000,000									
2003D	3,548,000,000									
2003S	(3,298,439)									
2004	3,379,600,000									
2004D	3,456,400,000									
2004S	(2,965,422)									
2005	3,935,600,000									
2005D	3,764,450,500									

Date	Quantity Minted	MS-60	MS-63	MS-65	PF-65				Notes
2005S	(3,344,679)								
2006	4,290,000,000								
2006D	3,944,000,000								
2006S	(3,054,436)								
2007	3,762,400,000								
2007D	3,638,800,000								
2007S	(2,577,166)								
2008	2,558,800,000								
2008D	2,849,600,000								
2008S	(2,169,561)								

Lincoln, Bicentennial (2009)

Date	Quantity Minted	MS-60	MS-63	MS-65	PF-65				Notes
2009, Birth and Early Childhood	284,400,000								
2009, Birth and Early Childhood, copper, Satin finish									
2009D, Birth and Early Childhood	350,400,000								
2009D, Birth and Early Childhood, copper, Satin finish	784,614								
2009S, Birth and Early Childhood, copper	(2,995,615)								
2009, Formative Years	376,000,000								
2009, Formative Years, copper, Satin finish	784,614								
2009D, Formative Years	363,600,000								
2009D, Formative Years, copper, Satin finish	784,614								
2009S, Formative Years, copper	(2,995,615)								
2009, Professional Life	316,000,000								
2009, Professional Life, copper, Satin finish	784,614								
2009D, Professional Life	336,000,000								
2009D, Professional Life, copper, Satin finish	784,614								
2009S, Professional Life, copper	(2,995,615)								
2009, Presidency	129,600,000								
2009, Presidency, copper, Satin finish	784,614								

Date	Quantity Minted	MS-60	MS-63	MS-65	PF-65				Notes
2009D, Presidency	198,000,000								
2009D, Presidency, copper, Satin finish	784,614								
2009S, Presidency, copper	(2,995,615)								

Lincoln, Shield Reverse (2010 to Date)

Date	Quantity Minted	MS-60	MS-63	MS-65	PF-65				Notes
2010	1,963,630,000								
2010D	2,047,200,000								
2010S	(1,689,216)								
2011	2,402,400,000								
2011D	2,536,140,000								
2011S	(1,673,010)								
2012	3,132,000,000								
2012D	2,883,200,000								
2012S	(1,237,415)								
2013	3,750,400,000								
2013D	3,319,600,000								
2013S	(1,274,505)								
2014	3,990,800,000								
2014D	4,155,600,000								
2014S	(1,190,369)								
2015									
2015D									
2015S									
2016	4,698,000,000								
2016D	4,420,400,000								
2016S	(1,011,624)								
2017P	4,361,220,000								
2017D	4,272,800,000								
2017S	(979,477)								
2018	4,066,800,000								
2018D	3,736,400,000								
2018S	(844,220)								
2019	3,542,800,000								
2019D	3,497,600,000								
2019S	(1,052,553)								
2019W	341,560								
2019W	(591,772)								

Date	Quantity Minted	MS-60	MS-63	MS-65	PF-65				Notes
2019W, Reverse Proof	(412,622)								
2020									
2020D									
2020S									
2021									
2021D									
2021S									
2022									
2022D									
2022S									

TWO-CENT PIECES

Two-Cent Piece (1864–1873)

Date		Quantity Minted	G-4	VG-8	F-12	EF-40	MS-60	PF-63	Notes
1864, Small Motto		19,822,500							
1864, Large Motto	(100+)								
1865	(500+)	13,640,000							
1866	(725+)	3,177,000							
1867	(625+)	2,938,750							
1867, Doubled-Die Obv									
1868	(600+)	2,803,750							
1869	(600+)	1,546,500							
1870	(1,000+)	861,250							
1871	(960+)	721,250							
1872	(950+)	65,000							
1873, Close 3, Pf only	(600)								
1873, Open 3, Restrike									

SILVER THREE-CENT PIECES (TRIMES)

Variety 1 (1851–1853)

Date	Quantity Minted	G-4	VG-8	F-12	EF-40	MS-60	PF-63	Notes
1851	5,447,400							
18510	720,000							
1852, 1 Over Inverted 2	18,663,500							
1852								
1853	11,400,000							

Variety 2 (1854–1858)

Date		Quantity Minted	G-4	VG-8	F-12	EF-40	MS-60	PF-63		Notes
1854		671,000								
1855		139,000								
1856		1,458,000								
1857		1,042,000								
1858	*(210)*	1,603,700								

Variety 3 (1859–1873)

Date		Quantity Minted	G-4	VG-8	F-12	EF-40	MS-60	PF-63		Notes
1859	(800)	364,200								
1860	(1,000)	286,000								
1861	(1,000)	497,000								
1862, 2 Over 1		343,000								
1862	(550)									
1863, So-called 3/2		21,000								
1863	(460)									
1864	(470)	12,000								
1865	(500)	8,000								
1866	(725)	22,000								
1867	(625)	4,000								
1868	(600)	3,500								
1869	(600)	4,500								
1870	(1,000)	3,000								
1871	(960)	3,400								
1872	(950)	1,000								
1873 (Close 3, Pf only)	(600)									

NICKEL THREE-CENT PIECES

Nickel Three-Cent Piece (1865–1889)

Date		Quantity Minted	VG-8	F-12	VF-20	EF-40	MS-60	PF-63		Notes
1865	(500+)	11,382,000								
1866	(725+)	4,801,000								
1867	(625+)	3,915,000								
1868	(600+)	3,252,000								
1869	(600+)	1,604,000								
1870	(1,000+)	1,335,000								
1871	(960+)	604,000								
1872	(950+)	862,000								
1873, Close 3	(1,100+)	390,000								
1873, Open 3		783,000								
1874	(700+)	790,000								
1875	(700+)	228,000								
1876	(1,150+)	162,000								
1877, Proof only	(900)									
1878, Proof only	(2,350)									
1879	(3,200)	38,000								
1880	(3,955)	21,000								
1881	(3,575)	1,077,000								
1882	(3,100)	22,200								
1883	(6,609)	4,000								
1884	(3,942)	1,700								
1885	(3,790)	1,000								
1886, Proof only	(4,290)									
1887	(2,960)	5,001								
1887, 7 Over 6										
1888	(4,582)	36,501								
1889	(3,436)	18,125								

NICKEL FIVE-CENT PIECES

Shield (1866–1883)

Date		Quantity Minted	VG-8	F-12	VF-20	EF-40	MS-60	PF-63	Notes
1866, Rays	*(600+)*	14,742,500							
1866, Repunched Date									
1867, Rays	*(25+)*	2,019,000							
1867, Without Rays	*(600+)*	28,890,500							
1867, Without Rays, Pattern Reverse									
1868	*(600+)*	28,817,000							
1869	*(600+)*	16,395,000							
1870	*(1,000+)*	4,806,000							
1871	*(960+)*	561,000							
1872	*(950+)*	6,036,000							
1873, Close 3	*(1,100+)*	436,050							
1873, Open 3		4,113,950							
1873, Lg Over Sm 3									
1874	*(700+)*	3,538,000							
1875	*(700+)*	2,097,000							
1876	*(1,150+)*	2,530,000							
1877, Proof only	(900)								
1878, Proof only	(2,350)								
1879		25,900							
1879, 9 Over 8	(3,200)								
1880	(3,955)	16,000							
1881	(3,575)	68,800							
1882	(3,100)	11,472,900							
1883	(5,419)	1,451,500							
1883, 3 Over 2									

Liberty Head, Variety 1, Without CENTS (1883)

Date		Quantity Minted	VG-8	F-12	VF-20	EF-40	MS-60	PF-63	Notes
1883, Without CENTS	(5,219)	5,474,300							

Liberty Head, Variety 2, With CENTS (1883–1913)

Date		Quantity Minted	VG-8	F-12	VF-20	EF-40	MS-60	PF-63	Notes
1883, With CENTS	(6,783)	16,026,200							
1884	(3,942)	11,270,000							
1885	(3,790)	1,472,700							
1886	(4,290)	3,326,000							
1887	(2,960)	15,260,692							
1888	(4,582)	10,167,901							
1889	(3,336)	15,878,025							
1890	(2,740)	16,256,532							
1891	(2,350)	16,832,000							
1892	(2,745)	11,696,897							
1893	(2,195)	13,368,000							
1894	(2,632)	5,410,500							
1895	(2,062)	9,977,822							
1896	(1,862)	8,841,058							
1897	(1,938)	20,426,797							
1898	(1,795)	12,530,292							
1899	(2,031)	26,027,000							
1900	(2,262)	27,253,733							
1901	(1,985)	26,478,228							
1902	(2,018)	31,487,561							
1903	(1,790)	28,004,935							
1904	(1,817)	21,403,167							
1905	(2,152)	29,825,124							
1906	(1,725)	38,612,000							
1907	(1,475)	39,213,325							
1908	(1,620)	22,684,557							
1909	(4,763)	11,585,763							
1910	(2,405)	30,166,948							
1911	(1,733)	39,557,639							
1912	(2,145)	26,234,569							
1912D		8,474,000							
1912S		238,000							
1913, Liberty Head *(5 known)*									

Indian Head or Buffalo, Variety 1, FIVE CENTS on Raised Ground (1913)

Date		Quantity Minted	VG-8	F-12	VF-20	EF-40	MS-60	PF-63	Notes
1913, Variety 1	(1,520)	30,992,000							
1913D, Variety 1		5,337,000							
1913S, Variety 1		2,105,000							

Note: Nickel five-cent Proofs of 1913 through 1916 have a "Matte Proof" finish.

Indian Head or Buffalo, Variety 2, FIVE CENTS in Recess (1913–1938)

Date		Quantity Minted	VG-8	F-12	VF-20	EF-40	MS-60	PF-63	Notes
1913, Variety 2	(1,514)	29,857,186							
1913D, Variety 2		4,156,000							
1913S, Variety 2		1,209,000							
1914	(1,275)	20,664,463							
1914, 4 Over 3									
1914D		3,912,000							
1914S		3,470,000							
1915	(1,050)	20,986,220							
1915D		7,569,000							
1915S		1,505,000							
1916	(600)	63,497,466							
1916, Doubled-Die Obverse									
1916D		13,333,000							
1916S		11,860,000							
1917		51,424,019							
1917D		9,910,000							
1917S		4,193,000							
1918		32,086,314							
1918D, 8 Over 7		8,362,000							
1918D									
1918S		4,882,000							
1919		60,868,000							
1919D		8,006,000							
1919S		7,521,000							
1920		63,093,000							
1920D		9,418,000							
1920S		9,689,000							

Note: Nickel five-cent Proofs of 1913 through 1916 have a "Matte Proof" finish.

Date	Quantity Minted	VG-8	F-12	VF-20	EF-40	MS-60	PF-63	Notes
1921	10,663,000							
1921S	1,557,000							
1923	35,715,000							
1923S	6,142,000							
1924	21,620,000							
1924D	5,258,000							
1924S	1,437,000							
1925	35,565,100							
1925D	4,450,000							
1925S	6,256,000							
1926	44,693,000							
1926D	5,638,000							
1926S	970,000							
1927	37,981,000							
1927D	5,730,000							
1927S	3,430,000							
1928	23,411,000							
1928D	6,436,000							
1928S	6,936,000							
1929	36,446,000							
1929D	8,370,000							
1929S	7,754,000							
1930	22,849,000							
1930S	5,435,000							
1931S	1,200,000							
1934	20,213,003							
1934D	7,480,000							
1935 1935, Doubled-Die Reverse	58,264,000							
1935D	12,092,000							
1935S	10,300,000							
1936 (4,420)	118,997,000							
1936D 1936D, 3-1/2 Legs	24,814,000							
1936S	14,930,000							
1937 (5,769)	79,480,000							
1937D 1937D, 3-Legged	17,826,000							
1937S	5,635,000							
1938D 1938D, D Over S	7,020,000							

Jefferson, Prewar Composition (1938–1942)

Date		Quantity Minted	VG-8	F-12	VF-20	EF-40	MS-63	PF-65		Notes
1938	(19,365)	19,496,000								
1938D		5,376,000								
1938S		4,105,000								
1939	(12,535)									
1939, Doubled MONTICELLO, FIVE CENTS		120,615,000								
1939D		3,514,000								
1939S		6,630,000								
1940	(14,158)	176,485,000								
1940D		43,540,000								
1940S		39,690,000								
1941	(18,720)	203,265,000								
1941D		53,432,000								
1941S		43,445,000								
1942	(29,600)	49,789,000								
1942D		13,938,000								
1942D, D Over Horizontal D										

Jefferson, Wartime Silver Alloy (1942–1945)

Date		Quantity Minted	VG-8	F-12	VF-20	EF-40	MS-63	PF-65		Notes
1942P	(27,600)	57,873,000								
1942S		32,900,000								
1943P, 3 Over 2										
1943P		271,165,000								
1943P, Doubled Eye										
1943D		15,294,000								
1943S		104,060,000								
1944P		119,150,000								
1944D		32,309,000								
1944S		21,640,000								
1945P		119,408,100								
1945P, Doubled-Die Reverse										
1945D		37,158,000								
1945S		58,939,000								

Jefferson, Prewar Composition, Mintmark Style Resumed (1946–1967)

Date		Quantity Minted	VF-20	EF-40	AU-50	MS-63	PF-65		Notes
1946		161,116,000							
1946D		45,292,200							
1946S		13,560,000							
1947		95,000,000							
1947D		37,822,000							
1947S		24,720,000							
1948		89,348,000							
1948D		44,734,000							
1948S		11,300,000							
1949		60,652,000							
1949D 1949D, D Over S		36,498,000							
1949S		9,716,000							
1950	(51,386)	9,796,000							
1950D		2,630,030							
1951	(57,500)	28,552,000							
1951D		20,460,000							
1951S		7,776,000							
1952	(81,980)	63,988,000							
1952D		30,638,000							
1952S		20,572,000							
1953	(128,800)	46,644,000							
1953D		59,878,600							
1953S		19,210,900							
1954	(233,300)	47,684,050							
1954D		117,183,060							
1954S 1954S, S Over D		29,384,000							
1955	(378,200)	7,888,000							
1955D 1955D, D Over S		74,464,100							
1956	(669,384)	35,216,000							
1956D		67,222,940							
1957	(1,247,952)	38,408,000							
1957D		136,828,900							
1958	(875,652)	17,088,000							
1958D		168,249,120							
1959	(1,149,291)	27,248,000							
1959D		160,738,240							
1960	(1,691,602)	55,416,000							
1960D		192,582,180							
1961	(3,028,144)	73,640,100							
1961D		229,342,760							

Date		Quantity Minted	VF-20	EF-40	AU-50	MS-63	PF-65			Notes
1962	(3,218,019)	97,384,000								
1962D		280,195,720								
1963	(3,075,645)	175,776,000								
1963D		276,829,460								
1964	(3,950,762)	1,024,672,000								
1964D		1,787,297,160								
1965		136,131,380								

Jefferson, Designer's Initials Added (1966–2003)

Date		Quantity Minted	MS-63	MS-65	PF-65					Notes
1966		156,208,283								
1967		107,325,800								
1968D		91,227,880								
1968S	(3,041,506)	100,396,004								
1969D		202,807,500								
1969S	(2,934,631)	120,165,000								
1970D		515,485,380								
1970S	(2,632,810)	238,832,004								
1971		106,884,000								
1971D		316,144,800								
1971, No S	(3,220,733)									
1971S										
1972		202,036,000								
1972D		351,694,600								
1972S	(3,260,996)									
1973		384,396,000								
1973D		261,405,000								
1973S	(2,760,339)									
1974		601,752,000								
1974D		277,373,000								
1974S	(2,612,568)									
1975		181,772,000								
1975D		401,875,300								
1975S	(2,845,450)									
1976		367,124,000								
1976D		563,964,147								
1976S	(4,149,730)									
1977		585,376,000								
1977D		297,313,422								
1977S	(3,251,152)									
1978		391,308,000								
1978D		313,092,780								
1978S	(3,127,781)									

Date		Quantity Minted	MS-63	MS-65	PF-65					Notes
1979		463,188,000								
1979D		325,867,672								
1979S, Type 1	(3,677,175)									
1979S, Type 2										
1980P		593,004,000								
1980D		502,323,448								
1980S	(3,554,806)									
1981P		657,504,000								
1981D		364,801,843								
1981S, Type 1	(4,063,083)									
1981S, Type 2										
1982P		292,355,000								
1982D		373,726,544								
1982S	(3,857,479)									
1983P		561,615,000								
1983D		536,726,276								
1983S	(3,279,126)									
1984P		746,769,000								
1984D		517,675,146								
1984S	(3,065,110)									
1985P		647,114,962								
1985D		459,747,446								
1985S	(3,362,821)									
1986P		536,883,483								
1986D		361,819,140								
1986S	(3,010,497)									
1987P		371,499,481								
1987D		410,590,604								
1987S	(4,227,728)									
1988P		771,360,000								
1988D		663,771,652								
1988S	(3,262,948)									
1989P		898,812,000								
1989D		570,842,474								
1989S	(3,220,194)									
1990P		661,636,000								
1990D		663,938,503								
1990S	(3,299,559)									
1991P		614,104,000								
1991D		436,496,678								
1991S	(2,867,787)									
1992P		399,552,000								
1992D		450,565,113								
1992S	(4,176,560)									
1993P		412,076,000								
1993D		406,084,135								

Date	Quantity Minted	MS-63	MS-65	PF-65					Notes
1993S	(3,394,792)								
1994P	722,160,000								
1994P, Special Unc	167,703								
1994D	715,762,110								
1994S	(3,269,923)								
1995P	774,156,000								
1995D	888,112,000								
1995S	(2,797,481)								
1996P	829,332,000								
1996D	817,736,000								
1996S	(2,525,265)								
1997P	470,972,000								
1997P, Special Unc	25,000								
1997D	466,640,000								
1997S	(2,796,678)								
1998P	688,272,000								
1998D	635,360,000								
1998S	(2,086,507)								
1999P	1,212,000,000								
1999D	1,066,720,000								
1999S	(3,347,966)								
2000P	846,240,000								
2000D	1,509,520,000								
2000S	(4,047,993)								
2001P	675,704,000								
2001D	627,680,000								
2001S	(3,184,606)								
2002P	539,280,000								
2002D	691,200,000								
2002S	(3,211,995)								
2003P	441,840,000								
2003D	383,040,000								
2003S	(3,298,439)								

Westward Journey (2004–2005)

Date	Quantity Minted	MS-63	MS-65	PF-65					Notes
2004P, Peace Medal	361,440,000								
2004D, Peace Medal	372,000,000								
2004S, Peace Medal	(2,992,069)								
2004P, Keelboat	366,720,000								
2004D, Keelboat	344,880,000								
2004S, Keelboat	(2,965,422)								
2005P, American Bison	448,320,000								
2005D, American Bison	487,680,000								
2005S, American Bison	(3,344,679)								
2005P, Ocean in View	394,080,000								
2005D, Ocean in View	411,120,000								
2005S, Ocean in View	(3,344,679)								

New Jefferson Portrait, Monticello Reverse Resumed (2006 to Date)

Date	Quantity Minted	MS-63	MS-65	PF-65					Notes
2006P	693,120,000								
2006D	809,280,000								
2006S	(3,054,436)								
2007P	571,680,000								
2007D	626,160,000								
2007S	(2,577,166)								
2008P	279,840,000								
2008D	345,600,000								
2008S	(2,169,561)								
2009P	39,840,000								
2009D	46,800,000								
2009S	(2,179,867)								
2010P	260,640,000								
2010D	229,920,000								
2010S	(1,689,216)								
2011P	450,000,000								
2011D	540,240,000								
2011S	(1,673,010)								
2012P	464,640,000								
2012D	558,960,000								
2012S	(1,237,415)								
2013P	607,440,000								
2013D	615,600,000								
2013S	(1,274,505)								

Date	Quantity Minted	MS-63	MS-65	PF-65					Notes
2014P	635,520,000								
2014D	570,720,000								
2014S	(1,190,369)								
2015P									
2015D									
2015S									
2016P	786,960,000								
2016D	759,600,000								
2016S	(1,011,624)								
2017P	710,160,000								
2017D	663,120,000								
2017S	(979,477)								
2018P	629,520,000								
2018D	626,880,000								
2018S	(844,220)								
2019P	567,854,400								
2019D	527,040,000								
2019S									
2020P									
2020D									
2020S									
2020W									
2020W, Reverse Proof									
2021P									
2021D									
2021S									
2022P									
2022D									
2022S									

HALF DIMES

Flowing Hair (1794–1795)

Date	Quantity Minted	G-4	VG-8	F-12	VF-20	EF-40	MS-60	Notes
1794	86,416							
1795								

Draped Bust, Small Eagle Reverse (1796–1797)

Date	Quantity Minted	G-4	VG-8	F-12	VF-20	EF-40	MS-60	Notes
1796, 6 Over 5	10,230							
1796								
1796, LIKERTY								
1797, 15 Stars	44,527							
1797, 16 Stars								
1797, 13 Stars								

Draped Bust, Heraldic Eagle Reverse (1800–1805)

Date	Quantity Minted	G-4	VG-8	F-12	VF-20	EF-40	MS-60	Notes
1800	24,000							
1800, LIBEKTY	16,000							
1801	27,760							
1802	3,060							
1803, Large 8	37,850							
1803, Small 8								
1805	15,600							

Capped Bust (1829–1837)

Date	Quantity Minted	G-4	VG-8	F-12	VF-20	EF-40	MS-60	Notes
1829	1,230,000							
1830	1,240,000							

Date	Quantity Minted	G-4	VG-8	F-12	VF-20	EF-40	MS-60		Notes
1831	1,242,700								
1832	965,000								
1833	1,370,000								
1834	1,480,000								
1834, 3 Over Inverted 3									
1835, Large Date and 5 C.	2,760,000								
1835, Large Date, Small 5 C.									
1835, Small Date, Large 5 C.									
1835, Small Date and 5 C.									
1836, Small 5 C.	1,900,000								
1836, Large 5 C.									
1836, 3 Over Inverted 3									
1837, Small 5 C.	871,000								
1837, Large 5 C.									

Liberty Seated, Variety 1, No Stars on Obverse (1837–1838)

Date	Quantity Minted	G-4	VG-8	F-12	VF-20	EF-40	MS-60		Notes
1837, Small Date	1,405,000								
1837, Large Date									
1838O, No Stars	70,000								

Liberty Seated, Variety 2, Stars on Obverse (1838–1853)

Date	Quantity Minted	G-4	VG-8	F-12	VF-20	EF-40	MS-60		Notes
1838, No Drapery, Large Stars	2,225,000								
1838, No Drapery, Small Stars									
1839, No Drapery	1,069,150								
1839O, No Drapery	1,060,000								
1840, No Drapery	1,034,000								
1840O, No Drapery	695,000								
1840, Drapery	310,085								
1840O, Drapery	240,000								
1841	1,150,000								
1841O	815,000								
1842	815,000								
1842O	350,000								
1843	1,165,000								
1844	430,000								
1844O	220,000								

Date	Quantity Minted	G-4	VG-8	F-12	VF-20	EF-40	MS-60		Notes
1845	1,564,000								
1846	27,000								
1847	1,274,000								
1848, Medium Date	668,000								
1848, Large Date									
18480	600,000								
1849, 9 Over 6	1,309,000								
1849, 9 Over Widely Placed 6									
1849, Normal Date									
18490	140,000								
1850	955,000								
18500	690,000								
1851	781,000								
18510	860,000								
1852	1,000,500								
18520	260,000								
1853, No Arrows	135,000								
18530, No Arrows	160,000								

Liberty Seated, Variety 3, Arrows at Date (1853–1855)

Date	Quantity Minted	VG-8	F-12	VF-20	EF-40	MS-60	PF-60		Notes
1853	13,210,020								
18530	2,200,000								
1854	5,740,000								
18540	1,560,000								
1855	1,750,000								
18550	600,000								

Liberty Seated, Variety 2 Resumed, With Weight Standard of Variety 3 (1856–1859)

Date	Quantity Minted	VG-8	F-12	VF-20	EF-40	MS-60	PF-60		Notes
1856	4,880,000								
18560	1,100,000								
1857	7,280,000								
18570	1,380,000								
1858 (300)	3,500,000								
1858, Repunched High Dt									
1858, Over Inverted Date									
18580	1,660,000								
1859 (800)	340,000								
18590	560,000								

Transitional Patterns (1859 and 1860)

Date	Quantity Minted	MS-60	MS-63	PF-63				Notes
1859, Obverse of 1859, Reverse of 1860	20							
1860, Obverse of 1859 (With Stars), Reverse of 1860	100							

Liberty Seated, Variety 4, Legend on Obverse (1860–1873)

Date		Quantity Minted	VG-8	F-12	VF-20	EF-40	MS-60	PF-60	Notes
1860, Legend	(1,000)	798,000							
18600		1,060,000							
1861	(1,000)	3,360,000							
1861, "1 Over 0"									
1862	(550)	1,492,000							
1863	(460)	18,000							
1863S		100,000							
1864	(470)	48,000							
1864S		90,000							
1865	(500)	13,000							
1865S		120,000							
1866	(725)	10,000							
1866S		120,000							
1867	(625)	8,000							
1867S		120,000							
1868	(600)	88,600							
1868S		280,000							
1869	(600)	208,000							
1869S		230,000							
1870	(1,000)	535,000							
1870S (unique)									
1871	(960)	1,873,000							
1871S		161,000							
1872	(950)	2,947,000							
1872S, Mintmk above bow		837,000							
1872S, Mintmk below bow									
1873 (Close 3 only)	(600)	712,000							
1873S (Close 3 only)		324,000							

DIMES

Draped Bust, Small Eagle Reverse (1796–1797)

Date	Quantity Minted	G-4	VG-8	F-12	VF-20	EF-40	MS-60	Notes
1796	22,135							
1797, 16 Stars	25,261							
1797, 13 Stars								

Draped Bust, Heraldic Eagle Reverse (1798–1807)

Date	Quantity Minted	G-4	VG-8	F-12	VF-20	EF-40	MS-60	Notes
1798, 8 Over 7, 16 Stars on Reverse	27,550							
1798, 8 Over 7, 13 Stars on Reverse								
1798, Large 8								
1798, Small 8								
1800	21,760							
1801	34,640							
1802	10,975							
1803	33,040							
1804, 13 Stars on Reverse	8,265							
1804, 14 Stars on Reverse								
1805, 4 Berries	120,780							
1805, 5 Berries								
1807	165,000							

Capped Bust, Variety 1, Wide Border (1809–1828)

Date	Quantity Minted	G-4	VG-8	F-12	VF-20	EF-40	MS-60	Notes
1809	51,065							
1811, 11 Over 09	65,180							
1814, Small Date	421,500							
1814, Large Date								
1814, STATESOFAMERICA								

Date	Quantity Minted	G-4	VG-8	F-12	VF-20	EF-40	MS-60	Notes
1820, Large 0								
1820, Small 0	942,587							
1820, STATESOFAMERICA								
1821, Small Date	1,186,512							
1821, Large Date								
1822	100,000							
1823, 3 Over 2, Small E's	440,000							
1823, 3 Over 2, Large E's								
1824, 4 Over 2, Flat Top 1 in 10 C.	510,000							
1824, 4 Over 2, Pointed Top 1 in 10 C.								
1825								
1827, Flat Top 1 in 10 C.	1,215,000							
1827, Pointed Top 1 in 10 C.								
1828, Large Date, Curl Base 2	125,000							
1828, Small Date, Square Base 2								

1829, Small 10 C.   1829, Large 10 C.

Capped Bust, Variety 2, Modified Design (1828–1837)

Date	Quantity Minted	G-4	VG-8	F-12	VF-20	EF-40	MS-60	Notes
1829, Curl Base 2								
1829, Small 10 C.	770,000							
1829, Medium 10 C.								
1829, Large 10 C.								
1830, 30 Over 29								
1830, Large 10 C.	510,000							
1830, Small 10 C.								
1831	771,350							
1832	522,500							
1833	485,000							
1833, Last 3 High								
1834, Small 4	635,000							
1834, Large 4								
1835	1,410,000							
1836	1,190,000							
1837	359,500							

Liberty Seated, Variety 1, No Stars on Obverse (1837–1838)

Date	Quantity Minted	G-4	VG-8	F-12	VF-20	EF-40	MS-60	Notes
1837, Large Date	682,500							
1837, Small Date								
18380	406,034							

No Drapery, Small Stars   No Drapery, Large Stars   Drapery

Liberty Seated, Variety 2, Stars on Obverse (1838–1853)

Date	Quantity Minted	G-4	VG-8	F-12	VF-20	EF-40	MS-60	Notes
1838, Small Stars								
1838, Large Stars	1,992,500							
1838, Partial Drapery								
1839, No Drapery	1,053,115							
18390, No Drapery	1,291,600							
1840, No Drapery	981,500							
18400, No Drapery	1,175,000							
1840, Drapery	377,500							
1841	1,622,500							
18410	2,007,500							
1842	1,887,500							
18420	2,020,000							
1843	1,370,000							
18430	150,000							
1844	72,500							
1845	1,755,000							
18450	230,000							
1846	31,300							
1847	245,000							
1848	451,500							
1849	839,000							
18490	300,000							
1850	1,931,500							
18500	510,000							
1851	1,026,500							
18510	400,000							
1852	1,535,500							
18520	430,000							
1853, No Arrows	95,000							

Liberty Seated, Variety 3, Arrows at Date (1853–1855)

Date	Quantity Minted	G-4	VG-8	F-12	VF-20	EF-40	MS-60	Notes
1853, With Arrows	12,078,010							
1853O	1,100,000							
1854	4,470,000							
1854O	1,770,000							
1855	2,075,000							

Liberty Seated, Variety 2 Resumed, With Weight Standard of Variety 3 (1856–1860)

Date		Quantity Minted	VG-8	F-12	VF-20	EF-40	MS-60	PF-60	Notes
1856, Large Date		5,780,000							
1856, Small Date									
1856O		1,180,000							
1856S		70,000							
1857		5,580,000							
1857O		1,540,000							
1858	(300+)	1,540,000							
1858O		290,000							
1858S		60,000							
1859	(800)	429,200							
1859O		480,000							
1859S		60,000							
1860S		140,000							

Liberty Seated, Variety 4, Legend on Obverse (1860–1873)

Date		Quantity Minted	VG-8	F-12	VF-20	EF-40	MS-60	PF-60	Notes
1859, Obverse of 1859 (With Stars), Reverse of 1860									
1860	(1,000)	606,000							
1860O		40,000							
1861	(1,000)	1,883,000							
1861S		172,500							

Date		Quantity Minted	VG-8	F-12	VF-20	EF-40	MS-60	PF-60		Notes
1862	(550)	847,000								
1862S		180,750								
1863	(460)	14,000								
1863S		157,500								
1864	(470)	11,000								
1864S		230,000								
1865	(500)	10,000								
1865S		175,000								
1866	(725)	8,000								
1866S		135,000								
1867	(625)	6,000								
1867S		140,000								
1868	(600)	464,000								
1868S		260,000								
1869	(600)	256,000								
1869S		450,000								
1870	(1,000)	470,500								
1870S		50,000								
1871	(960)	906,750								
1871CC		20,100								
1871S		320,000								
1872 (950) 1872, Doubled-Die Rev *(rare)*		2,395,500								
1872CC		35,480								
1872S		190,000								
1873, Close 3	(600)	1,507,400								
1873, Open 3		60,000								
1873CC *(unique)*		12,400								

Liberty Seated, Variety 5, Arrows at Date (1873–1874)

Date		Quantity Minted	VG-8	F-12	VF-20	EF-40	MS-60	PF-60		Notes
1873 (500) 1873, Doubled-Die Obverse		2,378,000								
1873CC		*18,791*								
1873S		455,000								
1874	(700)	2,939,300								
1874CC		10,817								
1874S		240,000								

Liberty Seated, Variety 4 Resumed, With Weight Standard of Variety 5 (1875–1891)

Date		Quantity Minted	VG-8	F-12	VF-20	EF-40	MS-60	PF-60		Notes
1875	(700)	10,350,000								
1875CC, Above Bow		4,645,000								
1875CC, Below Bow										
1875S, Below Bow		9,070,000								
1875S, Above Bow										
1876	(1,150)	11,450,000								
1876CC		8,270,000								
1876S		10,420,000								
1877	(510)	7,310,000								
1877CC		7,700,000								
1877S		2,340,000								
1878	(800)	1,677,200								
1878CC		200,000								
1879	(1,100)	14,000								
1880	(1,355)	36,000								
1881	(975)	24,000								
1882	(1,100)	3,910,000								
1883	(1,039)	7,674,673								
1884	(875)	3,365,505								
1884S		564,969								
1885	(930)	2,532,497								
1885S		43,690								
1886	(886)	6,376,684								
1886S		206,524								
1887	(710)	11,283,229								
1887S		4,454,450								
1888	(832)	5,495,655								
1888S		1,720,000								
1889	(711)	7,380,000								
1889S		972,678								
1890	(590)	9,910,951								
1890S, Large S		1,423,076								
1890S, Small S *(rare)*										
1891	(600)	15,310,000								
1891O		4,540,000								
1891O, O Over Horizontal O										
1891S		3,196,116								

Barber or Liberty Head (1892–1916)

Date		Quantity Minted	VG-8	F-12	VF-20	EF-40	MS-60	PF-63	Notes
1892	(1,245)	12,120,000							
18920		3,841,700							
1892S		990,710							
1893, "3 Over 2"		3,339,940							
1893	(792)								
18930		1,760,000							
1893S		2,491,401							
1894	(972)	1,330,000							
18940		720,000							
1894S		24							
1895	(880)	690,000							
18950		440,000							
1895S		1,120,000							
1896	(762)	2,000,000							
18960		610,000							
1896S		575,056							
1897	(731)	10,868,533							
18970		666,000							
1897S		1,342,844							
1898	(735)	16,320,000							
18980		2,130,000							
1898S		1,702,507							
1899	(846)	19,580,000							
18990		2,650,000							
1899S		1,867,493							
1900	(912)	17,600,000							
19000		2,010,000							
1900S		5,168,270							
1901	(813)	18,859,665							
19010		5,620,000							
1901S		593,022							
1902	(777)	21,380,000							
19020		4,500,000							
1902S		2,070,000							
1903	(755)	19,500,000							
19030		8,180,000							
1903S		613,300							
1904	(670)	14,600,357							
1904S		800,000							

Date		Quantity Minted	VG-8	F-12	VF-20	EF-40	MS-60	PF-63		Notes
1905	(727)	14,551,623								
1905O		3,400,000								
1905O, Micro O										
1905S		6,855,199								
1906	(675)	19,957,731								
1906D		4,060,000								
1906O		2,610,000								
1906S		3,136,640								
1907	(575)	22,220,000								
1907D		4,080,000								
1907O		5,058,000								
1907S		3,178,470								
1908	(545)	10,600,000								
1908D		7,490,000								
1908O		1,789,000								
1908S		3,220,000								
1909	(650)	10,240,000								
1909D		954,000								
1909O		2,287,000								
1909S		1,000,000								
1910	(551)	11,520,000								
1910D		3,490,000								
1910S		1,240,000								
1911	(543)	18,870,000								
1911D		11,209,000								
1911S		3,520,000								
1912	(700)	19,349,300								
1912D		11,760,000								
1912S		3,420,000								
1913	(622)	19,760,000								
1913S		510,000								
1914	(425)	17,360,230								
1914D		11,908,000								
1914S		2,100,000								
1915	(450)	5,620,000								
1915S		960,000								
1916		18,490,000								
1916S		5,820,000								

Winged Liberty Head or "Mercury" (1916–1945)

Date	Quantity Minted	VG-8	F-12	VF-20	EF-40	MS-60	MS-65	Notes
1916	22,180,080							
1916D	264,000							
1916S	10,450,000							
1917	55,230,000							
1917D	9,402,000							
1917S	27,330,000							
1918	26,680,000							
1918D	22,674,800							
1918S	19,300,000							
1919	35,740,000							
1919D	9,939,000							
1919S	8,850,000							
1920	59,030,000							
1920D	19,171,000							
1920S	13,820,000							
1921	11,230,000							
1921D	1,080,000							
1923	50,130,000							
1923S	6,440,000							
1924	24,010,000							
1924D	6,810,000							
1924S	7,120,000							
1925	25,610,000							
1925D	5,117,000							
1925S	5,850,000							
1926	32,160,000							
1926D	6,828,000							
1926S	1,520,000							
1927	28,080,000							
1927D	4,812,000							
1927S	4,770,000							
1928	19,480,000							
1928D	4,161,000							
1928S	7,400,000							
1929	25,970,000							
1929D	5,034,000							
1929S	4,730,000							

Date	Quantity Minted	VG-8	F-12	VF-20	EF-40	MS-60	MS-65		Notes
1930	6,770,000								
1930S	1,843,000								
1931	3,150,000								
1931D	1,260,000								
1931S	1,800,000								

Date	Quantity Minted	F-12	VF-20	EF-40	MS-60	MS-65	PF-65		Notes
1934	24,080,000								
1934D	6,772,000								
1935	58,830,000								
1935D	10,477,000								
1935S	15,840,000								
1936 (4,130)	87,500,000								
1936D	16,132,000								
1936S	9,210,000								
1937 (5,756)	56,860,000								
1937D	14,146,000								
1937S	9,740,000								
1938 (8,728)	22,190,000								
1938D	5,537,000								
1938S	8,090,000								
1939 (9,321)	67,740,000								
1939D	24,394,000								
1939S	10,540,000								
1940 (11,827)	65,350,000								
1940D	21,198,000								
1940S	21,560,000								
1941 (16,557)	175,090,000								
1941D	45,634,000								
1941S	43,090,000								
1942, 42 Over 41 / 1942 (22,329)	205,410,000								
1942D, 42 Over 41 / 1942D	60,740,000								
1942S	49,300,000								
1943	191,710,000								
1943D	71,949,000								
1943S	60,400,000								
1944	231,410,000								
1944D	62,224,000								
1944S	49,490,000								
1945	159,130,000								
1945D	40,245,000								
1945S / 1945S, Micro S	41,920,000								

Roosevelt, Silver Coinage (1946–1964)

Date		Quantity Minted	EF-40	AU-50	MS-60	MS-63	MS-65	PF-65	Notes
1946		255,250,000							
1946D		61,043,500							
1946S		27,900,000							
1947		121,520,000							
1947D		46,835,000							
1947S		34,840,000							
1948		74,950,000							
1948D		52,841,000							
1948S		35,520,000							
1949		30,940,000							
1949D		26,034,000							
1949S		13,510,000							
1950	(51,386)	50,130,114							
1950D		46,803,000							
1950S		20,440,000							
1951	(57,500)	103,880,102							
1951D		56,529,000							
1951S		31,630,000							
1952	(81,980)	99,040,093							
1952D		122,100,000							
1952S		44,419,500							
1953	(128,800)	53,490,120							
1953D		136,433,000							
1953S		39,180,000							
1954	(233,300)	114,010,203							
1954D		106,397,000							
1954S		22,860,000							
1955	(378,200)	12,450,181							
1955D		13,959,000							
1955S		18,510,000							
1956	(669,384)	108,640,000							
1956D		108,015,100							
1957	(1,247,952)	160,160,000							
1957D		113,354,330							
1958	(875,652)	31,910,000							
1958D		136,564,600							
1959	(1,149,291)	85,780,000							
1959D		164,919,790							

Date		Quantity Minted	EF-40	AU-50	MS-60	MS-63	MS-65	PF-65		Notes
1960	(1,691,602)	70,390,000								
1960, DblDie Obv										
1960D		200,160,400								
1961	(3,028,244)	93,730,000								
1961D		209,146,550								
1962	(3,218,019)	72,450,000								
1962D		334,948,380								
1963	(3,075,645)	123,650,000								
1963, DblDie Rev										
1963D		421,476,530								
1964	(3,950,762)	929,360,000								
1964D		1,357,517,180								
1964D, DblDie Rev										

Roosevelt, Clad Coinage and Silver Proofs (1965 to Date)

Date		Quantity Minted	AU-50	MS-60	MS-63	MS-65	PF-65			Notes
1965		1,652,140,570								
1966		1,382,734,540								
1967		2,244,007,320								
1968		424,470,400								
1968D		480,748,280								
1968S	(3,041,506)									
1969		145,790,000								
1969D		563,323,870								
1969S	(2,394,631)									
1970		345,570,000								
1970D		754,942,100								
1970S	(2,632,810)									
1971		162,690,000								
1971D		377,914,240								
1971S	(3,220,733)									
1972		431,540,000								
1972D		330,290,000								
1972S	(3,260,996)									
1973		315,670,000								
1973D		455,032,426								
1973S	(2,760,339)									
1974		470,248,000								
1974D		571,083,000								
1974S	(2,612,568)									
1975		585,673,900								
1975D		313,705,300								
1975S	(2,845,450)									

Date		Quantity Minted	AU-50	MS-60	MS-63	MS-65	PF-65			Notes
1976		568,760,000								
1976D		695,222,774								
1976S	(4,149,730)									
1977		796,930,000								
1977D		376,607,228								
1977S	(3,251,152)									
1978		663,980,000								
1978D		282,847,540								
1978S	(3,127,781)									
1979		315,440,000								
1979D		390,921,184								
1979S, Type 1	(3,677,175)									
1979S, Type 2										
1980P		735,170,000								
1980D		719,354,321								
1980S	(3,554,806)									
1981P		676,650,000								
1981D		712,284,143								
1981S, Type 1	(4,063,083)									
1981S, Type 2										
1982, No Mintmark, Strong Strike										
1982, No Mintmark, Weak Strike										
1982P		519,475,000								
1982D		542,713,584								
1982S	(3,857,479)									
1983P		647,025,000								
1983D		730,129,224								
1983S	(3,279,126)									
1984P		856,669,000								
1984D		704,803,976								
1984S	(3,065,110)									
1985P		705,200,962								
1985D		587,979,970								
1985S	(3,362,821)									
1986P		682,649,693								
1986D		473,326,970								
1986S	(3,010,497)									
1987P		762,709,481								
1987D		653,203,402								
1987S	(4,227,728)									
1988P		1,030,550,000								
1988D		962,385,489								
1988S	(3,262,948)									
1989P		1,298,400,000								

Date	Quantity Minted	AU-50	MS-60	MS-63	MS-65	PF-65			Notes
1989D	896,535,597								
1989S	(3,220,194)								
1990P	1,034,340,000								
1990D	839,995,824								
1990S	(3,299,559)								
1991P	927,220,000								
1991D	601,241,114								
1991S	(2,867,787)								
1992P	593,500,000								
1992D	616,273,932								
1992S	(2,858,981)								
1992S, Silver	(1,317,579)								
1993P	766,180,000								
1993D	750,110,166								
1993S	(2,633,439)								
1993S, Silver	(761,353)								
1994P	1,189,000,000								
1994D	1,303,268,110								
1994S	(2,484,594)								
1994S, Silver	(785,329)								
1995P	1,125,500,000								
1995D	1,274,890,000								
1995S	(2,117,496)								
1995S, Silver	(679,985)								
1996P	1,421,163,000								
1996D	1,400,300,000								
1996W	1,457,000								
1996S	(1,750,244)								
1996S, Silver	(775,021)								
1997P	991,640,000								
1997D	979,810,000								
1997S	(2,055,000)								
1997S, Silver	(741,678)								
1998P	1,163,000,000								
1998D	1,172,250,000								
1998S	(2,086,507)								
1998S, Silver	(878,792)								
1999P	2,164,000,000								
1999D	1,397,750,000								
1999S	(2,543,401)								
1999S, Silver	(804,565)								
2000P	1,842,500,000								
2000D	1,818,700,000								
2000S	(3,082,572)								
2000S, Silver	(965,421)								

Date		Quantity Minted	AU-50	MS-60	MS-63	MS-65	PF-65			Notes
2001P		1,369,590,000								
2001D		1,412,800,000								
2001S	(2,294,909)									
2001S, Silver	(889,697)									
2002P		1,187,500,000								
2002D		1,379,500,000								
2002S	(2,319,766)									
2002S, Silver	(892,229)									
2003P		1,085,500,000								
2003D		986,500,000								
2003S	(2,172,684)									
2003S, Silver	(1,125,755)									
2004P		1,328,000,000								
2004D		1,159,500,000								
2004S	(1,789,488)									
2004S, Silver	(1,175,934)									
2005P		1,412,000,000								
2005D		1,423,500,000								
2005S	(2,275,000)									
2005S, Silver	(1,069,679)									
2006P		1,381,000,000								
2006D		1,447,000,000								
2006S	(2,000,428)									
2006S, Silver	(1,054,008)									
2007P		1,047,500,000								
2007D		1,042,000,000								
2007S	(1,702,116)									
2007S, Silver	(875,050)									
2008P		391,000,000								
2008D		624,500,000								
2008S	(1,405,674)									
2008S, Silver	(763,887)									
2009P		96,500,000								
2009D		49,500,000								
2009S	(1,482,502)									
2009S, Silver	(697,365)									
2010P		557,000,000								
2010D		562,000,000								
2010S	(1,103,815)									
2010S, Silver	(585,401)									
2011P		748,000,000								
2011D		754,000,000								
2011S	(1,098,835)									
2011S, Silver	(574,175)									

2016-W Mercury Dime Centennial Gold Coin

Date	Quantity Minted	AU-50	MS-60	MS-63	MS-65	PF-65			Notes
2012P	808,000,000								
2012D	868,000,000								
2012S	(794,002)								
2012S, Silver	(495,315)								
2013P	1,086,500,000								
2013D	1,025,500,000								
2013S	(854,785)								
2013S, Silver	(467,691)								
2014P	1,125,500,000								
2014D	1,177,000,000								
2014S	(760,876)								
2014S, Silver	(491,157)								
2015P	1,497,510,000								
2015P, RevPf, Silver	(74,430)								
2015D	1,543,500,000								
2015S	(662,854)								
2015S, Silver	(387,310)								
2015W, Silver	(74,430)								
2016W, Mercury Dime Centennial Gold Coin	124,885								
2016P	1,517,000,000								
2016D	1,437,000,000								
2016S	(641,775)								
2016S, Silver	(419,496)								
2017P	1,437,500,000								
2017D	1,290,500,000								
2017S	(621,384)								
2017S, Silver	(406,994)								
2018P	1,193,000,000								
2018D	1,006,000,000								
2018S	(535,221)								
2018S, Silver	(350,820)								
2019P	1,147,500,000								
2019D	1,001,500,000								
2019S									
2019S, Silver									
2020P									
2020D									
2020S									
2020S, Silver									

Date	Quantity Minted	AU-50	MS-60	MS-63	MS-65	PF-65		Notes

TWENTY-CENT PIECES

Liberty Seated (1875–1878)

Date	Quantity Minted		VG-8	F-12	VF-20	EF-40	MS-60	PF-63		Notes
1875	(1,200)	38,500								
1875CC		133,290								
1875S		1,155,000								
1876	(1,500)	14,400								
1876CC		10,000								
1877	(510)									
1878	(600)									

QUARTER DOLLARS

Draped Bust, Small Eagle Reverse (1796)

Date	Quantity Minted	G-4	VG-8	F-12	VF-20	EF-40	MS-60	Notes
1796	6,146							

Draped Bust, Heraldic Eagle Reverse (1804–1807)

Date	Quantity Minted	G-4	VG-8	F-12	VF-20	EF-40	MS-60	Notes
1804	6,738							
1805	121,394							
1806, 6 Over 5	206,124							
1806								
1807	220,643							

Capped Bust, Variety 1, Large Diameter (1815–1828)

Date	Quantity Minted	G-4	VG-8	F-12	VF-20	EF-40	MS-60	Notes
1815	89,235							
1818, 8 Over 5	361,174							
1818, Normal Date								

Date	Quantity Minted	G-4	VG-8	F-12	VF-20	EF-40	MS-60	Notes
1819, Small 9	144,000							
1819, Large 9								
1820, Small 0	127,444							
1820, Large 0								
1821	216,851							
1822	64,080							
1822, 25 Over 50 C.								
1823, 3 Over 2	17,800							
1824, 4 Over 2	168,000							
1825, 5 Over 2								
1825, 5 Over 4								
1827, Original (Curl Base 2 in 25 C.)	4,000							
1827, Restrike (Sq Base 2 in 25 C.)								
1828	102,000							
1828, 25 Over 50 C.								

Capped Bust, Variety 2, Reduced Diameter, Motto Removed (1831–1838)

Date	Quantity Minted	G-4	VG-8	F-12	VF-20	EF-40	MS-60	Notes
1831, Small Letters	398,000							
1831, Large Letters								
1832	320,000							
1833	156,000							
1833, O Over F in OF								
1834	286,000							
1834, O Over F in OF								
1835	1,952,000							
1836	472,000							
1837	252,400							
1838	366,000							

Liberty Seated, Variety 1, No Motto Above Eagle (1838–1853)

Date	Quantity Minted	G-4	VG-8	F-12	VF-20	EF-40	MS-60	Notes
1838, No Drapery	466,000							
1839, No Drapery	491,146							
18400, No Drapery	382,200							
1840, Drapery	188,127							
18400, Drapery	43,000							
1841	120,000							
18410	452,000							
1842, Small Date (Proof only)								
1842, Large Date	88,000							
18420, Small Date	769,000							
18420, Large Date								
1843	645,600							
18430	968,000							
1844	421,200							
18440	740,000							
1845	922,000							
1846	510,000							
1847	734,000							
18470	368,000							
1848	146,000							
1849	340,000							
18490	*							
1850	190,800							
18500	412,000							
1851	160,000							
18510	88,000							
1852	177,060							
18520	96,000							
1853, Recut Date, No Arrows or Rays	44,200							

* Included in 1850-O mintage.

Liberty Seated, Variety 2, Arrows at Date, Rays Around Eagle (1853)

Date	Quantity Minted	G-4	VG-8	F-12	VF-20	EF-40	MS-60	Notes
1853	15,210,020							
1853, 3 Over 4								
18530	1,332,000							

Liberty Seated, Variety 3, Arrows at Date, No Rays (1854–1855)

Date	Quantity Minted	G-4	VG-8	F-12	VF-20	EF-40	MS-60	Notes
1854	12,380,000							
18540	1,484,000							
18540, Huge O								
1855	2,857,000							
18550	176,000							
1855S	396,400							

Liberty Seated, Variety 1 Resumed, With Weight Standard of Variety 2 (1856–1865)

Date		Quantity Minted	G-4	VG-8	F-12	VF-20	EF-40	MS-60	Notes
1856		7,264,000							
18560		968,000							
1856S		286,000							
1856S, S Over Small S									
1857		9,644,000							
18570		1,180,000							
1857S		82,000							
1858	(300)	7,368,000							
18580		520,000							
1858S		121,000							
1859	(800)	1,343,200							
18590		260,000							
1859S		80,000							
1860	(1,000)	804,400							
18600		388,000							
1860S		56,000							
1861	(1,000)	4,853,600							
1861S		96,000							
1862	(550)	932,000							
1862S		67,000							
1863	(460)	191,600							
1864	(470)	93,600							
1864S		20,000							
1865	(500)	58,800							
1865S		41,000							
1866 (unique, not a regular issue)									

Liberty Seated, Variety 4, Motto Above Eagle (1866–1873)

Date		Quantity Minted	VG-8	F-12	VF-20	EF-40	MS-60	PF-60	Notes
1866	(725)	16,800							
1866S		28,000							
1867	(625)	20,000							
1867S		48,000							
1868	(600)	29,400							
1868S		96,000							
1869	(600)	16,000							
1869S		76,000							
1870	(1,000)	86,400							
1870CC		8,340							
1871	(960)	118,200							
1871CC		10,890							
1871S		30,900							
1872	(950)	182,000							
1872CC		22,850							
1872S		83,000							
1873, Close 3	(600)	40,000							
1873, Open 3		172,000							
1873CC *(5 known)*		4,000							

Liberty Seated, Variety 5, Arrows at Date (1873–1874)

Date		Quantity Minted	VG-8	F-12	VF-20	EF-40	MS-60	PF-60	Notes
1873	(500)	1,271,200							
1873CC		12,462							
1873S		156,000							
1874	(700)	471,200							
1874S		392,000							

Liberty Seated, Variety 4 Resumed, With Weight Standard of Variety 5 (1875–1891)

Date		Quantity Minted	VG-8	F-12	VF-20	EF-40	MS-60	PF-60	Notes
1875	(700)	4,292,800							
1875CC		140,000							
1875S		680,000							
1876	(1,150)	17,816,000							
1876CC		4,944,000							
1876S		8,596,000							
1877	(510)	10,911,200							
1877CC		4,192,000							
1877S 1877S, S Over Horizontal S		8,996,000							
1878	(800)	2,260,000							
1878CC		996,000							
1878S		140,000							
1879	(1,100)	13,600							
1880	(1,355)	13,600							
1881	(975)	12,000							
1882	(1,100)	15,200							
1883	(1,039)	14,400							
1884	(875)	8,000							
1885	(930)	13,600							
1886	(886)	5,000							
1887	(710)	10,000							
1888	(832)	10,001							
1888S		1,216,000							
1889	(711)	12,000							
1890	(590)	80,000							
1891	(600)	3,920,000							
18910		6,800							
1891S		2,216,000							

Barber or Liberty Head (1892–1916)

Date		Quantity Minted	VG-8	F-12	VF-20	EF-40	MS-60	PF-63	Notes
1892	(1,245)	8,236,000							
1892O		2,460,000							
1892S		964,079							
1893	(792)	5,444,023							
1893O		3,396,000							
1893S		1,454,535							
1894	(972)	3,432,000							
1894O		2,852,000							
1894S		2,648,821							
1895	(880)	4,440,000							
1895O		2,816,000							
1895S		1,764,681							
1896	(762)	3,874,000							
1896O		1,484,000							
1896S		188,039							
1897	(731)	8,140,000							
1897O		1,414,800							
1897S		542,229							
1898	(735)	11,100,000							
1898O		1,868,000							
1898S		1,020,592							
1899	(846)	12,624,000							
1899O		2,644,000							
1899S		708,000							
1900	(912)	10,016,000							
1900O		3,416,000							
1900S		1,858,585							
1901	(813)	8,892,000							
1901O		1,612,000							
1901S		72,664							
1902	(777)	12,196,967							
1902O		4,748,000							
1902S		1,524,612							
1903	(755)	9,759,309							
1903O		3,500,000							
1903S		1,036,000							

Date	Quantity Minted		VG-8	F-12	VF-20	EF-40	MS-60	PF-63		Notes
1904	(670)	9,588,143								
19040		2,456,000								
1905	(727)	4,967,523								
19050		1,230,000								
1905S		1,884,000								
1906	(675)	3,655,760								
1906D		3,280,000								
19060		2,056,000								
1907	(575)	7,132,000								
1907D		2,484,000								
19070		4,560,000								
1907S		1,360,000								
1908	(545)	4,232,000								
1908D		5,788,000								
19080		6,244,000								
1908S		784,000								
1909	(650)	9,268,000								
1909D		5,114,000								
19090		712,000								
1909S		1,348,000								
1910	(551)	2,244,000								
1910D		1,500,000								
1911	(543)	3,720,000								
1911D		933,600								
1911S		988,000								
1912	(700)	4,400,000								
1912S		708,000								
1913	(613)	484,000								
1913D		1,450,800								
1913S		40,000								
1914	(380)	6,244,230								
1914D		3,046,000								
1914S		264,000								
1915	(450)	3,480,000								
1915D		3,694,000								
1915S		704,000								
1916		1,788,000								
1916D		6,540,800								

Standing Liberty, Variety 1, No Stars Below Eagle (1916–1917)

Date	Quantity Minted	VG-8	F-12	VF-20	EF-40	MS-60	PF-63	Notes
1916	52,000							
1917, Variety 1	8,740,000							
1917D, Variety 1	1,509,200							
1917S, Variety 1	1,952,000							

Standing Liberty, Variety 2, Stars Below Eagle, Pedestal Date (1917–1924)

Date	Quantity Minted	VG-8	F-12	VF-20	EF-40	MS-60	PF-63	Notes
1917, Variety 2	13,880,000							
1917D, Variety 2	6,224,400							
1917S, Variety 2	5,552,000							
1918	14,240,000							
1918D	7,380,000							
1918S, Normal Date	11,072,000							
1918S, 8 Over 7								
1919	11,324,000							
1919D	1,944,000							
1919S	1,836,000							
1920	27,860,000							
1920D	3,586,400							
1920S	6,380,000							
1921	1,916,000							
1923	9,716,000							
1923S	1,360,000							
1924	10,920,000							
1924D	3,112,000							
1924S	2,860,000							

Standing Liberty, Variety 2, Stars Below Eagle, Recessed Date (1925–1930)

Date	Quantity Minted	VG-8	F-12	VF-20	EF-40	MS-60	PF-63		Notes
1925	12,280,000								
1926	11,316,000								
1926D	1,716,000								
1926S	2,700,000								
1927	11,912,000								
1927D	976,000								
1927S	396,000								
1928	6,336,000								
1928D	1,627,600								
1928S	2,644,000								
1929	11,140,000								
1929D	1,358,000								
1929S	1,764,000								
1930	5,632,000								
1930S	1,556,000								

Washington, Silver Coinage (1932–1964)

Date	Quantity Minted	F-12	VF-20	EF-40	MS-60	MS-65	PF-65		Notes
1932	5,404,000								
1932D	436,800								
1932S	408,000								
1934, Doubled Die									
1934, Light Motto	31,912,052								
1934, Heavy Motto									
1934D	3,527,200								
1935	32,484,000								
1935D	5,780,000								
1935S	5,660,000								
1936 (3,837)	41,300,000								
1936D	5,374,000								
1936S	3,828,000								
1937 (5,542)	19,696,000								
1937, Doubled-Die Obverse									
1937D	7,189,600								
1937S	1,652,000								
1938 (8,045)	9,472,000								

Date	Quantity Minted	F-12	VF-20	EF-40	MS-60	MS-65	PF-65		Notes
1938S	2,832,000								
1939 (8,795)	33,540,000								
1939D	7,092,000								
1939S	2,628,000								
1940 (11,246)	35,704,000								
1940D	2,797,600								
1940S	8,244,000								
1941 (15,287)	79,032,000								
1941D	16,714,800								
1941S	16,080,000								
1942 (21,123)	102,096,000								
1942D 1942D, Doubled-Die Obverse	17,487,200								
1942S	19,384,000								
1943 1943, Doubled-Die Obverse	99,700,000								
1943D	16,095,600								
1943S 1943S, Doubled-Die Obverse	21,700,000								
1944	104,956,000								
1944D	14,600,800								
1944S	12,560,000								
1945	74,372,000								
1945D	12,341,600								
1945S	17,004,001								
1946	53,436,000								
1946D	9,072,800								
1946S	4,204,000								
1947	22,556,000								
1947D	15,338,400								
1947S	5,532,000								
1948	35,196,000								
1948D	16,766,800								
1948S	15,960,000								
1949	9,312,000								
1949D	10,068,400								
1950 (51,386)	24,920,126								
1950D 1950D, D Over S	21,075,600								
1950S 1950S, S Over D	10,284,004								
1951 (57,500)	43,448,102								
1951D	35,354,800								
1951S	9,048,000								
1952 (81,980)	38,780,093								
1952D	49,795,200								

Date	Quantity Minted	F-12	VF-20	EF-40	MS-60	MS-65	PF-65	Notes
1952S	13,707,800							
1953	(128,800) 18,536,120							
1953D	56,112,400							
1953S	14,016,000							
1954	(233,300) 54,412,203							
1954D	42,305,500							
1954S	11,834,722							
1955	(378,200) 18,180,181							
1955D	3,182,400							
1956	(669,384) 44,144,000							
1956D	32,334,500							
1957	(1,247,952) 46,532,000							
1957D	77,924,160							
1958	(875,652) 6,360,000							
1958D	78,124,900							
1959	(1,149,291) 24,384,000							
1959D	62,054,232							
1960	(1,691,602) 29,164,000							
1960D	63,000,324							
1961	(3,028,244) 37,036,000							
1961D	83,656,928							
1962	(3,218,019) 36,156,000							
1962D	127,554,756							
1963	(3,075,645) 74,316,000							
1963D	135,288,184							
1964	(3,950,762) 560,390,585							
1964D	704,135,528							

Washington, Clad Coinage (1965–1974)

Date	Quantity Minted	VF-20	EF-40	MS-60	MS-65	PF-65	Notes
1965	1,819,717,540						
1966	821,101,500						
1967	1,524,031,848						
1968	220,731,500						
1968D	101,534,000						
1968S	(3,041,506)						
1969	176,212,000						
1969D	114,372,000						
1969S	(2,934,631)						
1970	136,420,000						
1970D	417,341,364						
1970S	(2,632,810)						
1971	109,284,000						
1971D	258,634,428						
1971S	(3,220,733)						

Date	Quantity Minted	VF-20	EF-40	MS-60	MS-65	PF-65			Notes
1972	215,048,000								
1972D	311,067,732								
1972S	(3,260,996)								
1973	346,924,000								
1973D	232,977,400								
1973S	(2,760,339)								
1974	801,456,000								
1974D	353,160,300								
1974S	(2,612,568)								

Washington, Bicentennial (Dated 1776–1976)

Date	Quantity Minted	VF-20	EF-40	MS-60	MS-65	PF-65			Notes
1776–1976, Copper-Nickel Clad	809,784,016								
1776–1976D, Copper-Nickel Clad	860,118,839								
1776–1976S, Copper-Nickel Clad	(7,059,099)								
1776–1976S, Silver Clad	*11,000,000*								
1776–1976S, Silver Clad	*(4,000,000)*								

Washington, Eagle Reverse Resumed (1977–1998)

Date	Quantity Minted	AU-50	MS-60	MS-65	PF-65			Notes
1977	468,556,000							
1977D	256,524,978							
1977S	(3,251,152)							
1978	521,452,000							
1978D	287,373,152							
1978S	(3,127,781)							
1979	515,708,000							
1979D	489,789,780							
1979S, Type 1	(3,677,175)							
1979S, Type 2								
1980P	635,832,000							
1980D	518,327,487							
1980S	(3,554,806)							
1981P	601,716,000							
1981D	575,722,833							
1981S, Type 1	(4,063,083)							
1981S, Type 2								
1982P	500,931,000							

Date	Quantity Minted	AU-50	MS-60	MS-65	PF-65				Notes
1982D	480,042,788								
1982S	(3,857,479)								
1983P	673,535,000								
1983D	617,806,446								
1983S	(3,279,126)								
1984P	676,545,000								
1984D	546,483,064								
1984S	(3,065,110)								
1985P	775,818,962								
1985D	519,962,888								
1985S	(3,362,821)								
1986P	551,199,333								
1986D	504,298,660								
1986S	(3,010,497)								
1987P	582,499,481								
1987D	655,594,696								
1987S	(4,227,728)								
1988P	562,052,000								
1988D	596,810,688								
1988S	(3,262,948)								
1989P	512,868,000								
1989D	896,535,597								
1989S	(3,220,194)								
1990P	613,792,000								
1990D	927,638,181								
1990S	(3,299,559)								
1991P	570,968,000								
1991D	630,966,693								
1991S	(2,867,787)								
1992P	384,764,000								
1992D	389,777,107								
1992S	(2,858,981)								
1992S, Silver	(1,317,579)								
1993P	639,276,000								
1993D	645,476,128								
1993S	(2,633,439)								
1993S, Silver	(761,353)								
1994P	825,600,000								
1994D	880,034,110								
1994S	(2,484,594)								
1994S, Silver	(785,329)								
1995P	1,004,336,000								
1995D	1,103,216,000								
1995S	(2,117,496)								
1995S, Silver	(679,985)								
1996P	925,040,000								

Date		Quantity Minted	AU-50	MS-60	MS-65	PF-65			Notes
1996D		906,868,000							
1996S	(1,750,244)								
1996S, Silver	(775,021)								
1997P		595,740,000							
1997D		599,680,000							
1997S	(2,055,000)								
1997S, Silver	(741,678)								
1998P		896,268,000							
1998D		821,000,000							
1998S	(2,086,507)								
1998S, Silver	(878,792)								

Obverse, State Quarter Dollars

State Quarters (1999–2008)

Date		Quantity Minted	MS-63	MS-65	PF-65				Notes
1999P, Delaware		373,400,000							
1999D, Delaware		401,424,000	-						
1999S, Delaware	(3,713,359)								
1999S, Delaware, Silver	(804,565)								
1999P, Pennsylvania		349,000,000							
1999D, Pennsylvania		358,332,000							
1999S, Pennsylvania	(3,713,359)								
1999S, Pennsylvania, Silver	(804,565)								
1999P, New Jersey		363,200,000							
1999D, New Jersey		299,028,000							
1999S, New Jersey	(3,713,359)								
1999S, New Jersey, Silver	(804,565)								
1999P, Georgia		451,188,000							
1999D, Georgia		488,744,000							
1999S, Georgia	(3,713,359)								
1999S, Georgia, Silver	(804,565)								
1999P, Connecticut		688,744,000							
1999D, Connecticut		657,880,000							

73

Date	Quantity Minted	MS-63	MS-65	PF-65			Notes
1999S, Connecticut	(3,713,359)						
1999S, Connecticut, Silver	(804,565)						

Date	Quantity Minted	MS-63	MS-65	PF-65			Notes
2000P, Massachusetts	628,600,000						
2000D, Massachusetts	535,184,000						
2000S, Massachusetts	(4,020,172)						
2000S, Massachusetts, Silver	(965,421)						
2000P, Maryland	678,200,000						
2000D, Maryland	556,532,000						
2000S, Maryland	(4,020,172)						
2000S, Maryland, Silver	(965,421)						
2000P, South Carolina	742,576,000						
2000D, South Carolina	566,208,000						
2000S, South Carolina	(4,020,172)						
2000S, South Carolina, Silver	(965,421)						
2000P, New Hampshire	673,040,000						
2000D, New Hampshire	495,976,000						
2000S, New Hampshire	(4,020,172)						
2000S, New Hampshire, Silver	(965,421)						
2000P, Virginia	943,000,000						
2000D, Virginia	651,616,000						
2000S, Virginia	(4,020,172)						
2000S, Virginia, Silver	(965,421)						

Date	Quantity Minted	MS-63	MS-65	PF-65			Notes
2001P, New York	655,400,000						
2001D, New York	619,640,000						
2001S, New York	(3,094,140)						
2001S, New York, Silver	(889,697)						
2001P, North Carolina	627,600,000						
2001D, North Carolina	427,876,000						

Date	Quantity Minted	MS-63	MS-65	PF-65				Notes
2001S, North Carolina	(3,094,140)							
2001S, North Carolina, Silver	(889,697)							
2001P, Rhode Island	423,000,000							
2001D, Rhode Island	447,100,000							
2001S, Rhode Island	(3,094,140)							
2001S, Rhode Island, Silver	(889,697)							
2001P, Vermont	423,400,000							
2001D, Vermont	459,404,000							
2001S, Vermont	(3,094,140)							
2001S, Vermont, Silver	(889,697)							
2001P, Kentucky	353,000,000							
2001D, Kentucky	370,564,000							
2001S, Kentucky	(3,094,140)							
2001S, Kentucky, Silver	(889,697)							

Date	Quantity Minted	MS-63	MS-65	PF-65				Notes
2002P, Tennessee	361,600,000							
2002D, Tennessee	286,468,000							
2002S, Tennessee	(3,084,245)							
2002S, Tennessee, Silver	(892,229)							
2002P, Ohio	217,200,000							
2002D, Ohio	414,832,000							
2002S, Ohio	(3,084,245)							
2002S, Ohio, Silver	(892,229)							
2002P, Louisiana	362,000,000							
2002D, Louisiana	402,204,000							
2002S, Louisiana	(3,084,245)							
2002S, Louisiana, Silver	(892,229)							
2002P, Indiana	362,600,000							
2002D, Indiana	327,200,000							
2002S, Indiana	(3,084,245)							
2002S, Indiana, Silver	(892,229)							
2002P, Mississippi	290,000,000							
2002D, Mississippi	289,600,000							
2002S, Mississippi	(3,084,245)							
2002S, Mississippi, Silver	(892,229)							

Date	Quantity Minted	MS-63	MS-65	PF-65		Notes
2003P, Illinois	225,800,000					
2003D, Illinois	237,400,000					
2003S, Illinois	(3,408,516)					
2003S, Illinois, Silver	(1,125,755)					
2003P, Alabama	225,000,000					
2003D, Alabama	232,400,000					
2003S, Alabama	(3,408,516)					
2003S, Alabama, Silver	(1,125,755)					
2003P, Maine	217,400,000					
2003D, Maine	231,400,000					
2003S, Maine	(3,408,516)					
2003S, Maine, Silver	(1,125,755)					
2003P, Missouri	225,000,000					
2003D, Missouri	228,200,000					
2003S, Missouri	(3,408,516)					
2003S, Missouri, Silver	(1,125,755)					
2003P, Arkansas	228,000,000					
2003D, Arkansas	229,800,000					
2003S, Arkansas	(3,408,516)					
2003S, Arkansas, Silver	(1,125,755)					

Date	Quantity Minted	MS-63	MS-65	PF-65		Notes
2004P, Michigan	233,800,000					
2004D, Michigan	225,800,000					
2004S, Michigan	(2,740,684)					
2004S, Michigan, Silver	(1,769,786)					
2004P, Florida	240,200,000					
2004D, Florida	241,600,000					
2004S, Florida	(2,740,684)					
2004S, Florida, Silver	(1,769,786)					
2004P, Texas	278,800,000					
2004D, Texas	263,000,000					

Date		Quantity Minted	MS-63	MS-65	PF-65				Notes
2004S, Texas	(2,740,684)								
2004S, Texas, Silver	(1,769,786)								
2004P, Iowa		213,800,000							
2004D, Iowa		251,400,000							
2004S, Iowa	(2,740,684)								
2004S, Iowa, Silver	(1,769,786)								
2004P, Wisconsin		226,400,000							
2004D, Wisconsin		226,800,000							
2004D, Wisconsin, Extra Leaf High									
2004D, Wisconsin, Extra Leaf Low									
2004S, Wisconsin	(2,740,684)								
2004S, Wisconsin, Silver	(1,769,786)								

Date		Quantity Minted	MS-63	MS-65	PF-65				Notes
2005P, California		257,200,000							
2005D, California		263,200,000							
2005S, California	(3,262,960)								
2005S, California, Silver	(1,678,649)								
2005P, Minnesota		239,600,000							
2005D, Minnesota		248,400,000							
2005S, Minnesota	(3,262,960)								
2005S, Minnesota, Silver	(1,678,649)								
2005P, Oregon		316,200,000							
2005D, Oregon		404,000,000							
2005S, Oregon	(3,262,960)								
2005S, Oregon, Silver	(1,678,649)								
2005P, Kansas		263,400,000							
2005D, Kansas		300,000,000							
2005S, Kansas	(3,262,960)								
2005S, Kansas, Silver	(1,678,649)								
2005P, West Virginia		365,400,000							
2005D, West Virginia		356,200,000							
2005S, West Virginia	(3,262,960)								
2005S, West Virginia, Silver	(1,678,649)								

Date	Quantity Minted	MS-63	MS-65	PF-65				Notes
2006P, Nevada	277,000,000							
2006D, Nevada	312,800,000							
2006S, Nevada	(2,882,428)							
2006S, Nevada, Silver	(1,585,008)							
2006P, Nebraska	318,000,000							
2006D, Nebraska	273,000,000							
2006S, Nebraska	(2,882,428)							
2006S, Nebraska, Silver	(1,585,008)							
2006P, Colorado	274,800,000							
2006D, Colorado	294,200,000							
2006S, Colorado	(2,882,428)							
2006S, Colorado, Silver	(1,585,008)							
2006P, North Dakota	305,800,000							
2006D, North Dakota	359,000,000							
2006S, North Dakota	(2,882,428)							
2006S, North Dakota, Silver	(1,585,008)							
2006P, South Dakota	245,000,000							
2006D, South Dakota	265,800,000							
2006S, South Dakota	(2,882,428)							
2006S, South Dakota, Silver	(1,585,008)							

Date	Quantity Minted	MS-63	MS-65	PF-65				Notes
2007P, Montana	257,000,000							
2007D, Montana	256,240,000							
2007S, Montana	(2,374,778)							
2007S, Montana, Silver	(1,313,481)							
2007P, Washington	265,200,000							
2007D, Washington	280,000,000							
2007S, Washington	(2,374,778)							
2007S, Washington, Silver	(1,313,481)							
2007P, Idaho	294,600,000							
2007D, Idaho	286,800,000							

Date	Quantity Minted	MS-63	MS-65	PF-65			Notes
2007S, Idaho	(2,374,778)						
2007S, Idaho, Silver	(1,313,481)						
2007P, Wyoming	243,600,000						
2007D, Wyoming	320,800,000						
2007S, Wyoming	(2,374,778)						
2007S, Wyoming, Silver	(1,313,481)						
2007P, Utah	255,000,000						
2007D, Utah	253,200,000						
2007S, Utah	(2,374,778)						
2007S, Utah, Silver	(1,313,481)						

Date	Quantity Minted	MS-63	MS-65	PF-65			Notes
2008P, Oklahoma	222,000,000						
2008D, Oklahoma	194,600,000						
2008S, Oklahoma	(2,078,112)						
2008S, Oklahoma, Silver	(1,192,908)						
2008P, New Mexico	244,200,000						
2008D, New Mexico	244,400,000						
2008S, New Mexico	(2,078,112)						
2008S, New Mexico, Silver	(1,192,908)						
2008P, Arizona	244,600,000						
2008D, Arizona	265,000,000						
2008S, Arizona	(2,078,112)						
2008S, Arizona, Silver	(1,192,908)						
2008P, Alaska	251,800,000						
2008D, Alaska	254,000,000						
2008S, Alaska	(2,078,112)						
2008S, Alaska, Silver	(1,192,908)						
2008P, Hawaii	254,000,000						
2008D, Hawaii	263,600,000						
2008S, Hawaii	(2,078,112)						
2008S, Hawaii, Silver	(1,192,908)						

District of Columbia and U.S. Territories (2009)

Date	Quantity Minted	MS-63	MS-65	PF-65				Notes
2009P, District of Columbia	83,600,000							
2009D, District of Columbia	88,800,000							
2009S, District of Columbia	(2,113,478)							
2009S, District of Columbia, Silver	(996,548)							
2009P, Puerto Rico	53,200,000							
2009D, Puerto Rico	86,000,000							
2009S, Puerto Rico	(2,113,478)							
2009S, Puerto Rico, Silver	(996,548)							
2009P, Guam	45,000,000							
2009D, Guam	42,600,000							
2009S, Guam	(2,113,478)							
2009S, Guam, Silver	(996,548)							
2009P, American Samoa	42,600,000							
2009D, American Samoa	39,600,000							
2009S, American Samoa	(2,113,478)							
2009S, American Samoa, Silver	(996,548)							
2009P, U.S. Virgin Islands	41,000,000							
2009D, U.S. Virgin Islands	41,000,000							
2009S, U.S. Virgin Islands	(2,113,478)							
2009S, U.S. Virgin Islands, Silver	(996,548)							
2009P, Northern Mariana Islands	35,200,000							
2009D, Northern Mariana Islands	37,600,000							
2009S, Northern Mariana Islands	(2,113,478)							
2009S, Northern Mariana Islands, Silver	(996,548)							

America the Beautiful™ (2010–2021)

Date	Quantity Minted	MS-63	MS-65	PF-65			Notes
2010P, Hot Springs National Park (AR)	35,600,000						
2010D, Hot Springs National Park (AR)	34,000,000						
2010S, Hot Springs National Park (AR)	(1,402,889)						
2010S, Hot Springs Nat'l Park (AR), Silver	(859,417)						
2010P, Yellowstone National Park (WY)	33,600,000						
2010D, Yellowstone National Park (WY)	34,800,000						
2010S, Yellowstone National Park (WY)	(1,404,259)						
2010S, Yellowstone Nat'l Park (WY), Silver	(859,417)						
2010P, Yosemite National Park (CA)	35,200,000						
2010D, Yosemite National Park (CA)	34,800,000						
2010S, Yosemite National Park (CA)	(1,401,522)						
2010S, Yosemite National Park (CA), Silver	(859,417)						
2010P, Grand Canyon National Park (AZ)	34,800,000						
2010D, Grand Canyon Nat'l Park (AZ)	35,400,000						
2010S, Grand Canyon Nat'l Park (AZ)	(1,401,462)						
2010S, Grand Canyon Nat'l Park (AZ), Silv	(859,417)						
2010P, Mt. Hood National Forest (OR)	34,400,000						
2010D, Mt. Hood National Forest (OR)	34,400,000						
2010S, Mt. Hood National Forest (OR)	(1,398,106)						
2010S, Mt. Hood Nat'l Forest (OR), Silver	(859,417)						

Date	Quantity Minted	MS-63	MS-65	PF-65			Notes
2011P, Gettysburg Nat'l Mil Park (PA)	30,800,000						
2011D, Gettysburg Nat'l Mil Park (PA)	30,400,000						
2011S, Gettysburg Nat'l Mil Park (PA)	(1,273,068)						
2011S, Gettysburg Nat'l Mil Park (PA), Silver	(722,076)						
2011P, Glacier National Park (MT)	30,400,000						
2011D, Glacier National Park (MT)	31,200,000						
2011S, Glacier National Park (MT)	(1,269,422)						
2011S, Glacier National Park (MT), Silver	(722,076)						
2011P, Olympic National Park (WA)	30,400,000						
2011D, Olympic National Park (WA)	30,600,000						

Date	Quantity Minted	MS-63	MS-65	PF-65				Notes
2011S, Olympic National Park (WA)	(1,268,231)							
2011S, Olympic National Park (WA), Silver	(722,076)							
2011P, Vicksburg Nat'l Mil Park (MS)	30,800,000							
2011D, Vicksburg Nat'l Mil Park (MS)	33,400,000							
2011S, Vicksburg Nat'l Mil Park (MS)	(1,268,623)							
2011S, Vicksburg Nat'l Mil Park (MS), Silver	(722,076)							
2011P, Chickasaw Nat'l Rec Area (OK)	73,800,000							
2011D, Chickasaw Nat'l Rec Area (OK)	69,400,000							
2011S, Chickasaw Nat'l Rec Area (OK)	(1,266,825)							
2011S, Chickasaw Nat'l Rec Area (OK), Silv	(722,076)							

Date	Quantity Minted	MS-63	MS-65	PF-65				Notes
2012P, El Yunque Nat'l Forest (PR)	25,800,000							
2012D, El Yunque Nat'l Forest (PR)	25,000,000							
2012S, El Yunque Nat'l Forest (PR)	1,680,140							
2012S, El Yunque Nat'l Forest (PR)	(1,012,094)							
2012S, El Yunque Nat'l Forest (PR), Silver	(608,060)							
2012P, Chaco Culture Nat'l Historical Park (NM)	22,000,000							
2012D, Chaco Culture Nat'l Historical Park (NM)	22,000,000							
2012S, Chaco Culture Nat'l Historical Park (NM)	1,389,020							
2012S, Chaco Culture Nat'l Historical Park (NM)	(961,464)							
2012S, Chaco Culture Nat'l Historical Park (NM), Silver	(608,060)							
2012P, Acadia Nat'l Park (Maine)	24,800,000							
2012D, Acadia Nat'l Park (Maine)	21,606,000							
2012S, Acadia Nat'l Park (Maine)	1,409,120							
2012S, Acadia Nat'l Park (Maine)	(962,038)							
2012S, Acadia Nat'l Park (Maine), Silver	(608,060)							
2012P, Hawai'i Volcanoes Nat'l Park (HI)	46,200,000							
2012D, Hawai'i Volcanoes Nat'l Park (HI)	78,600,000							
2012S, Hawai'i Volcanoes Nat'l Park (HI)	1,409,120							
2012S, Hawai'i Volcanoes Nat'l Park (HI)	(962,447)							
2012S, Hawai'i Volcanoes Nat'l Park (HI), Silver	(608,060)							
2012P, Denali Nat'l Park and Preserve (AK)	135,400,000							
2012D, Denali Nat'l Park and Preserve (AK)	166,600,000							
2012S, Denali Nat'l Park and Preserve (AK)	1,409,220							
2012S, Denali Nat'l Park and Preserve (AK)	(959,602)							
2012S, Denali Nat'l Park and Preserve (AK), Silver	(608,060)							

Date	Quantity Minted	MS-63	MS-65	PF-65			Notes
2013P, White Mountain National Forest (NH)	68,800,000						
2013D, White Mountain National Forest (NH)	107,600,000						
2013S, White Mountain National Forest (NH)	1,606,900						
2013S, White Mountain National Forest (NH)	(989,803)						
2013S, White Mountain National Forest (NH), Silver	(467,691)						
2013P, Perry's Victory and Int'l Peace Memorial (OH)	107,800,000						
2013D, Perry's Victory and Int'l Peace Memorial (OH)	131,600,000						
2013S, Perry's Victory and Int'l Peace Memorial (OH)	1,425,860						
2013S, Perry's Victory and Int'l Peace Memorial (OH)	(947,815)						
2013S, Perry's Victory and Int'l Peace Memorial (OH), Silver	(467,691)						
2013P, Great Basin National Park (NV)	122,400,000						
2013D, Great Basin National Park (NV)	141,400,000						
2013S, Great Basin National Park (NV)	1,316,500						
2013S, Great Basin National Park (NV)	(945,777)						
2013S, Great Basin National Park (NV), Silver	(467,691)						
2013P, Ft. McHenry National Monument / Historic Shrine (MD)	120,000,000						
2013D, Ft. McHenry National Monument / Historic Shrine (MD)	151,400,000						
2013S, Ft. McHenry National Monument / Historic Shrine (MD)	1,313,680						
2013S, Ft. McHenry National Monument / Historic Shrine (MD)	(946,380)						
2013S, Ft. McHenry National Monument / Historic Shrine (MD), Silver	(467,691)						
2013P, Mount Rushmore National Memorial (SD)	231,800,000						
2013D, Mount Rushmore National Memorial (SD)	272,400,000						
2013S, Mount Rushmore National Memorial (SD)	1,373,260						
2013S, Mount Rushmore National Memorial (SD)	(958,853)						
2013S, Mount Rushmore National Memorial (SD), Silver	(467,691)						

Date	Quantity Minted	MS-63	MS-65	PF-65		Notes
2014P, Great Smoky Mountains National Park (TN)	73,200,000					
2014D, Great Smoky Mountains National Park (TN)	99,400,000					
2014S, Great Smoky Mountains National Park (TN)	1,360,780					
2014S, Great Smoky Mountains National Park (TN)	(881,896)					
2014S, Great Smoky Mountains National Park (TN), Silver	(472,107)					
2014P, Shenandoah National Park (VA)	112,800,000					
2014D, Shenandoah National Park (VA)	197,800,000					
2014S, Shenandoah National Park (VA)	1,266,720					
2014S, Shenandoah National Park (VA)	(846,441)					
2014S, Shenandoah National Park (VA), Silver	(472,107)					
2014P, Arches National Park (UT)	214,200,000					
2014D, Arches National Park (UT)	251,400,000					
2014S, Arches National Park (UT)	1,235,940					
2014S, Arches National Park (UT)	(844,775)					
2014S, Arches National Park (UT), Silver	(472,107)					
2014P, Great Sand Dunes National Park (CO)	159,600,000					
2014D, Great Sand Dunes National Park (CO)	171,800,000					
2014S, Great Sand Dunes National Park (CO)	1,176,760					
2014S, Great Sand Dunes National Park (CO)	(843,238)					
2014S, Great Sand Dunes National Park (CO), Silver	(472,107)					
2014P, Everglades National Park (FL)	157,601,200					
2014D, Everglades National Park (FL)	142,400,000					
2014S, Everglades National Park (FL)	1,180,900					
2014S, Everglades National Park (FL)	(856,139)					
2014S, Everglades National Park (FL), Silver	(472,107)					

Date	Quantity Minted	MS-63	MS-65	PF-65			Notes
2015P, Homestead National Monument of America (NE)	214,400,000						
2015D, Homestead National Monument of America (NE)	248,600,000						
2015S, Homestead National Monument of America (NE)	1,153,840						
2015S, Homestead National Monument of America (NE)	(831,503)						
2015S, Homestead National Monument of America (NE), Silver	(490,829)						
2015P, Kisatchie National Forest (LA)	397,200,000						
2015D, Kisatchie National Forest (LA)	379,600,000						
2015S, Kisatchie National Forest (LA)	1,099,380						
2015S, Kisatchie National Forest (LA)	(762,407)						
2015S, Kisatchie National Forest (LA), Silver	(490,829)						
2015P, Blue Ridge Parkway (NC)	325,616,000						
2015D, Blue Ridge Parkway (NC)	505,200,000						
2015S, Blue Ridge Parkway (NC)	1,096,620						
2015S, Blue Ridge Parkway (NC)	(762,407)						
2015S, Blue Ridge Parkway (NC), Silver	(490,829)						
2015P, Bombay Hook National Wildlife Refuge (DE)	275,000,000						
2015D, Bombay Hook National Wildlife Refuge (DE)	206,400,000						
2015S, Bombay Hook National Wildlife Refuge (DE)	1,013,920						
2015S, Bombay Hook National Wildlife Refuge (DE)	(762,407)						
2015S, Bombay Hook National Wildlife Refuge (DE), Silver	(490,829)						
2015P, Saratoga National Historical Park (NY)	223,000,000						
2015D, Saratoga National Historical Park (NY)	215,800,000						
2015S, Saratoga National Historical Park (NY)	1,045,500						
2015S, Saratoga National Historical Park (NY)	(791,347)						
2015S, Saratoga National Historical Park (NY), Silver	(490,829)						

2016-W Standing Liberty Centennial Gold Coin

Date	Quantity Minted	MS-63	MS-65	PF-65		Notes
2016W, Standing Liberty Centennial Gold Coin	91,752					
2016P, Shawnee National Forest (IL)	155,600,000					
2016D, Shawnee National Forest (IL)	151,800,000					
2016S, Shawnee National Forest (IL)	1,066,440					
2016S, Shawnee National Forest (IL)	(732,039)					
2016S, Shawnee National Forest (IL), Silver	(515,205)					
2016P, Cumberland Gap National Historical Park (KY)	215,400,000					
2016D, Cumberland Gap National Historical Park (KY)	223,200,000					
2016S, Cumberland Gap National Historical Park (KY)	1,021,120					
2016S, Cumberland Gap National Historical Park (KY)	(701,831)					
2016S, Cumberland Gap National Historical Park (KY), Silver	(515,205)					
2016P, Harpers Ferry National Historical Park (WV)	434,630,000					
2016D, Harpers Ferry National Historical Park (WV)	424,000,000					
2016S, Harpers Ferry National Historical Park (WV)	1,035,840					
2016S, Harpers Ferry National Historical Park (WV)	(701,203)					
2016S, Harpers Ferry National Historical Park (WV), Silver	(515,205)					
2016P, Theodore Roosevelt National Park (ND)	231,600,000					
2016D, Theodore Roosevelt National Park (ND)	223,200,000					
2016S, Theodore Roosevelt National Park (ND)	1,057,020					
2016S, Theodore Roosevelt National Park (ND)	(702,930)					
2016S, Theodore Roosevelt National Park (ND), Silver	(515,205)					
2016P, Fort Moultrie (Fort Sumter National Monument) (SC)	154,400,000					
2016D, Fort Moultrie (Fort Sumter National Monument) (SC)	142,200,000					
2016S, Fort Moultrie (Fort Sumter National Monument) (SC)	966,260					

Date	Quantity Minted	MS-63	MS-65	PF-65			Notes
2016S, Fort Moultrie (Fort Sumter National Monument) (SC)	(717,049)						
2016S, Fort Moultrie (Fort Sumter National Monument) (SC), Silver	(515,205)						

Date	Quantity Minted	MS-63	MS-65	PF-65			Notes
2017P, Effigy Mounds National Monument (IA)	271,200,000						
2017D, Effigy Mounds National Monument (IA)	210,800,000						
2017S, Effigy Mounds National Monument (IA)	931,340						
2017S, Effigy Mounds National Monument (IA), Enhanced Unc.							
2017S, Effigy Mounds National Monument (IA)	(706,042)						
2017S, Effigy Mounds National Monument (IA), Silver	(496,626)						
2017P, Frederick Douglass National Historic Site (DC)	184,800,000						
2017D, Frederick Douglass National Historic Site (DC)	185,800,000						
2017S, Frederick Douglass National Historic Site (DC)	934,940						
2017S, Frederick Douglass National Historic Site (DC), Enhanced Unc.							
2017S, Frederick Douglass National Historic Site (DC)	(672,188)						
2017S, Frederick Douglass National Historic Site (DC), Silver	(496,626)						
2017P, Ozark National Scenic Riverways (MO)	203,000,000						
2017D, Ozark National Scenic Riverways (MO)	200,000,000						
2017S, Ozark National Scenic Riverways (MO)	906,840						
2017S, Ozark National Scenic Riverways (MO), Enhanced Unc.							
2017S, Ozark National Scenic Riverways (MO)	(671,902)						
2017S, Ozark National Scenic Riverways (MO), Silver	(496,626)						
2017P, Ellis Island (Statue of Liberty National Monument) (NJ)	234,000,000						
2017D, Ellis Island (Statue of Liberty National Monument) (NJ)	254,000,000						
2017S, Ellis Island (Statue of Liberty National Monument) (NJ)	956,200						
2017S, Ellis Island (Statue of Liberty National Monument) (NJ), Enhanced Unc.							
2017S, Ellis Island (Statue of Liberty National Monument) (NJ)	(674,537)						
2017S, Ellis Island (Statue of Liberty National Monument) (NJ), Silver	(496,626)						

Date	Quantity Minted	MS-63	MS-65	PF-65			Notes
2017P, George Rogers Clark National Historical Park (IN)	191,600,000						
2017D, George Rogers Clark National Historical Park (IN)	180,800,000						
2017S, George Rogers Clark National Historical Park (IN)	919,060						
2017S, George Rogers Clark National Historical Park (IN), Enhanced Unc.							
2017S, George Rogers Clark National Historical Park (IN)	(689,235)						
2017S, George Rogers Clark National Historical Park (IN), Silver	(496,626)						

Date	Quantity Minted	MS-63	MS-65	PF-65			Notes
2018P, Pictured Rocks National Lakeshore (MI)	186,714,000						
2018D, Pictured Rocks National Lakeshore (MI)	182,600,000						
2018S, Pictured Rocks National Lakeshore (MI)	917,580						
2018S, Pictured Rocks National Lakeshore (MI)	(688,538)						
2018S, Pictured Rocks National Lakeshore (MI), Silver	(350,820)						
2018P, Apostle Islands National Lakeshore (WI)	223,200,000						
2018D, Apostle Islands National Lakeshore (WI)	216,600,000						
2018S, Apostle Islands National Lakeshore (WI)	871,820						
2018S, Apostle Islands National Lakeshore (WI)	(659,633)						
2018S, Apostle Islands National Lakeshore (WI), Silver	(350,820)						
2018P, Voyageurs National Park (MN)	237,400,000						
2018D, Voyageurs National Park (MN)	197,800,000						
2018S, Voyageurs National Park (MN)	831,560						
2018S, Voyageurs National Park (MN)	(659,448)						
2018S, Voyageurs National Park (MN), Silver	(350,820)						
2018P, Cumberland Island National Seashore (GA)	138,000,000						
2018D, Cumberland Island National Seashore (GA)	151,600,000						
2018S, Cumberland Island National Seashore (GA)	816,660						
2018S, Cumberland Island National Seashore (GA)	(658,438)						
2018S, Cumberland Island National Seashore (GA), Silver	(350,820)						
2018P, Block Island National Wildlife Refuge (RI)	159,600,000						
2018D, Block Island National Wildlife Refuge (RI)	159,600,000						

Date	Quantity Minted	MS-63	MS-65	PF-65			Notes
2018S, Block Island National Wildlife Refuge (RI)	764,660						
2018S, Block Island National Wildlife Refuge (RI)	(675,567)						
2018S, Block Island National Wildlife Refuge (RI), Silver	(350,820)						

Date	Quantity Minted	MS-63	MS-65	PF-65			Notes
2019P, Lowell National Historical Park (MA)							
2019D, Lowell National Historical Park (MA)							
2019S, Lowell National Historical Park (MA)							
2019S, Lowell National Historical Park (MA)							
2019S, Lowell National Historical Park (MA), Silver							
2019W, Lowell National Historical Park (MA)							
2019P, American Memorial Park (Northern Mariana Islands)							
2019D, American Memorial Park (Northern Mariana Islands)							
2019S, American Memorial Park (Northern Mariana Islands)							
2019S, American Memorial Park (Northern Mariana Islands)							
2019S, American Memorial Park (Northern Mariana Islands), Silver							
2019W, American Memorial Park (Northern Mariana Islands)							
2019P, San Antonio Missions National Historical Park (TX)							
2019D, San Antonio Missions National Historical Park (TX)							
2019S, San Antonio Missions National Historical Park (TX)							
2019S, San Antonio Missions National Historical Park (TX)							
2019S, San Antonio Missions National Historical Park (TX), Silver							
2019W, San Antonio Missions National Historical Park (TX)							
2019P, War in the Pacific National Historical Park (Guam)							
2019D, War in the Pacific National Historical Park (Guam)							
2019S, War in the Pacific National Historical Park (Guam)							
2019S, War in the Pacific National Historical Park (Guam)							

Date	Quantity Minted	MS-63	MS-65	PF-65		Notes
2019S, War in the Pacific National Historical Park (Guam), Silver						
2019W, War in the Pacific National Historical Park (Guam)						
2019P, Frank Church River of No Return Wilderness (ID)						
2019D, Frank Church River of No Return Wilderness (ID)						
2019S, Frank Church River of No Return Wilderness (ID)						
2019S, Frank Church River of No Return Wilderness (ID)						
2019S, Frank Church River of No Return Wilderness (ID), Silver						
2019W, Frank Church River of No Return Wilderness (ID)						

Date	Quantity Minted	MS-63	MS-65	PF-65		Notes
2020P, National Park of American Samoa (American Samoa)						
2020D, National Park of American Samoa (American Samoa)						
2020S, National Park of American Samoa (American Samoa)						
2020S, National Park of American Samoa (American Samoa)						
2020S, National Park of American Samoa (American Samoa), Silver						
2020W, National Park of American Samoa (American Samoa)						
2020P, Weir Farm National Historic Site (CT)						
2020D, Weir Farm National Historic Site (CT)						
2020S, Weir Farm National Historic Site (CT)						
2020S, Weir Farm National Historic Site (CT)						
2020S, Weir Farm National Historic Site (CT), Silver						
2020W, Weir Farm National Historic Site (CT)						
2020P, Salt River Bay National Historical Park and Ecological Preserve (USVI)						
2020D, Salt River Bay National Historical Park and Ecological Preserve (USVI)						
2020S, Salt River Bay National Historical Park and Ecological Preserve (USVI)						
2020S, Salt River Bay National Historical Park and Ecological Preserve (USVI)	.					
2020S, Salt River Bay National Historical Park and Ecological Preserve (USVI), Silver						

Date	Quantity Minted	MS-63	MS-65	PF-65			Notes
2020W, Salt River Bay National Historical Park and Ecological Preserve (USVI)							
2020P, Marsh-Billings-Rockefeller National Historical Park (VT)							
2020D, Marsh-Billings-Rockefeller National Historical Park (VT)							
2020S, Marsh-Billings-Rockefeller National Historical Park (VT)							
2020S, Marsh-Billings-Rockefeller National Historical Park (VT)							
2020S, Marsh-Billings-Rockefeller National Historical Park (VT), Silver							
2020W, Marsh-Billings-Rockefeller National Historical Park (VT)							
2020P, Tallgrass Prairie National Preserve (KS)							
2020D, Tallgrass Prairie National Preserve (KS)							
2020S, Tallgrass Prairie National Preserve (KS)							
2020S, Tallgrass Prairie National Preserve (KS)							
2020S, Tallgrass Prairie National Preserve (KS), Silver							
2020W, Tallgrass Prairie National Preserve (KS)							

Date	Quantity Minted	MS-63	MS-65	PF-65			Notes
2021P, Tuskegee Airmen National Historic Site (AL)							
2021D, Tuskegee Airmen National Historic Site (AL)							
2021S, Tuskegee Airmen National Historic Site (AL)							
2021S, Tuskegee Airmen National Historic Site (AL)							
2021S, Tuskegee Airmen National Historic Site (AL), Silver							
2021W, Tuskegee Airmen National Historic Site (AL)							
2022P							
2022D							
2022S							
2022S, Silver							

HALF DOLLARS

Flowing Hair (1794–1795)

Date	Quantity Minted	AG-3	G-4	VG-8	F-12	VF-20	EF-40	Notes
1794	23,464							
1795, Normal Date								
1795, Recut Date	299,680							
1795, 3 Leaves Under Each Wing								

Draped Bust, Small Eagle Reverse (1796–1797)

Date	Quantity Minted	AG-3	G-4	VG-8	F-12	VF-20	EF-40	Notes
1796, 15 Stars								
1796, 16 Stars	3,918							
1797, 15 Stars								

Draped Bust, Heraldic Eagle Reverse (1801–1807)

Date	Quantity Minted	G-4	VG-8	F-12	VF-20	EF-40	MS-60	Notes
1801	30,289							
1802	29,890							

Date	Quantity Minted	G-4	VG-8	F-12	VF-20	EF-40	MS-60	Notes
1803, Small 3	188,234							
1803, Large 3								
1805, 5 Over 4	211,722							
1805, Normal Date								
1806, 6 Over 5	839,576							
1806, 6 Over Inverted 6								
1806, Knobbed 6, Large Stars (Traces of Overdate)								
1806, Knobbed 6, Small Stars								
1806, Knobbed 6, Stem Not Through Claw								
1806, Pointed 6, Stem Through Claw								
1806, E Over A in STATES								
1806, Pointed 6, Stem Not Through Claw								
1807	301,076							

Capped Bust, Lettered Edge, First Style (1807–1808)

Date	Quantity Minted	G-4	VG-8	F-12	VF-20	EF-40	MS-60	Notes
1807, Small Stars	750,500							
1807, Large Stars								
1807, Large Stars, 50 Over 20								
1807, "Bearded" Liberty								
1808, 8 Over 7	1,368,600							
1808								

Capped Bust, Lettered Edge, Remodeled Portrait and Eagle (1809–1836)

Date	Quantity Minted	G-4	VG-8	F-12	VF-20	EF-40	MS-60	Notes
1809, Normal Edge								
1809, xxxx Edge	1,405,810							
1809, lllll Edge								
1810	1,276,276							
1811, (18.11), 11 Over 10								
1811, Small 8	1,203,644							
1811, Large 8								
1812, 2 Over 1, Small 8								
1812, 2 Over 1, Large 8								
1812	1,628,059							
1812, Single Leaf Below Wing								
1813								
1813, 50 C. Over UNI	1,241,903							
1814, 4 Over 3								
1814, E Over A in STATES								
1814	1,039,075							
1814, Single Leaf Below Wing								
1815, 5 Over 2	47,150							
1817, 7 Over 3								
1817, 7 Over 4 (8 known)								
1817, Dated 181.7	1,215,567							
1817								
1817, Single Leaf Below Wing								
1818, 8 Over 7, Small 8								
1818, 8 Over 7, Large 8	1,960,322							
1818								
1819, Small 9 Over 8								
1819, Large 9 Over 8	2,208,000							
1819								
1820, 20 Over 19, Square 2								
1820, 20 Over 19, Curl Base 2								
1820, Curl Base 2, Small Date								
1820, Square Base Knob 2, Large Date	751,122							
1820, Square Base No Knob 2, Large Date								
1820, No Serifs on E's								

Date	Quantity Minted	G-4	VG-8	F-12	VF-20	EF-40	MS-60	Notes
1821	1,305,797							
1822	1,559,573							
1822, 2 Over 1								
1823, Broken 3	1,694,200							
1823, Patched 3								
1823, Ugly 3								
1823, Normal								
1824, 4 Over Various Dates	3,504,954							
1824, 4 Over 1								
1824, 4 Over 4 (2 varieties)								
1824, Normal								
1825	2,943,166							
1826	4,004,180							
1827, 7 Over 6	5,493,400							
1827, Square Base 2								
1827, Curl Base 2								
1828, Curl Base No Knob 2	3,075,200							
1828, Curl Base Knob 2								
1828, Square Base 2, Large 8's								
1828, Square Base 2, Small 8's, Large Letters								
1828, Square Base 2, Small 8's and Letters								
1829, 9 Over 7	3,712,156							
1829								
1829, Large Letters								
1830, Small 0	4,764,800							
1830, Large 0								
1830, Large Letters								
1831	5,873,660							
1832	4,797,000							
1832, Large Letters								
1833	5,206,000							
1834, Large Date and Letters	6,412,004							
1834, Large Date, Small Letters								
1834, Small Date, Stars, Letters								
1835	5,352,006							
1836	6,545,000							
1836, 1836 Over 1336								
1836, 50 Over 00								
1836, Beaded Border on Reverse								

Capped Bust, Reeded Edge, Reverse 50 CENTS (1836–1837)

Date	Quantity Minted	G-4	VG-8	F-12	VF-20	EF-40	MS-60	Notes
1836	*1,200+*							
1837	3,629,820							

Capped Bust, Reeded Edge, Reverse HALF DOL. (1838–1839)

Date	Quantity Minted	G-4	VG-8	F-12	VF-20	EF-40	MS-60	Notes
1838	3,546,000							
1838O	20							
1839	1,392,976							
1839, Small Letters Reverse *(extremely rare)*								
1839O	116,000							

Liberty Seated, Variety 1, No Motto Above Eagle (1839–1853)

Date	Quantity Minted	G-4	VG-8	F-12	VF-20	EF-40	MS-60	Notes
1839, No Drapery From Elbow	1,972,400							
1839, Drapery From Elbow								

Date	Quantity Minted	G-4	VG-8	F-12	VF-20	EF-40	MS-60		Notes
1840, Small Letters	1,435,008								
1840, Medium Letters									
1840O	855,100								
1841	310,000								
1841O	401,000								
1842, Small Date, Small Letters	*								
1842O, Small Date, Small Letters	203,000								
1842, Medium Date	2,012,764								
1842, Small Date									
1842O, Medium Date	754,000								
1843	3,844,000								
1843O	2,268,000								
1844	1,766,000								
1844O	2,005,000								
1844O, Doubled Date									
1845	589,000								
1845O	2,094,000								
1845O, No Drapery									
1846, Medium Date	2,210,000								
1846, Tall Date									
1846, 6 Over Horizontal 6									
1846O, Medium Date	2,304,000								
1846O, Tall Date									
1847, 7 Over 6	1,156,000								
1847									
1847O	2,584,000								
1848	580,000								
1848O	3,180,000								
1849	1,252,000								
1849O	2,310,000								
1850	227,000								
1850O	2,456,000								
1851	200,750								
1851O	402,000								
1852	77,130								
1852O	144,000								
1853O (4 known)									

* Included in 1842, Medium Date mintage.

Liberty Seated, Variety 2, Arrows at Date, Rays Around Eagle (1853)

Date	Quantity Minted	G-4	VG-8	F-12	VF-20	EF-40	MS-60	Notes
1853	3,532,708							
1853O	1,328,000							

Liberty Seated, Variety 3, Arrows at Date, No Rays (1854–1855)

Date	Quantity Minted	G-4	VG-8	F-12	VF-20	EF-40	MS-60	Notes
1854	2,982,000							
1854O	5,240,000							
1855 Over 1854	759,500							
1855, Normal Date								
1855O	3,688,000							
1855S	129,950							

Liberty Seated, Variety 1 Resumed, With Weight Standard of Variety 2 (1856–1866)

Date	Quantity Minted	VG-8	F-12	VF-20	EF-40	MS-60	PF-60	Notes
1856	938,000							
1856O	2,658,000							
1856S	211,000							
1857	1,988,000							
1857O	818,000							
1857S	158,000							
1858 *(300+)*	4,225,700							
1858O	7,294,000							
1858S	476,000							
1859 *(800)*	747,200							
1859O	2,834,000							
1859S	566,000							
1860 *(1,000)*	302,700							
1860O	1,290,000							
1860S	472,000							
1861 *(1,000)*	2,887,400							
1861O	2,532,633							
1861O, Cracked Obverse								
1861S	939,500							

Date		Quantity Minted	VG-8	F-12	VF-20	EF-40	MS-60	PF-60		Notes
1862	(550)	253,000								
1862S		1,352,000								
1863	(460)	503,200								
1863S		916,000								
1864	(470)	379,100								
1864S		658,000								
1865	(500)	511,400								
1865S		675,000								
1866S, No Motto		60,000								
1866 *(unique, not a regular issue)*										

Liberty Seated, Variety 4, Motto Above Eagle (1866–1873)

Date		Quantity Minted	VG-8	F-12	VF-20	EF-40	MS-60	PF-63		Notes
1866	(725)	744,900								
1866S		994,000								
1867	(625)	449,300								
1867S		1,196,000								
1868	(600)	417,600								
1868S		1,160,000								
1869	(600)	795,300								
1869S		656,000								
1870	(1,000)	633,900								
1870CC		54,617								
1870S		1,004,000								
1871	(960)	1,203,600								
1871CC		153,950								
1871S		2,178,000								
1872	(950)	880,600								
1872CC		257,000								
1872S		580,000								
1873, Close 3	(600)	587,000								
1873, Open 3		214,200								
1873CC		122,500								
1873S, No Arrows *(unknown in any collection)*		5,000								

Liberty Seated, Variety 5, Arrows at Date (1873–1874)

Date		Quantity Minted	VG-8	F-12	VF-20	EF-40	MS-60	PF-63		Notes
1873	(550)	1,815,150								
1873CC		214,560								
1873S		228,000								
1874	(700)	2,359,600								
1874CC		59,000								
1874S		394,000								

Liberty Seated, Variety 4 Resumed, With Weight Standard of Variety 5 (1875–1891)

Date		Quantity Minted	VG-8	F-12	VF-20	EF-40	MS-60	PF-63		Notes
1875	(700)	6,026,800								
1875CC		1,008,000								
1875S		3,200,000								
1876	(1,150)	8,418,000								
1876CC		1,956,000								
1876S		4,528,000								
1877	(510)	8,304,000								
1877, 7 Over 6										
1877CC		1,420,000								
1877S		5,356,000								
1878	(800)	1,377,600								
1878CC		62,000								
1878S		12,000								
1879	(1,100)	4,800								
1880	(1,355)	8,400								
1881	(975)	10,000								
1882	(1,100)	4,400								
1883	(1,039)	8,000								
1884	(875)	4,400								
1885	(930)	5,200								
1886	(886)	5,000								
1887	(710)	5,000								
1888	(832)	12,001								
1889	(711)	12,000								
1890	(590)	12,000								
1891	(600)	200,000								

Barber or Liberty Head (1892–1915)

Date		Quantity Minted	VG-8	F-12	VF-20	EF-40	MS-60	PF-63		Notes
1892	(1,245)	934,000								
1892O		390,000								
1892O, Micro O										
1892S		1,029,028								
1893	(792)	1,826,000								
1893O		1,389,000								
1893S		740,000								
1894	(972)	1,148,000								
1894O		2,138,000								
1894S		4,048,690								
1895	(880)	1,834,338								
1895O		1,766,000								
1895S		1,108,086								
1896	(762)	950,000								
1896O		924,000								
1896S		1,140,948								
1897	(731)	2,480,000								
1897O		632,000								
1897S		933,900								
1898	(735)	2,956,000								
1898O		874,000								
1898S		2,358,550								
1899	(846)	5,538,000								
1899O		1,724,000								
1899S		1,686,411								
1900	(912)	4,762,000								
1900O		2,744,000								
1900S		2,560,322								
1901	(813)	4,268,000								
1901O		1,124,000								
1901S		847,044								
1902	(777)	4,922,000								
1902O		2,526,000								
1902S		1,460,670								
1903	(755)	2,278,000								
1903O		2,100,000								

Date		Quantity Minted	VG-8	F-12	VF-20	EF-40	MS-60	PF-63		Notes
1903S		1,920,772								
1904	(670)	2,992,000								
1904O		1,117,600								
1904S		553,038								
1905	(727)	662,000								
1905O		505,000								
1905S		2,494,000								
1906	(675)	2,638,000								
1906D		4,028,000								
1906O		2,446,000								
1906S		1,740,154								
1907	(575)	2,598,000								
1907D		3,856,000								
1907O		3,946,600								
1907S		1,250,000								
1908	(545)	1,354,000								
1908D		3,280,000								
1908O		5,360,000								
1908S		1,644,828								
1909	(650)	2,368,000								
1909O		925,400								
1909S		1,764,000								
1910	(551)	418,000								
1910S		1,948,000								
1911	(543)	1,406,000								
1911D		695,080								
1911S		1,272,000								
1912	(700)	1,550,000								
1912D		2,300,800								
1912S		1,370,000								
1913	(627)	188,000								
1913D		534,000								
1913S		604,000								
1914	(380)	124,230								
1914S		992,000								
1915	(450)	138,000								
1915D		1,170,400								
1915S		1,604,000								

Liberty Walking (1916–1947)

Date	Quantity Minted	VG-8	F-12	VF-20	EF-40	MS-60	PF-63		Notes
1916	608,000								
1916D, Obverse Mintmark	1,014,400								
1916S, Obverse Mintmark	508,000								
1917	12,292,000								
1917D, Obverse Mintmark	765,400								
1917D, Reverse Mintmark	1,940,000								
1917S, Obverse Mintmark	952,000								
1917S, Reverse Mintmark	5,554,000								
1918	6,634,000								
1918D	3,853,040								
1918S	10,282,000								
1919	962,000								
1919D	1,165,000								
1919S	1,552,000								
1920	6,372,000								
1920D	1,551,000								
1920S	4,624,000								
1921	246,000								
1921D	208,000								
1921S	548,000								
1923S	2,178,000								
1927S	2,392,000								
1928S	1,940,000								
1929D	1,001,200								
1929S	1,902,000								
1933S	1,786,000								
1934	6,964,000								
1934D	2,361,000								
1934S	3,652,000								
1935	9,162,000								

Date		Quantity Minted	VG-8	F-12	VF-20	EF-40	MS-60	PF-63		Notes
1935D		3,003,800								
1935S		3,854,000								
1936	(3,901)	12,614,000								
1936D		4,252,400								
1936S		3,884,000								
1937	(5,728)	9,522,000								
1937D		1,676,000								
1937S		2,090,000								
1938	(8,152)	4,110,000								
1938D		491,600								
1939	(8,808)	6,812,000								
1939D		4,267,800								
1939S		2,552,000								
1940	(11,279)	9,156,000								
1940S		4,550,000								
1941	(15,412)	24,192,000								
1941D		11,248,400								
1941S		8,098,000								
1942	(21,120)	47,818,000								
1942D		10,973,800								
1942S		12,708,000								
1943		53,190,000								
1943D		11,346,000								
1943S		13,450,000								
1944		28,206,000								
1944D		9,769,000								
1944S		8,904,000								
1945		31,502,000								
1945D		9,966,800								
1945S		10,156,000								
1946 1946, Doubled-Die Reverse		12,118,000								
1946D		2,151,000								
1946S		3,724,000								
1947		4,094,000								
1947D		3,900,600								

Franklin (1948–1963)

Date		Quantity Minted	VF-20	EF-40	MS-60	MS-63	MS-65	PF-65		Notes
1948		3,006,814								
1948D		4,028,600								
1949		5,614,000								
1949D		4,120,600								
1949S		3,744,000								
1950	(51,386)	7,742,123								
1950D		8,031,600								
1951	(57,500)	16,802,102								
1951D		9,475,200								
1951S		13,696,000								
1952	(81,980)	21,192,093								
1952D		25,395,600								
1952S		5,526,000								
1953	(128,800)	2,668,120								
1953D		20,900,400								
1953S		4,148,000								
1954	(233,300)	13,188,202								
1954D		25,445,580								
1954S		4,993,400								
1955	(378,200)	2,498,181								
1956	(669,384)	4,032,000								
1957	(1,247,952)	5,114,000								
1957D		19,966,850								
1958	(875,652)	4,042,000								
1958D		23,962,412								
1959	(1,149,291)	6,200,000								
1959D		13,053,750								
1960	(1,691,602)	6,024,000								
1960D		18,215,812								
1961		8,290,000								
1961, Doubled-Die Proof	(3,028,244)									
1961D		20,276,442								
1962	(3,218,019)	9,714,000								
1962D		35,473,281								
1963	(3,075,645)	22,164,000								
1963D		67,069,292								

Kennedy, Silver Coinage (1964)

Date		Quantity Minted	MS-60	MS-63	MS-65	PF-65			Notes
1964	(3,950,762)	273,304,004							
1964, Hv Acc Hair									
1964D		156,205,446							

Kennedy, Silver Clad Coinage (1965–1970)

Date		Quantity Minted	MS-60	MS-63	MS-65	PF-65			Notes
1965		65,879,366							
1966		108,984,932							
1967		295,046,978							
1968D		246,951,930							
1968S	(3,041,506)								
1969D		129,881,800							
1969S	(2,934,631)								
1970D		2,150,000							
1970S	(2,632,810)								

Kennedy, Clad Coinage (1971–1974)

Date		Quantity Minted	MS-60	MS-63	MS-65	PF-65			Notes
1971		155,164,000							
1971D		302,097,424							
1971S	(3,220,733)								
1972		153,180,000							
1972D		141,890,000							
1972S	(3,260,996)								
1973		64,964,000							
1973D		83,171,400							
1973S	(2,760,339)								
1974		201,596,000							
1974D		79,066,300							
1974D, DblDie Obv									
1974S	(2,612,568)								

Kennedy, Bicentennial (Dated 1776–1976)

Date	Quantity Minted	MS-60	MS-63	MS-65	PF-65			Notes
1976	234,308,000							
1976D	287,565,248							
1976S	(7,059,099)							
1976S, Silver Clad	11,000,000							
1976S, Silver Clad	(4,000,000)							

Kennedy, Eagle Reverse Resumed (1977 to Date)

Date	Quantity Minted	MS-60	MS-63	MS-65	PF-65			Notes
1977	43,598,000							
1977D	31,449,106							
1977S	(3,251,152)							
1978	14,350,000							
1978D	13,765,799							
1978S	(3,127,781)							
1979	68,312,000							
1979D	15,815,422							
1979S, Type 1	(3,677,175)							
1979S, Type 2								
1980P	44,134,000							
1980D	33,456,449							
1980S	(3,554,806)							
1981P	29,544,000							
1981D	27,839,533							
1981S, Type 1	(4,063,083)							
1981S, Type 2								
1982P	10,819,000							
1982D	13,140,102							
1982S	(3,857,479)							
1983P	34,139,000							
1983D	32,472,244							
1983S	(3,279,126)							
1984P	26,029,000							
1984D	26,262,158							
1984S	(3,065,110)							

Date	Quantity Minted	MS-60	MS-63	MS-65	PF-65				Notes
1985P	18,706,962								
1985D	19,814,034								
1985S	(3,362,821)								
1986P	13,107,633								
1986D	15,336,145								
1986S	(3,010,497)								
1987P	2,890,758								
1987D	2,890,758								
1987S	(4,227,728)								
1988P	13,626,000								
1988D	12,000,096								
1988S	(3,262,948)								
1989P	24,542,000								
1989D	23,000,216								
1989S	(3,220,194)								
1990P	22,278,000								
1990D	20,096,242								
1990S	(3,299,559)								
1991P	14,874,000								
1991D	15,054,678								
1991S	(2,867,787)								
1992P	17,628,000								
1992D	17,000,106								
1992S	(2,858,981)								
1992S, Silver	(1,317,579)								
1993P	15,510,000								
1993D	15,000,006								
1993S	(2,633,439)								
1993S, Silver	(761,353)								
1994P	23,718,000								
1994D	23,828,110								
1994S	(2,484,594)								
1994S, Silver	(785,329)								
1995P	26,496,000								
1995D	26,288,000								
1995S	(2,117,496)								
1995S, Silver	(679,985)								
1996P	24,442,000								
1996D	24,744,000								
1996S	(1,750,244)								
1996S, Silver	(775,021)								
1997P	20,882,000								
1997D	19,876,000								
1997S	(2,055,000)								
1997S, Silver	(741,678)								
1998P	15,646,000								

Date	Quantity Minted	MS-60	MS-63	MS-65	PF-65				Notes
1998D	15,064,000								
1998S	(2,086,507)								
1998S, Silver	(878,792)								
1998S, Silver, Matte Finish	(62,000)								
1999P	8,900,000								
1999D	10,682,000								
1999S	(2,543,401)								
1999S, Silver	(804,565)								
2000P	22,600,000								
2000D	19,466,000								
2000S	(3,082,483)								
2000S, Silver	(965,421)								
2001P	21,200,000								
2001D	19,504,000								
2001S	(2,294,909)								
2001S, Silver	(889,697)								
2002P	3,100,000								
2002D	2,500,000								
2002S	(2,319,766)								
2002S, Silver	(892,229)								
2003P	2,500,000								
2003D	2,500,000								
2003S	(2,172,684)								
2003S, Silver	(1,125,755)								
2004P	2,900,000								
2004D	2,900,000								
2004S	(1,789,488)								
2004S, Silver	(1,175,934)								
2005P	3,800,000								
2005D	3,500,000								
2005S	(2,275,000)								
2005S, Silver	(1,069,679)								
2006P	2,400,000								
2006D	2,000,000								
2006S	(2,000,428)								
2006S, Silver	(1,054,008)								
2007P	2,400,000								
2007D	2,400,000								
2007S	(1,702,116)								
2007S, Silver	(875,050)								
2008P	1,700,000								
2008D	1,700,000								
2008S	(1,405,674)								
2008S, Silver	(763,887)								
2009P	1,900,000								

2016-W Liberty Walking Centennial Gold Coin

Date	Quantity Minted	MS-60	MS-63	MS-65	PF-65				Notes
2009D	1,900,000								
2009S	(1,482,502)								
2009S, Silver	(697,365)								
2010P	1,800,000								
2010D	1,700,000								
2010S	(1,103,815)								
2010S, Silver	(585,401)								
2011P	1,750,000								
2011D	1,700,000								
2011S	(1,098,835)								
2011S, Silver	(574,175)								
2012P	1,800,000								
2012D	1,700,000								
2012S	(843,705)								
2012S, Silver	(445,612)								
2013P	5,000,000								
2013D	4,600,000								
2013S	(854,785)								
2013S, Silver	(467,691)								
2014P	2,500,000								
2014P, High Relief									
2014P, Silver	(219,173)								
2014D	2,100,000								
2014D, High Relief	197,608								
2014D, Silver	219,173								
2014S, Enhanced Uncirculated, Silver	219,173								
2014S	(767,977)								
2014S, Silver	(472,107)								
2014W, Rev. Proof, Silver	(219,173)								
2014W, 50th Anniv., Gold	(73,772)								
2015P	2,300,000								
2015D	2,300,000								
2015S	(662,854)								
2015S, Silver	(387,310)								
2016W, Liberty Walking Centennial Gold Coin	65,509								

Date	Quantity Minted		MS-60	MS-63	MS-65	PF-65				Notes
2016P		2,100,000								
2016D		2,100,000								
2016S	(641,775)									
2016S, Silver	(419,256)									
2017P		1,800,000								
2017D		2,900,000								
2017S	(621,384)									
2017S, Silver	(406,994)									
2018P		4,800,000								
2018D		6,100,000								
2018S	(535,221)									
2018S, Silver	(350,820)	1,800,000								
2019P										
2019D										
2019S										
2019S, Silver										
2019S, Enhanced Reverse Proof										
2020P										
2020D										
2020S										
2020S, Silver										
2021P										
2021D										
2021S										
2021S, Silver										
2022P										
2022D										
2022S										
2022S, Silver										

SILVER AND RELATED DOLLARS

Flowing Hair (1794–1795)

Date	Quantity Minted	G-4	VG-8	F-12	VF-20	EF-40	MS-60	Notes
1794	1,758							
1794, Silver Plug *(unique)*								
1795, Two Leaves	160,295							
1795, Three Leaves								
1795, Silver Plug								

Draped Bust, Small Eagle Reverse (1795–1798)

Date	Quantity Minted	G-4	VG-8	F-12	VF-20	EF-40	MS-60	Notes
1795, Uncentered Bust	42,738							
1795, Centered Bust								
1796, Small Date, Small Letters *(3 varieties)*	79,920							
1796, Small Date, Large Letters								
1796, Large Date, Small Letters								
1797, 10 Stars Left, 6 Right	7,776							
1797, 9 Stars Left, 7 Right, Large Letters								
1797, 9 Stars Left, 7 Right, Small Letters								
1798, 15 Stars on Obverse	*							
1798, 13 Stars on Obverse								

* Included in 1798, Knob 9, 5 Vertical Lines, mintage.

Draped Bust, Heraldic Eagle Reverse (1798–1804)

Date	Quantity Minted	G-4	VG-8	F-12	VF-20	EF-40	MS-60	Notes
1798, Knob 9, 5 Vertical Lines								
1798, Knob 9, 4 Vertical Lines								
1798, Knob 9, 10 Arrows								
1798, Pointed 9, Close Date	327,536							
1798, Pointed 9, Wide Date								
1798, Pointed 9, 5 Vertical Lines								
1798, Pointed 9, 10 Arrows								
1798, Pointed 9, 4 Berries								
1799, 99 Over 98, 15-Star Reverse								
1799, 99 Over 98, 13-Star Reverse								
1799, Irregular Date, 15-Star Reverse	423,515							
1799, Irregular Date, 13-Star Reverse								
1799, Normal Date								
1799, 8 Stars Left, 5 Right								
1800, Very Wide Date, Low 8								
1800, "Dotted Date" (from die breaks)	220,920							
1800, Only 12 Arrows								
1800, Normal Dies								
1800, AMERICAI								
1801	54,454							
1801, Proof Restrike (reverse struck from first die of 1804 dollar) (2 known)								
1802, 2 Over 1, Narrow Date								
1802, 2 Over 1, Wide Date								
1802, Narrow Normal Date	41,650							
1802, Wide Normal Date								
1802, Proof Restrike (4 known)								
1803, Small 3								
1803, Large 3	85,634							
1803, Proof Restrike (4 known)								

Date	Quantity Minted	G-4	VG-8	F-12	VF-20	EF-40	MS-60		Notes
1804, 1st Reverse, Class I *(8 known)*									
1804, 2nd Reverse, Class III *(6 known)*									
1804, Second Reverse, Class II (unique)									
1804, Mint-Made Electrotype of the Unique Plain-Edge Specimen *(4 known)*									

Gobrecht (1836–1839)

Date	Quantity Minted	G-4	VG-8	F-12	VF-20	EF-40	MS-60		Notes
1836, All kinds									
1838, All kinds									
1839, All kinds									

Liberty Seated, No Motto (1840–1865)

Date	Quantity Minted	VG-8	F-12	VF-20	EF-40	MS-60	PF-63		Notes
1840	61,005								
1841	173,000								
1842	184,618								
1843	165,100								
1844	20,000								
1845	24,500								
1846	110,600								
18460	59,000								
1847	140,750								
1848	15,000								
1849	62,600								

Date		Quantity Minted	VG-8	F-12	VF-20	EF-40	MS-60	PF-63		Notes
1850		7,500								
18500		40,000								
1851, Original, High Date		1,300								
1851, Restrike, Date Centered										
1852, Original		1,100								
1852, Restrike										
1853		46,110								
1854		33,140								
1855		26,000								
1856		63,500								
1857		94,000								
1858	(300)									
1859	(800)	255,700								
18590		360,000								
1859S		20,000								
1860	(1,330)	217,600								
18600		515,000								
1861	(1,000)	77,500								
1862	(550)	11,540								
1863	(460)	27,200								
1864	(470)	30,700								
1865	(500)	46,500								
1866, No Motto *(2 known)*										

Liberty Seated, With Motto (1866–1873)

Date		Quantity Minted	VG-8	F-12	VF-20	EF-40	MS-60	PF-63		Notes
1866	(725)	48,900								
1867	(625)	46,900								
1868	(600)	162,100								
1869	(600)	423,700								
1870	(1,000)	415,000								
1870CC		11,758								
1870S										
1871	(960)	1,073,800								
1871CC		1,376								
1872	(950)	1,105,500								

Date	Quantity Minted	VG-8	F-12	VF-20	EF-40	MS-60	PF-63	Notes
1872CC	3,150							
1872S	9,000							
1873 (600)	293,000							
1873CC	2,300							
1873S *(unknown in any collection)*	700							

Trade Dollars (1873–1885)

Date	Quantity Minted	VG-8	F-12	EF-40	MS-60	MS-63	PF-63	Notes
1873 (865)	396,635							
1873CC	124,500							
1873S	703,000							
1874 (700)	987,100							
1874CC	1,373,200							
1874S	2,549,000							
1875 (700)	218,200							
1875, Reverse 2								
1875CC	1,573,700							
1875CC, Reverse 2								
1875S	4,487,000							
1875S, Reverse 2								
1875S, S Over CC								
1876 (1,150)	455,000							
1876, Obv 2, Rev 2 *(extremely rare)*								
1876, Reverse 2								
1876CC	509,000							
1876CC, Reverse 1								
1876CC, DblDie Rev								
1876S	5,227,000							
1876S, Reverse 2								
1876S, Obv 2, Rev 2								
1877 (510)	3,039,200							
1877CC	534,000							
1877S	9,519,000							

Date	Quantity Minted	VG-8	F-12	EF-40	MS-60	MS-63	PF-63	Notes
1878	(900)							
1878CC	97,000							
1878S	4,162,000							
1879	(1,541)							
1880	(1,987)							
1881	(960)							
1882	(1,097)							
1883	(979)							
1884	(10)							
1885	(5)							

Morgan (1878–1921)

Date	Quantity Minted		VF-20	EF-40	AU-50	MS-60	MS-63	PF-63	Notes
1878, 7 Feathers									
1878, 7 Over 8 Clear Doubled Feathers									
1878, 7 Feathers, 2nd Reverse	(250)	9,759,300							
1878, 7 Feathers, 3rd Reverse									
1878CC		2,212,000							
1878S		9,774,000							
1879	(1,100)	14,806,000							
1879CC, CC Over CC		756,000							
1879CC, Clear CC									
1879O		2,887,000							
1879S, 2nd Reverse		9,110,000							
1879S, 3rd Reverse									
1880	(1,355)	12,600,000							
1880, 80 Over 79									
1880CC, 80/79, 2nd Rev		495,000							
1880CC, 8/7, 2nd Rev									
1880CC, 8/High 7, 3rd Rev									
1880CC, 8/Low 7, 3rd Rev									
1880CC, 3rd Reverse									

Date		Quantity Minted	VF-20	EF-40	AU-50	MS-60	MS-63	PF-63		Notes
18800, 80 Over 79		5,305,000								
18800										
1880S, 80 Over 79		8,900,000								
1880S, 0 Over 9										
1880S										
1881	(984)	9,163,000								
1881CC		296,000								
18810		5,708,000								
1881S		12,760,000								
1882	(1,100)	11,100,000								
1882CC		1,133,000								
18820		6,090,000								
18820, 0 Over S										
1882S		9,250,000								
1883	(1,039)	12,290,000								
1883CC		1,204,000								
18830		8,725,000								
1883S		6,250,000								
1884	(875)	14,070,000								
1884CC		1,136,000								
18840		9,730,000								
1884S		3,200,000								
1885	(930)	17,787,000								
1885CC		228,000								
18850		9,185,000								
1885S		1,497,000								
1886	(886)	19,963,000								
18860		10,710,000								
1886S		750,000								
1887, 7 Over 6		20,290,000								
1887	(710)									
18870, 7 Over 6		11,550,000								
18870										
1887S		1,771,000								
1888	(833)	19,183,000								
18880		12,150,000								
18880, Doubled-Die Obv										
1888S		657,000								
1889	(811)	21,726,000								
1889CC		350,000								
18890		11,875,000								
1889S		700,000								
1890	(590)	16,802,000								
1890CC		2,309,041								
18900		10,701,000								
1890S		8,230,373								

Date		Quantity Minted	VF-20	EF-40	AU-50	MS-60	MS-63	PF-63		Notes
1891	(650)	8,693,556								
1891CC		1,618,000								
1891O		7,954,529								
1891S		5,296,000								
1892	(1,245)	1,036,000								
1892CC		1,352,000								
1892O		2,744,000								
1892S		1,200,000								
1893	(792)	378,000								
1893CC		677,000								
1893O		300,000								
1893S		100,000								
1894	(972)	110,000								
1894O		1,723,000								
1894S		1,260,000								
1895, Proof	(880)									
1895O		450,000								
1895S		400,000								
1896	(762)	9,976,000								
1896O		4,900,000								
1896S		5,000,000								
1897	(731)	2,822,000								
1897O		4,004,000								
1897S		5,825,000								
1898	(735)	5,884,000								
1898O		4,440,000								
1898S		4,102,000								
1899	(846)	330,000								
1899O		12,290,000								
1899S		2,562,000								
1900	(912)	8,830,000								
1900O		12,590,000								
1900O, O Over CC										
1900S		3,540,000								
1901	(813)	6,962,000								
1901, Doubled-Die Reverse										
1901O		13,320,000								
1901S		2,284,000								
1902	(777)	7,994,000								
1902O		8,636,000								
1902S		1,530,000								
1903	(755)	4,652,000								
1903O		4,450,000								
1903S		1,241,000								

Date	Quantity Minted	VF-20	EF-40	AU-50	MS-60	MS-63	PF-63		Notes
1904	(650) 2,788,000								
19040	3,720,000								
1904S	2,304,000								
1921	44,690,000								
1921D	20,345,000								
1921S	21,695,000								

Peace (1921–1935)

Date	Quantity Minted	VF-20	EF-40	AU-50	MS-60	MS-63		Notes
1921, High Relief	1,006,473							
1922, High Relief	35,401							
1922, Normal Relief	51,737,000							
1922D	15,063,000							
1922S	17,475,000							
1923	30,800,000							
1923D	6,811,000							
1923S	19,020,000							
1924	11,811,000							
1924S	1,728,000							
1925	10,198,000							
1925S	1,610,000							
1926	1,939,000							
1926D	2,348,700							
1926S	6,980,000							
1927	848,000							
1927D	1,268,900							
1927S	866,000							
1928	360,649							
1928S	1,632,000							
1934	954,057							
1934D 1934D, Doubled-Die Obverse	1,569,500							
1934S	1,011,000							
1935	1,576,000							
1935S	1,964,000							

Eisenhower, Eagle Reverse (1971–1974)

Date		Quantity Minted	VF-20	EF-40	AU-50	MS-60	MS-63	PF-65	Notes
1971, Copper-Nickel Clad		47,799,000							
1971D, Copper-Nickel Clad, Variety I		68,587,424							
1971D, Copper-Nickel Clad, Variety II									
1971S, Silver Clad	(4,265,234)	6,868,530							
1972, Copper-Nickel Clad, Variety I		75,890,000							
1972 , Copper-Nickel Clad, Variety II									
1972, Copper-Nickel Clad, Variety III									
1972D, Copper-Nickel Clad		92,548,511							
1972S, Silver Clad	(1,811,631)	2,193,056							
1973, Copper-Nickel Clad		2,000,056							
1973D, Copper-Nickel Clad		2,000,000							
1973S, Copper-Nickel Clad	(2,760,339)								
1973S, Silver Clad	(1,013,646)	1,883,140							
1974, Copper-Nickel Clad		27,366,000							
1974D, Copper-Nickel Clad		45,517,000							
1974S, Copper-Nickel Clad	(2,612,568)								
1974S, Silver Clad	(1,306,579)	1,900,156							

Eisenhower, Bicentennial (Dated 1776–1976)

Date	Quantity Minted	VF-20	EF-40	AU-50	MS-60	MS-63	PF-65		Notes
1776–1976, Copper-Nickel Clad, Variety 1	4,019,000								
1776–1976, Copper-Nickel Clad, Variety 2	113,318,000								
1776–1976D, Copper-Nickel Clad, Variety 1	21,048,710								
1776–1976D, Copper-Nickel Clad, Variety 2	82,179,564								
1776–1976S, Copper-Nickel Clad, Variety 1	(2,845,450)								
1776–1976S, Copper-Nickel Clad, Variety 2	(4,149,730)								
1776–1976, Silver Clad, Variety 2									
1776–1976S, Silver Clad, Variety 1	11,000,000								
1776–1976S, Silver Clad, Variety 1	(4,000,000)								

Eisenhower, Eagle Reverse Resumed (1977–1978)

Date	Quantity Minted	MS-63	MS-65	PF-65					Notes
1977, Copper-Nickel Clad	12,596,000								
1977D, Copper-Nickel Clad	32,983,006								
1977S, Copper-Nickel Clad	(3,251,152)								
1978, Copper-Nickel Clad	25,702,000								
1978D, Copper-Nickel Clad	33,012,890								
1978S, Copper-Nickel Clad	(3,127,781)								

Susan B. Anthony (1979–1999)

Date	Quantity Minted	MS-63	MS-65	PF-65					Notes
1979P, Narrow Rim	360,222,000								
1979P, Wide Rim									
1979D	288,015,744								
1979S	109,576,000								
1979S, Proof, Type 1	(3,677,175)								
1979S, Proof, Type 2									
1980P	27,610,000								
1980D	41,628,708								
1980S	20,422,000								
1980S, Proof	(3,554,806)								
1981P	3,000,000								
1981D	3,250,000								
1981S	3,492,000								
1981S, Proof, Type 1	(4,063,083)								
1981S, Proof, Type 2									
1999P	29,592,000								
1999P, Proof	(750,000)								
1999D	11,776,000								

Sacagawea (2000–2008)

Date	Quantity Minted	MS-63	MS-65	PF-65					Notes
2000P	767,140,000								
2000P, Goodacre Presentation Finish	5,000								
2000P, Boldly Detailed Tail Feathers	5,500								
2000D	518,916,000								
2000S	(4,047,904)								
2001P	62,468,000								
2001D	70,939,500								
2001S	(3,183,740)								
2002P	3,865,610								
2002D	3,732,000								
2002S	(3,211,995)								
2003P	3,080,000								
2003D	3,080,000								
2003S	(3,298,439)								
2004P	2,660,000								
2004D	2,660,000								
2004S	(2,965,422)								
2005P	2,520,000								
2005D	2,520,000								
2005S	(3,344,679)								
2006P	4,900,000								
2006D	2,800,000								
2006S	(3,054,436)								
2007P	3,640,000								
2007D	3,920,000								
2007S	(2,577,166)								
2008P	1,820,000								
2008D	1,820,000								
2008S	(2,169,561)								

Reverse

Date, Mintmark, and
Mottos Incused on Edge

Presidential (2007–2016)

Date	Quantity Minted	MS-65	PF-65						Notes
2007P, Washington	176,680,000								
2007D, Washington	163,680,000								
2007S, Washington	(3,965,989)								
2007P, J. Adams	112,420,000								
2007D, J. Adams	112,140,000								
2007S, J. Adams	(3,965,989)								
2007P, Jefferson	100,800,000								
2007D, Jefferson	102,810,000								
2007S, Jefferson	(3,965,989)								
2007P, Madison	84,560,000								
2007D, Madison	87,780,000								
2007S, Madison	(3,965,989)								

Date	Quantity Minted	MS-65	PF-65						Notes
2008P, Monroe	64,260,000								
2008D, Monroe	60,230,000								
2008S, Monroe	(3,083,940)								
2008P, J.Q. Adams	57,540,000								
2008D, J.Q. Adams	57,720,000								
2008S, J.Q. Adams	(3,083,940)								
2008P, Jackson	61,180,000								
2008D, Jackson	61,070,000								
2008S, Jackson	(3,083,940)								
2008P, Van Buren	51,520,000								
2008D, Van Buren	50,960,000								
2008S, Van Buren	(3,083,940)								

Date	Quantity Minted	MS-65	PF-65							Notes
2009P, W.H. Harrison	43,260,000									
2009D, W.H. Harrison	55,160,000									
2009S, W.H. Harrison (2,809,452)										
2009P, Tyler	43,540,000									
2009D, Tyler	43,540,000									
2009S, Tyler (2,809,452)										
2009P, Polk	46,620,000									
2009D, Polk	41,720,000									
2009S, Polk (2,809,452)										
2009P, Taylor	41,580,000									
2009D, Taylor	36,680,000									
2009S, Taylor (2,809,452)										

Date	Quantity Minted	MS-65	PF-65							Notes
2010P, Fillmore	37,520,000									
2010D, Fillmore	36,960,000									
2010S, Fillmore (2,224,613)										
2010P, Pierce	38,220,000									
2010D, Pierce	38,360,000									
2010S, Pierce (2,224,613)										
2010P, Buchanan	36,820,000									
2010D, Buchanan	36,540,000									
2010S, Buchanan (2,224,613)										
2010P, Lincoln	49,000,000									
2010D, Lincoln	48,020,000									
2010S, Lincoln (2,224,613)										

Date	Quantity Minted	MS-65	PF-65						Notes
2011P, Johnson	35,560,000								
2011D, Johnson	37,100,000								
2011S, Johnson	(1,972,863)								
2011P, Grant	38,080,000								
2011D, Grant	37,940,000								
2011S, Grant	(1,972,863)								
2011P, Hayes	37,660,000								
2011D, Hayes	36,820,000								
2011S, Hayes	(1,972,863)								
2011P, Garfield	37,100,000								
2011D, Garfield	37,100,000								
2011S, Garfield	(1,972,863)								

Date	Quantity Minted	MS-65	PF-65						Notes
2012P, Arthur	6,020,000								
2012D, Arthur	4,060,000								
2012S, Arthur	(1,438,743)								
2012P, Cleveland, Var 1	5,640,000								
2012D, Cleveland, Var 1	4,060,000								
2012S, Cleveland, Var 1	(1,438,743)								
2012P, B. Harrison	5,640,000								
2012D, B. Harrison	4,200,000								
2012S, B. Harrison	(1,438,743)								
2012P, Cleveland, Var 2	10,680,000								
2012D, Cleveland, Var 2	3,920,000								
2012S, Cleveland, Var 2	(1,438,743)								

Date	Quantity Minted	MS-65	PF-65						Notes
2013P, McKinley	4,760 000								
2013D, McKinley	3,365,100								
2013S, McKinley	(1,488,798)								
2013P, T. Roosevelt	5,310,700								
2013D, T. Roosevelt	3,920,000								
2013S, T. Roosevelt	(1,503,943)								
2013P, Taft	4,760,000								
2013D, Taft	3,360,000								
2013S, Taft	(1,488,798)								
2013P, Wilson	4,620,000								
2013D, Wilson	3,360,000								
2013S, Wilson	(1,488,798)								

Date	Quantity Minted	MS-65	PF-65						Notes
2014P, Harding	6,160,000								
2014D, Harding	3,780,000								
2014S, Harding	(1,373,569)								
2014P, Coolidge	4,480,000								
2014D, Coolidge	3,780,000								
2014S, Coolidge	(1,373,569)								
2014P, Hoover	4,480,000								
2014D, Hoover	3,780,000								
2014S, Hoover	(1,373,569)								
2014P, F.D. Roosevelt	4,760,000								
2014D, F.D. Roosevelt	3,920,000								
2014S, F.D. Roosevelt	(1,392,619)								
2015P, Truman	4,900,000								
2015P, Truman, Reverse Proof	(16,812)								
2015D, Truman	3,500,000								
2015S, Truman, Proof	(1,272,232)								
2015P, Eisenhower	4,900,000								

Date	Quantity Minted	MS-65	PF-65						Notes
2015P, Eisenhower, Reverse Proof	(16,744)								
2015D, Eisenhower	3,645,998								
2015S, Eisenhower, Proof	(1,272,232)								
2015P, Kennedy	6,160,000								
2015P, Kennedy, Reverse Proof	(49,501)								
2015D, Kennedy	5,180,000								
2015S, Kennedy, Proof	(1,272,232)								
2015P, L.B. Johnson	7,840,000								
2015P, L.B. Johnson, Reverse Proof	(23,905)								
2015D, L.B. Johnson	4,200,000								
2015S, L.B. Johnson, Proof	(1,272,232)								
2016P, Nixon	5,460,000								
2016D, Nixon	4,340,000								
2016S, Nixon, Proof	(1,163,415)								
2016P, Ford	5,460,000								
2016D, Ford	5,040,000								
2016S, Ford, Proof	(1,163,415)								
2016P, Reagan	7,140,000								
2016D, Reagan	5,880,000								
2016S, Reagan, Proof	(1,163,415)								
2016S, Reagan, Reverse Proof	(47,447)								

Date	Quantity Minted	MS-65	PF-65						Notes
2020P, G.H.W. Bush									
2020D, G.H.W. Bush									
2020S, G.H.W. Bush, Proof									

Native American Dollars (2009 to Date)

Date	Quantity Minted	MS-65	PF-65					Notes
2009P, Three Sisters	39,200,000							
2009D, Three Sisters	35,700,000							
2009S, Three Sisters	(2,179,867)							
2010P, Great Law	32,060,000							
2010D, Great Law	48,720,000							
2010S, Great Law	(1,689,216)							
2011P, Wampanoag Treaty	29,400,000							
2011D, Wampanoag Treaty	48,160,000							
2011S, Wampanoag Treaty	(1,673,410)							
2012P, Trade Routes	2,800,000							
2012D, Trade Routes	3,080,000							
2012S, Trade Routes	(1,189,445)							
2013P, Treaty, Delawares	1,820,000							
2013D, Treaty, Delawares	1,820,000							
2013S, Treaty, Delawares	(1,222,180)							
2014P, Native Hospitality	3,080,000							
2014D, Native Hospitality	2,800,000							
2014S, Native Hospitality, Proof	(1,144,154)							

Date	Quantity Minted	MS-65	PF-65						Notes
2014D, Native Hospitality, Enhanced Uncirculated	50,000								
2015P, Mohawk Ironworkers	2,800,000								
2015D, Mohawk Ironworkers	2,240,000								
2015S, Mohawk Ironworkers, Proof	(1,050,164)								
2015W, Mohawk Ironworkers, Enhanced Uncirculated	88,805								
2016P, Code Talkers	2,800,000								
2016D, Code Talkers	2,100,000								
2016S, Code Talkers, Proof	(931,866)								
2016S, Code Talkers, Enhanced Uncirculated	50,737								
2017P, Sequoyah	1,820,000								
2017D, Sequoyah	1,540,000								
2017S, Sequoyah, Proof	(926,763)								
2017S, Sequoyah, Enhanced Uncirculated	210,419								
2018P, Jim Thorpe	1,400,000								
2018D, Jim Thorpe	1,400,000								
2018S, Jim Thorpe, Proof	(848,726)								
2018S, Jim Thorpe, Reverse Proof	(199,116)								
2019P, American Indians in Space	1,400,000								
2019D, American Indians in Space	1,540,000								
2019S, American Indians in Space, Proof	(1,091,213)								
2019P, American Indians in Space, Enhanced Uncirculated	46,966								
2020P, Elizabeth Peratrovich and Alaska's Anti-Discrimination Law									
2020D, Elizabeth Peratrovich and Alaska's Anti-Discrimination Law									
2020S, Elizabeth Peratrovich and Alaska's Anti-Discrimination Law, Proof									
2021P, American Indians in the U.S. Military Service									
2021D, American Indians in the U.S. Military Service									
2021S, American Indians in the U.S. Military Service, Proof									
2022P, Ely Samuel Parker									
2022D, Ely Samuel Parker									
2022S, Ely Samuel Parker, Proof									

American Innovation Dollars (2018 to date)

Date	Quantity Minted	MS-65	PF-65					Notes
2018P, Innovators	750,875							
2018D, Innovators	724,475							
2018S, Innovators, Proof	(224,553)							
2018S, Innovators, Reverse Proof	(74,720)							
2019P, Delaware	410,300							
2019D, Delaware	421,375							
2019S, Delaware, Proof	(114,414)							
2019S, Delaware, Reverse Proof	(62,257)							
2019P, Pennsylvania	423,000							
2019D, Pennsylvania	390,850							
2019S, Pennsylvania, Proof	(114,414)							
2019S, Pennsylvania, Reverse Proof	(46,461)							
2019P, New Jersey	436,200							
2019D, New Jersey	400,900							
2019S, New Jersey, Proof	(114,414)							
2019S, New Jersey, Reverse Proof	(41,883)							
2019P, Georgia	397,150							
2019D, Georgia	371,225							
2019S, Georgia, Proof	(114,414)							
2019S, Georgia, Reverse Proof	(38,363)							
2020P, Connecticut								
2020D, Connecticut								
2020S, Connecticut, Proof								
2020S, Connecticut, Reverse Proof								

Date	Quantity Minted	MS-65	PF-65							Notes
2020P, Massachusetts										
2020D, Massachusetts										
2020S, Massachusetts, Proof										
2020S, Massachusetts, Reverse Proof										
2020P, Maryland										
2020D, Maryland										
2020S, Maryland, Proof										
2020S, Maryland, Reverse Proof										
2020P, South Carolina										
2020D, South Carolina										
2020S, South Carolina, Proof										
2020S, South Carolina, Reverse Proof										
2021P, New Hampshire										
2021D, New Hampshire										
2021S, New Hampshire, Proof										
2021S, New Hampshire, Reverse Proof										
2021P, Virginia										
2021D, Virginia										
2021S, Virginia, Proof										
2021S, Virginia, Reverse Proof										
2021P, New York										
2021D, New York										
2021S, New York, Proof										
2021S, New York, Reverse Proof										
2021P, North Carolina										
2021D, North Carolina										
2021S, North Carolina, Proof										
2021S, North Carolina, Reverse Proof										
2022P, Rhode Island										
2022D, Rhode Island										
2022S, Rhode Island, Proof										
2022S, Rhode Island, Reverse Proof										
2022P, Vermont										
2022D, Vermont										
2022S, Vermont, Proof										
2022S, Vermont, Reverse Proof										
2022P, Kentucky										
2022D, Kentucky										
2022S, Kentucky, Proof										
2022S, Kentucky, Reverse Proof										
2022P, Tennessee										
2022D, Tennessee										
2022S, Tennessee, Proof										
2022S, Tennessee, Reverse Proof										

GOLD DOLLARS

Liberty Head (Type 1) (1849–1854)

Date	Quantity Minted	VF-20	EF-40	AU-50	MS-60	MS-63		Notes
1849, Open Wreath, No L								
1849, Small Head, With L	688,567							
1849, Close Wreath (Ends Closer to Numeral)								
1849C, Close Wreath	11,634							
1849C, Open Wreath (ex. rare)								
1849D, Open Wreath	21,588							
18490, Open Wreath	215,000							
1850	481,953							
1850C	6,966							
1850D	8,382							
18500	14,000							
1851	3,317,671							
1851C	41,267							
1851D	9,882							
18510	290,000							
1852	2,045,351							
1852C	9,434							
1852D	6,360							
18520	140,000							
1853	4,076,051							
1853C	11,515							
1853D	6,583							
18530	290,000							
1854	855,502							
1854D	2,935							
1854S	14,632							

Indian Princess Head, Small Head (Type 2) (1854–1856)

Date	Quantity Minted	VF-20	EF-40	AU-50	MS-60	MS-63		Notes
1854	783,943							
1855	758,269							
1855C	9,803							
1855D	1,811							
1855O	55,000							
1856S	24,600							

Indian Princess Head, Large Head (Type 3) (1856–1889)

Date		Quantity Minted	VF-20	EF-40	AU-50	MS-60	MS-63	PF-63	Notes
1856, Upright 5		1,762,936							
1856, Slant 5									
1856D		1,460							
1857		774,789							
1857C		13,280							
1857D		3,533							
1857S		10,000							
1858		117,995							
1858D		3,477							
1858S		10,000							
1859	(80)	168,244							
1859C		5,235							
1859D		4,952							
1859S		15,000							
1860	(154)	36,514							
1860D		1,566							
1860S		13,000							
1861	(349)	527,150							
1861D		1,250							

Date	Quantity Minted		VF-20	EF-40	AU-50	MS-60	MS-63	PF-63	Notes
1862	(35)	1,361,355							
1863	(50)	6,200							
1864	(50)	5,900							
1865	(25)	3,725							
1866	(30)	7,100							
1867	(50)	5,200							
1868	(25)	10,500							
1869	(25)	5,900							
1870	(35)	6,300							
1870S		3,000							
1871	(30)	3,900							
1872	(30)	3,500							
1873, Close 3	(25)	1,800							
1873, Open 3		123,300							
1874	(20)	198,800							
1875	(20)	400							
1876	(45)	3,200							
1877	(20)	3,900							
1878	(20)	3,000							
1879	(30)	3,000							
1880	(36)	1,600							
1881	(87)	7,620							
1882	(125)	5,000							
1883	(207)	10,800							
1884	(1,006)	5,230							
1885	(1,105)	11,156							
1886	(1,016)	5,000							
1887	(1,043)	7,500							
1888	(1,079)	15,501							
1889	(1,779)	28,950							

QUARTER EAGLES

Capped Bust to Right (1796–1807)

Date	Quantity Minted	F-12	VF-20	EF-40	AU-50	MS-60		Notes
1796, No Stars on Obverse	963							
1796, Stars on Obverse	432							
1797	427							
1798	1,094							
1802	3,035							
1804, 13-Star Reverse	3,327							
1804, 14-Star Reverse								
1805	1,781							
1806, 6/4, 8 Stars Left, 5 Right	1,136							
1806, 6/5, 7 Stars Left, 6 Right	480							
1807	6,812							

Capped Bust to Left, Large Size (1808)

Date	Quantity Minted	F-12	VF-20	EF-40	AU-50	MS-60		Notes
1808	2,710							

Capped Head to Left, Large Diameter (1821–1827)

Date	Quantity Minted	F-12	VF-20	EF-40	AU-50	MS-60		Notes
1821	6,448							
1824, 4 Over 1	2,600							
1825	4,434							
1826, 6 Over 6	760							
1827	2,800							

Capped Head to Left, Reduced Diameter (1829–1834)

Date	Quantity Minted	VF-20	EF-40	AU-50	MS-60			Notes
1829	3,403							
1830	4,540							
1831	4,520							
1832	4,400							
1833	4,160							
1834, With Motto	4,000							

Classic Head, No Motto on Reverse (1834–1839)

Date	Quantity Minted	VF-20	EF-40	AU-50	MS-60			Notes
1834, No Motto	112,234							
1835	131,402							
1836, Script 8	547,986							
1836, Block 8								
1837	45,080							
1838	47,030							
1838C	7,880							
1839	27,021							
1839C	18,140							
1839D	13,674							
1839O	17,781							

Liberty Head (1840–1907)

Date	Quantity Minted	VF-20	EF-40	AU-50	MS-60			Notes
1840	18,859							
1840C	12,822							
1840D	3,532							
1840O	33,580							

Date	Quantity Minted	VF-20	EF-40	AU-50	MS-60					Notes
1841	(unknown)									
1841C	10,281									
1841D	4,164									
1842	2,823									
1842C	6,729									
1842D	4,643									
1842O	19,800									
1843, Large Date	100,546									
1843C, Small Date, Crosslet 4	2,988									
1843C, Large Date, Plain 4	23,076									
1843D, Small Date, Crosslet 4	36,209									
1843O, Small Date, Crosslet 4	288,002									
1843O, Large Date, Plain 4	76,000									
1844	6,784									
1844C	11,622									
1844D	17,332									
1845	91,051									
1845D	19,460									
1845O	4,000									
1846	21,598									
1846C	4,808									
1846D	19,303									
1846O	62,000									
1847	29,814									
1847C	23,226									
1847D	15,784									
1847O	124,000									
1848	6,500									
1848, CAL. Above Eagle	1,389									
1848C	16,788									
1848D	13,771									
1849	23,294									
1849C	10,220									
1849D	10,945									
1850	252,923									
1850C	9,148									
1850D	12,148									
1850O	84,000									
1851	1,372,748									
1851C	14,923									
1851D	11,264									
1851O	148,000									
1852	1,159,681									
1852C	9,772									
1852D	4,078									
1852O	140,000									

Date		Quantity Minted	VF-20	EF-40	AU-50	MS-60	PF-63			Notes
1853		1,404,668								
1853D		3,178								
1854		596,258								
1854C		7,295								
1854D		1,760								
1854O		153,000								
1854S		246								
1855		235,480								
1855C		3,677								
1855D		1,123								
1856		384,240								
1856C		7,913								
1856D		874								
1856O		21,100								
1856S		72,120								
1857		214,130								
1857D		2,364								
1857O		34,000								
1857S		69,200								
1858		47,377								
1858C		9,056								
1859, Old Reverse	(80)	39,364								
1859, New Reverse										
1859D		2,244								
1859S		15,200								
1860, Old Reverse	(112)	22,563								
1860, New Reverse										
1860C		7,469								
1860S		35,600								
1861, Old Reverse	(90)	1,283,788								
1861, New Reverse										
1861S		24,000								
1862, 2 Over 1		98,508								
1862	(35)									
1862S		8,000								
1863, Proof only	(30)									
1863S		10,800								
1864	(50)	2,824								
1865	(25)	1,520								
1865S		23,376								
1866	(30)	3,080								
1866S		38,960								
1867	(50)	3,200								
1867S		28,000								
1868	(25)	3,600								
1868S		34,000								

Date	Quantity Minted		VF-20	EF-40	AU-50	MS-60	PF-63			Notes
1869	(25)	4,320								
1869S		29,500								
1870	(35)	4,520								
1870S		16,000								
1871	(30)	5,320								
1871S		22,000								
1872	(30)	3,000								
1872S		18,000								
1873, Close 3	(25)	55,200								
1873, Open 3		122,800								
1873S		27,000								
1874	(20)	3,920								
1875	(20)	400								
1875S		11,600								
1876	(45)	4,176								
1876S		5,000								
1877	(20)	1,632								
1877S		35,400								
1878	(20)	286,240								
1878S		178,000								
1879	(30)	88,960								
1879S		43,500								
1880	(36)	2,960								
1881	(51)	640								
1882	(67)	4,000								
1883	(82)	1,920								
1884	(73)	1,950								
1885	(87)	800								
1886	(88)	4,000								
1887	(122)	6,160								
1888	(97)	16,001								
1889	(48)	17,600								
1890	(93)	8,720								
1891	(80)	10,960								
1892	(105)	2,440								
1893	(106)	30,000								
1894	(122)	4,000								
1895	(119)	6,000								
1896	(132)	19,070								
1897	(136)	29,768								
1898	(165)	24,000								
1899	(150)	27,200								
1900	(205)	67,000								
1901	(223)	91,100								
1902	(193)	133,540								
1903	(197)	201,060								

Date	Quantity Minted	VF-20	EF-40	AU-50	MS-60	PF-63		Notes
1904	(170) 160,790							
1905	(144) 217,800							
1906	(160) 176,330							
1907	(154) 336,294							

Indian Head (1908–1929)

Date	Quantity Minted	VF-20	EF-40	AU-50	MS-60	PF-63		Notes
1908	(236) 564,821							
1909	(139) 441,760							
1910	(682) 492,000							
1911	(191) 704,000							
1911D	55,680							
1912	(197) 616,000							
1913	(165) 722,000							
1914	(117) 240,000							
1914D	448,000							
1915	(100) 606,000							
1925D	578,000							
1926	446,000							
1927	388,000							
1928	416,000							
1929	532,000							

THREE-DOLLAR GOLD PIECES

Indian Princess Head (1854–1889)

Date	Quantity Minted	VF-20	EF-40	AU-50	MS-60	PF-63		Notes
1854	138,618							
1854D	1,120							
1854O	24,000							
1855	50,555							
1855S	6,600							
1856	26,010							

Date		Quantity Minted	VF-20	EF-40	AU-50	MS-60	PF-63			Notes
1856S		34,500								
1857		20,891								
1857S		14,000								
1858		2,133								
1859	(80)	15,558								
1860	(119)	7,036								
1860S		7,000								
1861	(113)	5,959								
1862	(35)	5,750								
1863	(39)	5,000								
1864	(50)	2,630								
1865	(25)	1,140								
1866	(30)	4,000								
1867	(50)	2,600								
1868	(25)	4,850								
1869	(25)	2,500								
1870	(35)	3,500								
1870S (unique)										
1871	(30)	1,300								
1872	(30)	2,000								
1873, Open 3 (Original)	(25)									
1873, Close 3		(unknown)								
1874	(20)	41,800								
1875, Proof only	(20)									
1876, Proof only	(45)									
1877	(20)	1,468								
1878	(20)	82,304								
1879	(30)	3,000								
1880	(36)	1,000								
1881	(54)	500								
1882	(76)	1,500								
1883	(89)	900								
1884	(106)	1,000								
1885	(109)	801								
1886	(142)	1,000								
1887	(160)	6,000								
1888	(291)	5,000								
1889	(129)	2,300								

FOUR-DOLLAR GOLD PIECES

Stella (1879–1880)

Date	Quantity Minted	VF-20	EF-40	AU-50	MS-60	PF-63			Notes
1879, Flowing Hair	*(425+)*								
1879, Coiled Hair *(12 known)*									
1880, Flowing Hair *(17 known)*									
1880, Coiled Hair *(8 known)*									

HALF EAGLES

Capped Bust to Right, Small Eagle Reverse (1795–1798)

Date	Quantity Minted	F-12	VF-20	EF-40	AU-50	MS-60			Notes
1795, Small Eagle Reverse	8,707								
1796, 6 Over 5	6,196								
1797, 15 Stars	3,609								
1797, 16 Stars									
1798, Small Eagle Reverse *(7 known)*									

Capped Bust to Right, Heraldic Eagle Reverse (1795–1807)

Date	Quantity Minted	F-12	VF-20	EF-40	AU-50	MS-60		Notes
1795, Heraldic Eagle Reverse*								
1797, 7 Over 5*								
1797, 16-Star Obverse* *(unique)*								
1797, 15-Star Obverse* *(unique)*	24,867							
1798, Small 8								
1798, Large 8, 13-Star Reverse								
1798, Large 8, 14-Star Reverse								
1799	7,451							
1800	37,628							
1802, 2 Over 1	53,176							
1803, 3 Over 2	33,506							
1804, Small 8	30,475							
1804, Small 8 Over Large 8								
1805	33,183							
1806, Pointed-Top 6	9,676							
1806, Round-Top 6	54,417							
1807	32,488							

* Thought to have been struck in 1798 and included in the mintage figure for that year.

Capped Bust to Left (1807–1812)

Date	Quantity Minted	F-12	VF-20	EF-40	AU-50	MS-60		Notes
1807	51,605							
1808, 8 Over 7	55,578							
1808								
1809, 9 Over 8	33,875							
1810, Small Date, Small 5	100,287							
1810, Small Date, Tall 5								
1810, Large Date, Small 5								
1810, Large Date, Large 5								
1811, Small 5	99,581							
1811, Tall 5								
1812	58,087							

Capped Head to Left, Large Diameter (1813–1829)

Date	Quantity Minted	F-12	VF-20	EF-40	AU-50	MS-60		Notes
1813	95,428							
1814, 4 Over 3	15,454							
1815 *(11 known)*	635							
1818								
1818, STATESOF one word	48,588							
1818, 5D Over 50								
1819								
1819, 5D Over 50	51,723							
1820, Curved-Base 2, Small Letters								
1820, Curved-Base 2, Large Letters	263,806							
1820, Square-Base 2								
1821	34,641							
1822 *(3 known)*	17,796							
1823	14,485							
1824	17,340							
1825, 5 Over Partial 4								
1825, 5 Over 4 *(2 known)*	29,060							
1826	18,069							
1827	24,913							
1828, 8 Over 7 *(5 known)*								
1828	28,029							
1829, Large Date								
1829, Small Date*	57,442							

* Reduced diameter.

Capped Head to Left, Reduced Diameter (1829–1834)

Date	Quantity Minted	F-12	VF-20	EF-40	AU-50	MS-60		Notes
1830, Small or Large 5D	126,351							
1831, Small or Large 5D	140,594							
1832, Curved-Base 2, 12 Stars *(5 known)*	157,487							
1832, Square-Base 2, 13 Stars								
1833, Large Date	193,630							
1833, Small Date								
1834, Plain 4	50,141							
1834, Crosslet 4								

Classic Head (1834–1838)

Date	Quantity Minted	F-12	VF-20	EF-40	AU-50	MS-60		Notes
1834, Plain 4	657,460							
1834, Crosslet 4								
1835	371,534							
1836	553,147							
1837	207,121							
1838	286,588							
1838C	17,179							
1838D	20,583							

Liberty Head, Variety 1, No Motto Above Eagle (1839–1866)

Date	Quantity Minted	F-12	VF-20	EF-40	AU-50	MS-60	PF-63	Notes
1839	118,143							
1839C	17,205							
1839D	18,939							
1840	137,382							
1840C	18,992							
1840D	22,896							
1840O	40,120							
1841	15,833							
1841C	21,467							
1841D	29,392							
1841O *(not known to exist)*	*50*							
1842, Small Letters 1842, Large Letters	27,578							
1842C, Small Date 1842C, Large Date	27,432							
1842D, Small Date 1842D, Large Date	59,608							
1842O	16,400							
1843	611,205							
1843C	44,277							
1843D	98,452							
1843O, Small Letters	19,075							
1843O, Large Letters	82,000							
1844	340,330							
1844C	23,631							
1844D	88,982							
1844O	364,600							
1845	417,099							
1845D	90,629							
1845O	41,000							
1846, Large Date 1846, Small Date	395,942							
1846C	12,995							
1846D 1846D, High 2nd D Over D	80,294							
1846O	58,000							
1847 1847, Top of Extra 7 Very Low at Border	915,981							

Date	Quantity Minted	F-12	VF-20	EF-40	AU-50	MS-60	PF-63		Notes
1847C	84,151								
1847D	64,405								
1847O	12,000								
1848	260,775								
1848C	64,472								
1848D	47,465								
1849	133,070								
1849C	64,823								
1849D	39,036								
1850	64,491								
1850C	63,591								
1850D	43,984								
1851	377,505								
1851C	49,176								
1851D	62,710								
1851O	41,000								
1852	573,901								
1852C	72,574								
1852D	91,584								
1853	305,770								
1853C	65,571								
1853D	89,678								
1854	160,675								
1854C	39,283								
1854D	56,413								
1854O	46,000								
1854S *(3 known)*	268								
1855	117,098								
1855C	39,788								
1855D	22,432								
1855O	11,100								
1855S	61,000								
1856	197,990								
1856C	28,457								
1856D	19,786								
1856O	10,000								
1856S	105,100								
1857	98,188								
1857C	31,360								
1857D	17,046								
1857O	13,000								
1857S	87,000								
1858	15,136								
1858C	38,856								
1858D	15,362								
1858S	18,600								

Date		Quantity Minted	F-12	VF-20	EF-40	AU-50	MS-60	PF-63		Notes
1859	(80)	16,734								
1859C		31,847								
1859D		10,366								
1859S		13,220								
1860	(62)	19,763								
1860C		14,813								
1860D		14,635								
1860S		21,200								
1861	(66)	688,084								
1861C		6,879								
1861D		1,597								
1861S		18,000								
1862	(35)	4,430								
1862S		9,500								
1863	(30)	2,442								
1863S		17,000								
1864	(50)	4,170								
1864S		3,888								
1865	(25)	1,270								
1865S		27,612								
1866S, No Motto		9,000								

Liberty Head, Variety 2, Motto Above Eagle (1866–1908)

Date		Quantity Minted	VF-20	EF-40	AU-50	MS-60	PF-63			Notes
1866	(30)	6,700								
1866S		34,920								
1867	(50)	6,870								
1867S		29,000								
1868	(25)	5,700								
1868S		52,000								
1869	(25)	1,760								
1869S		31,000								
1870	(35)	4,000								
1870CC		7,675								
1870S		17,000								
1871	(30)	3,200								
1871CC		20,770								
1871S		25,000								
1872	(30)	1,660								
1872CC		16,980								

Date		Quantity Minted	VF-20	EF-40	AU-50	MS-60	PF-63			Notes
1872S		36,400								
1873, Close 3	(25)	112,480								
1873, Open 3		112,505								
1873CC		7,416								
1873S		31,000								
1874	(20)	3,488								
1874CC		21,198								
1874S		16,000								
1875	(20)	200								
1875CC		11,828								
1875S		9,000								
1876	(45)	1,432								
1876CC		6,887								
1876S		4,000								
1877	(20)	1,132								
1877CC		8,680								
1877S		26,700								
1878	(20)	131,720								
1878CC		9,054								
1878S		144,700								
1879	(30)	301,920								
1879CC		17,281								
1879S		426,200								
1880	(36)	3,166,400								
1880CC		51,017								
1880S		1,348,900								
1881, Final 1 Over 0		5,708,802								
1881	(42)									
1881CC		13,886								
1881S		969,000								
1882	(48)	2,514,520								
1882CC		82,817								
1882S		969,000								
1883	(61)	233,400								
1883CC		12,598								
1883S		83,200								
1884	(48)	191,030								
1884CC		16,402								
1884S		177,000								
1885	(66)	601,440								
1885S		1,211,500								
1886	(72)	388,360								
1886S		3,268,000								
1887, Proof only	(87)									
1887S		1,912,000								
1888	(95)	18,201								

Date		Quantity Minted	VF-20	EF-40	AU-50	MS-60	PF-63			Notes
1888S		293,900								
1889	(45)	7,520								
1890	(88)	4,240								
1890CC		53,800								
1891	(53)	61,360								
1891CC		208,000								
1892	(92)	753,480								
1892CC		82,968								
1892O		10,000								
1892S		298,400								
1893	(77)	1,528,120								
1893CC		60,000								
1893O		110,000								
1893S		224,000								
1894	(75)	957,880								
1894O		16,600								
1894S		55,900								
1895	(81)	1,345,855								
1895S		112,000								
1896	(103)	58,960								
1896S		155,400								
1897	(83)	867,800								
1897S		354,000								
1898	(75)	633,420								
1898S		1,397,400								
1899	(99)	1,710,630								
1899S		1,545,000								
1900	(230)	1,405,500								
1900S		329,000								
1901	(140)	615,900								
1901S, Final 1 Over 0		3,648,000								
1901S										
1902	(162)	172,400								
1902S		939,000								
1903	(154)	226,870								
1903S		1,855,000								
1904	(136)	392,000								
1904S		97,000								
1905	(108)	302,200								
1905S		880,700								
1906	(85)	348,735								
1906D		320,000								
1906S		598,000								
1907	(92)	626,100								
1907D		888,000								
1908		421,874								

Indian Head (1908–1929)

Date		Quantity Minted	VF-20	EF-40	AU-50	MS-60	PF-63			Notes
1908	(167)	577,845								
1908D		148,000								
1908S		82,000								
1909	(78)	627,060								
1909D		3,423,560								
1909O		34,200								
1909S		297,200								
1910	(250)	604,000								
1910D		193,600								
1910S		770,200								
1911	(139)	915,000								
1911D		72,500								
1911S		1,416,000								
1912	(144)	790,000								
1912S		392,000								
1913	(99)	915,901								
1913S		408,000								
1914	(125)	247,000								
1914D		247,000								
1914S		263,000								
1915*	(75)	588,000								
1915S		164,000								
1916S		240,000								
1929		662,000								

* Pieces dated 1915-D are counterfeit.

EAGLES

Capped Bust to Right, Small Eagle Reverse (1795–1797)

Date	Quantity Minted	F-12	VF-20	EF-40	AU-50	MS-60		Notes
1795, 13 Leaves Below Eagle	5,583							
1795, 9 Leaves Below Eagle								
1796	4,146							
1797, Small Eagle Reverse	3,615							

Capped Bust to Right, Heraldic Eagle Reverse (1797–1804)

Date	Quantity Minted	F-12	VF-20	EF-40	AU-50	MS-60		Notes
1797, Heraldic Eagle Reverse	10,940							
1798, 8 Over 7, 9 Stars Left, 4 Right	900							
1798, 8 Over 7, 7 Stars Left, 6 Right	842							
1799, Small Obverse Stars	37,449							
1799, Large Obverse Stars								
1800	5,999							
1801	44,344							
1803, Small Reverse Stars	15,017							
1803, Large Reverse Stars								
1804, Crosslet 4	3,757							
1804, Plain 4, Proof, Restrike *(4 known)*								

Liberty Head, No Motto Above Eagle (1838–1866)

Date	Quantity Minted	VF-20	EF-40	AU-50	MS-60	PF-63		Notes
1838	7,200							
1839, Large Letters	25,801							
1839, 9 Over 8, Type of 1838								
1839, Small Letters	12,447							
1840	47,338							
1841	63,131							
1841O	2,500							
1842, Small Date, Plain 4	18,623							
1842, Large Date, Crosslet 4	62,884							
1842O	27,400							
1843	75,462							
1843O	175,162							
1844	6,361							
1844O	118,700							
1845	26,153							
1845O	47,500							
1846	20,095							
1846O	81,780							
1847	862,258							
1847O	571,500							
1848	145,484							
1848O	35,850							
1849	653,618							
1849O	23,900							
1850, Large Date	291,451							
1850, Small Date								
1850O	57,500							
1851	176,328							
1851O	263,000							
1852	263,106							
1852O	18,000							
1853, 3 Over 2	201,253							
1853								
1853O	51,000							
1854	54,250							

Date	Quantity Minted	VF-20	EF-40	AU-50	MS-60	PF-63		Notes
18540, Large or Small Date	52,500							
1854S	123,826							
1855	121,701							
18550	18,000							
1855S	9,000							
1856	60,490							
18560	14,500							
1856S	68,000							
1857	16,606							
18570	5,500							
1857S	26,000							
1858	2,521							
18580	20,000							
1858S	11,800							
1859 (80)	16,013							
18590	2,300							
1859S	7,000							
1860 (50)	15,055							
18600	11,100							
1860S	5,000							
1861 (69)	113,164							
1861S	15,500							
1862 (35)	10,960							
1862S	12,500							
1863 (30)	1,218							
1863S	10,000							
1864 (50)	3,530							
1864S	2,500							
1865 (25)	3,980							
1865S	16,700							
1865S, 865 Over Inverted 186								
1866S	8,500							

Liberty Head, Motto Above Eagle (1866–1907)

Date	Quantity Minted	VF-20	EF-40	AU-50	MS-60	PF-63		Notes
1866 (30)	3,750							
1866S	11,500							
1867 (50)	3,090							

Date		Quantity Minted	VF-20	EF-40	AU-50	MS-60	PF-63			Notes
1867S		9,000								
1868	(25)	10,630								
1868S		13,500								
1869	(25)	1,830								
1869S		6,430								
1870	(35)	3,990								
1870CC		5,908								
1870S		8,000								
1871	(30)	1,790								
1871CC		8,085								
1871S		16,500								
1872	(30)	1,620								
1872CC		4,600								
1872S		17,300								
1873	(25)	800								
1873CC		4,543								
1873S		12,000								
1874	(20)	53,140								
1874CC		16,767								
1874S		10,000								
1875	(20)	100								
1875CC		7,715								
1876	(45)	687								
1876CC		4,696								
1876S		5,000								
1877	(20)	797								
1877CC		3,332								
1877S		17,000								
1878	(20)	73,780								
1878CC		3,244								
1878S		26,100								
1879	(30)	384,740								
1879CC		1,762								
1879O		1,500								
1879S		224,000								
1880	(36)	1,644,840								
1880CC		11,190								
1880O		9,200								
1880S		506,250								
1881	(40)	3,877,220								
1881CC		24,015								
1881O		8,350								
1881S		970,000								
1882	(40)	2,324,440								
1882CC		6,764								
1882O		10,820								

Date		Quantity Minted	VF-20	EF-40	AU-50	MS-60	PF-63		Notes
1882S		132,000							
1883	(40)	208,700							
1883CC		12,000							
1883O		800							
1883S		38,000							
1884	(45)	76,860							
1884CC		9,925							
1884S		124,250							
1885	(65)	253,462							
1885S		228,000							
1886	(60)	236,100							
1886S		826,000							
1887	(80)	53,600							
1887S		817,000							
1888	(75)	132,921							
1888O		21,335							
1888S		648,700							
1889	(45)	4,440							
1889S		425,400							
1890	(63)	57,980							
1890CC		17,500							
1891	(48)	91,820							
1891CC		103,732							
1892	(72)	797,480							
1892CC		40,000							
1892O		28,688							
1892S		115,500							
1893	(55)	1,840,840							
1893CC		14,000							
1893O		17,000							
1893S		141,350							
1894	(43)	2,470,735							
1894O		107,500							
1894S		25,000							
1895	(56)	567,770							
1895O		98,000							
1895S		49,000							
1896	(78)	76,270							
1896S		123,750							
1897	(69)	1,000,090							
1897O		42,500							
1897S		234,750							
1898	(67)	812,130							
1898S		473,600							
1899	(86)	1,262,219							
1899O		37,047							

Date		Quantity Minted	VF-20	EF-40	AU-50	MS-60	PF-63			Notes
1899S		841,000								
1900	(120)	293,840								
1900S		81,000								
1901	(85)	1,718,740								
19010		72,041								
1901S		2,812,750								
1902	(113)	82,400								
1902S		469,500								
1903	(96)	125,830								
19030		112,771								
1903S		538,000								
1904	(108)	161,930								
19040		108,950								
1905	(86)	200,992								
1905S		369,250								
1906	(77)	165,420								
1906D		981,000								
19060		86,895								
1906S		457,000								
1907	(74)	1,203,899								
1907D		1,030,000								
1907S		210,500								

Indian Head, Variety 1, No Motto on Reverse (1907–1908)

Date	Quantity Minted	VF-20	EF-40	AU-50	MS-60	PF-63			Notes
1907, Wire Rim, Periods	500								
1907, Rounded Rim, Periods Before and After •E•PLURIBUS•UNUM•	50								
1907, No Periods	239,406								
1908, No Motto	33,500								
1908D, No Motto	210,000								

Indian Head, Variety 2, Motto on Reverse (1908–1933)

Date		Quantity Minted	VF-20	EF-40	AU-50	MS-60	MS-63	PF-63	Notes
1908	(116)	341,370							
1908D		836,500							
1908S		59,850							
1909	(74)	184,789							
1909D		121,540							
1909S		292,350							
1910	(204)	318,500							
1910D		2,356,640							
1910S		811,000							
1911	(95)	505,500							
1911D		30,100							
1911S		51,000							
1912	(83)	405,000							
1912S		300,000							
1913	(71)	442,000							
1913S		66,000							
1914	(50)	151,000							
1914D		343,500							
1914S		208,000							
1915	(75)	351,000							
1915S		59,000							
1916S		138,500							
1920S		126,500							
1926		1,014,000							
1930S		96,000							
1932		4,463,000							
1933		312,500							

DOUBLE EAGLES

Liberty Head, Without Motto on Reverse (1849–1866)

Date		Quantity Minted	VF-20	EF-40	AU-50	MS-60	PF-63		Notes
1849 *(pattern)*		1							
1850		1,170,261							
18500		141,000							
1851		2,087,155							
18510		315,000							
1852		2,053,026							
18520		190,000							
1853, "3 Over 2"		1,261,326							
1853									
18530		71,000							
1854, Small Date		757,899							
1854, Large Date									
18540		3,250							
1854S		141,468							
1855		364,666							
18550		8,000							
1855S		879,675							
1856		329,878							
18560		2,250							
1856S		1,189,750							
1857		439,375							
18570		30,000							
1857S		970,500							
1858		211,714							
18580		35,250							
1858S		846,710							
1859	(80)	43,597							
18590		9,100							
1859S		636,445							
1860	(59)	577,670							
18600		6,600							

Date		Quantity Minted	VF-20	EF-40	AU-50	MS-60	PF-63			Notes
1860S		544,950								
1861	(66)	2,976,453								
18610		17,741								
1861S		768,000								
1861, Paquet Reverse (Tall Letters)										
1861S, Paquet Reverse (Tall Letters)		19,250								
1862	(35)	92,133								
1862S		854,173								
1863	(30)	142,790								
1863S		966,570								
1864	(50)	204,235								
1864S		793,660								
1865	(25)	351,175								
1865S		1,042,500								
1866S		120,000								

Liberty Head, Motto Above Eagle, Value TWENTY D. (1866–1876)

Date		Quantity Minted	VF-20	EF-40	AU-50	MS-60	PF-63			Notes
1866	(30)	698,745								
1866S		842,250								
1867	(50)	251,015								
1867S		920,750								
1868	(25)	98,575								
1868S		837,500								
1869	(25)	175,130								
1869S		686,750								
1870	(35)	155,150								
1870CC		3,789								
1870S		982,000								
1871	(30)	80,120								
1871CC		17,387								
1871S		928,000								
1872	(30)	251,850								
1872CC		26,900								

Date		Quantity Minted	VF-20	EF-40	AU-50	MS-60	PF-63			Notes
1872S		780,000								
1873, Close 3	(25)	1,709,825								
1873, Open 3										
1873CC, Close 3		22,410								
1873S, Close 3		1,040,600								
1873S, Open 3										
1874	(20)	366,780								
1874CC		115,085								
1874S		1,214,000								
1875	(20)	295,720								
1875CC		111,151								
1875S		1,230,000								
1876	(45)	583,860								
1876CC		138,441								
1876S		1,597,000								

Liberty Head, Motto Above Eagle, Value TWENTY DOLLARS (1877–1907)

Date		Quantity Minted	VF-20	EF-40	AU-50	MS-60	PF-63			Notes
1877	(20)	397,650								
1877CC		42,565								
1877S		1,735,000								
1878	(20)	543,625								
1878CC		13,180								
1878S		1,739,000								
1879	(30)	207,600								
1879CC		10,708								
1879O		2,325								
1879S		1,223,800								
1880	(36)	51,420								
1880S		836,000								
1881	(61)	2,199								
1881S		727,000								
1882	(59)	571								
1882CC		39,140								
1882S		1,125,000								
1883, Proof only	(92)									

Date		Quantity Minted	VF-20	EF-40	AU-50	MS-60	PF-63		Notes
1883CC		59,962							
1883S		1,189,000							
1884, Proof only	(71)								
1884CC		81,139							
1884S		916,000							
1885	(77)	751							
1885CC		9,450							
1885S		683,500							
1886	(106)	1,000							
1887, Proof only	(121)								
1887S		283,000							
1888	(105)	226,161							
1888S		859,600							
1889	(41)	44,070							
1889CC		30,945							
1889S		774,700							
1890	(55)	75,940							
1890CC		91,209							
1890S		802,750							
1891	(52)	1,390							
1891CC		5,000							
1891S		1,288,125							
1892	(93)	4,430							
1892CC		27,265							
1892S		930,150							
1893	(59)	344,280							
1893CC		18,402							
1893S		996,175							
1894	(50)	1,368,940							
1894S		1,048,550							
1895	(51)	1,114,605							
1895S		1,143,500							
1896	(128)	792,535							
1896S		1,403,925							
1897	(86)	1,383,175							
1897S		1,470,250							
1898	(75)	170,395							
1898S		2,575,175							
1899	(84)	1,669,300							
1899S		2,010,300							
1900	(124)	1,874,460							
1900S		2,459,500							
1901	(96)	111,430							
1901S		1,596,000							
1902	(114)	31,140							
1902S		1,753,625							

Date		Quantity Minted	VF-20	EF-40	AU-50	MS-60	PF-63		Notes
1903	(158)	287,270							
1903S		954,000							
1904	(98)	6,256,699							
1904S		5,134,175							
1905	(92)	58,919							
1905S		1,813,000							
1906	(94)	69,596							
1906D		620,250							
1906S		2,065,750							
1907	(78)	1,451,786							
1907D		842,250							
1907S		2,165,800							

Saint-Gaudens, Ultra High Relief Pattern, MCMVII (1907)

Date	Quantity Minted	PF-67						Notes
1907, Ultra High Relief, Plain Edge *(unique)*								
1907, Ultra High Relief, Lettered Edge								

Saint-Gaudens, Without Motto IN GOD WE TRUST, High Relief, MCMVII (1907)

Date	Quantity Minted	VF-20	EF-40	AU-50	MS-60			Notes
1907, High Relief, Roman Numerals (MCMVII), Wire Rim	12,367							
1907, Same, Flat Rim								

Saint-Gaudens, Without Motto IN GOD WE TRUST, Arabic Numerals (1907–1908)

Date	Quantity Minted	VF-20	EF-40	AU-50	MS-60		Notes
1907, Arabic Numerals	361,667						
1908	4,271,551						
1908D	663,750						

Saint-Gaudens, With Motto IN GOD WE TRUST (1908–1933)

Date		Quantity Minted	VF-20	EF-40	AU-50	MS-60	PF-63		Notes
1908	(101)	156,258							
1908D		349,500							
1908S		22,000							
1909, 9 Over 8		161,282							
1909	(67)								
1909D		52,500							
1909S		2,774,925							
1910	(167)	482,000							
1910D		429,000							
1910S		2,128,250							
1911	(100)	197,250							
1911D		846,500							
1911S		775,750							
1912	(74)	149,750							
1913	(58)	168,780							
1913D		393,500							
1913S		34,000							

Date		Quantity Minted	VF-20	EF-40	AU-50	MS-60	PF-63			Notes
1914	(70)	95,250								
1914D		453,000								
1914S		1,498,000								
1915	(50)	152,000								
1915S		567,500								
1916S		796,000								
1920		228,250								
1920S		558,000								
1921		528,500								
1922		1,375,500								
1922S		2,658,000								
1923		566,000								
1923D		1,702,250								
1924		4,323,500								
1924D		3,049,500								
1924S		2,927,500								
1925		2,831,750								
1925D		2,938,500								
1925S		3,776,500								
1926		816,750								
1926D		481,000								
1926S		2,041,500								
1927		2,946,750								
1927D		180,000								
1927S		3,107,000								
1928		8,816,000								
1929		1,779,750								
1930S		74,000								
1931		2,938,250								
1931D		106,500								
1932		1,101,750								
1933 *(extremely rare)*		445,500								

COMMEMORATIVES

Classic Commemorative Silver and Gold

Date	Distribution	AU-50	MS-60	MS-65	Notes
1892, World's Columbian Exposition half dollar	950,000				
1893, Same type	1,550,405				
1893, World's Columbian Exposition quarter	24,214				
1900, Lafayette	36,026				
1903, Louisiana Purchase / Thomas Jefferson	17,500				
1903, Louisiana Purchase / William McKinley	17,500				
1904, Lewis and Clark Exposition	10,025				
1905, Lewis and Clark Exposition	10,041				
1915S, Panama-Pacific Exposition half dollar	27,134				
1915S, Panama-Pacific Exposition gold dollar	15,000				
1915S, Panama-Pacific Exposition $2.50	6,749				
1915S, Panama-Pacific Exposition $50, Round	483				
1915S, Panama-Pacific Exposition $50, Octagonal	645				
1916, McKinley Memorial	15,000				
1917, McKinley Memorial	5,000				

Date	Distribution	AU-50	MS-60	MS-65		Notes
1918, Illinois Centennial	100,058					
1920, Maine Centennial	50,028					
1920, Pilgrim Tercentenary	152,112					
1921, Same, With Date Added in Field	20,053					
1921, Missouri Centennial, "2 ★ 4" in Field	9,400					
1921, Missouri Centennial, Plain	11,400					
1921, Alabama Centennial, With "2X2" in Field of Obverse	*6,006*					
1921, Alabama Centennial, Plain	*16,014*					
1922, Grant Memorial half dollar, With Star	4,256					
1922, Same type, No Star	67,405					
1922, Grant Memorial dollar, With Star	5,016					
1922, Grant Memorial dollar, No Star	5,016					
1923S, Monroe Doctrine Centennial	274,077					
1924, Huguenot-Walloon Tercentenary	142,080					
1925, Lexington-Concord Sesquicentennial	162,013					
1925, Stone Mountain Memorial	1,314,709					
1925S, California Diamond Jubilee	86,594					
1925, Fort Vancouver Centennial	14,994					
1926, Sesquicentennial of American Independence half dollar	141,120					
1926, Sesquicentennial of American Independence $2.50	46,019					
1926, Oregon Trail Memorial	47,955					
1926S, Same type, S Mint	83,055					
1928, Oregon Trail Memorial (same as 1926)	6,028					
1933D, Oregon Trail Memorial	5,008					
1934D, Oregon Trail Memorial	7,006					
1936, Oregon Trail Memorial	10,006					
1936S, Same type, S Mint	5,006					
1937D, Oregon Trail Memorial	12,008					
1938, Oregon Trail Memorial (same as 1926)	6,006					
1938D, Same type, D Mint	6,005					
1938S, Same type, S Mint	6,006					
1939, Oregon Trail Memorial (same as 1926)	3,004					
1939D, Same type, D Mint	3,004					
1939S, Same type, S Mint	3,005					
1927, Vermont Sesquicentennial	28,142					
1928, Hawaiian Sesquicentennial	10,008					
1928, Hawaiian Sesquicentennial Sandblast Proof Presentation Piece	(50)					
1934, Maryland Tercentenary	25,015					
1934, Texas Independence Centennial	61,463					
1935, Texas Independence Centennial (same as 1934)	9,996					
1935D, Same type, D Mint	10,007					
1935S, Same type, S Mint	10,008					

Date	Distribution	AU-50	MS-60	MS-65		Notes
1936, Texas Independence Centennial (same as 1934)	8,911					
1936D, Same type, D Mint	9,039					
1936S, Same type, S Mint	9,055					
1937, Texas Independence Centennial (same as 1934)	6,571					
1937D, Same type, D Mint	6,605					
1937S, Same type, S Mint	6,637					
1938, Texas Independence Centennial (same as 1934)	3,780					
1938D, Same type, D Mint	3,775					
1938S, Same type, S Mint	3,814					
1934, Daniel Boone Bicentennial	10,007					
1935, Same type	10,010					
1935D, Same type, D Mint	5,005					
1935S, Same type, S Mint	5,005					
1935, Same as 1934, Same 1934 on Reverse	10,008					
1935D, Same type, D Mint	2,003					
1935S, Same type, S Mint	2,004					
1936, Daniel Boone Bicentennial (same as above)	12,012					
1936D, Same type, D Mint	5,005					
1936S, Same type, S Mint	5,006					
1937, Daniel Boone Bicentennial (same as above)	9,810					
1937D, Same type, D Mint	2,506					
1937S, Same type, S Mint	2,506					
1938, Daniel Boone Bicentennial (same as above)	2,100					
1938D, Same type, D Mint	2,100					
1938S, Same type, S Mint	2,100					
1935, Connecticut Tercentenary	25,018					
1935, Arkansas Centennial	13,012					
1935D, Same type, D Mint	5,505					
1935, Same type, S Mint	5,506					
1936, Arkansas Centennial (same as 1935; date 1936 on reverse)	9,660					
1936, Same type, D Mint	9,660					
1936S, Same type, S Mint	9,662					
1937, Arkansas Centennial (same as 1935)	5,505					
1937, Same type, D Mint	5,505					
1937S, Same type S Mint	5,506					
1938, Arkansas Centennial (same as 1935)	3,156					
1938, Same type, D Mint	3,155					
1938S, Same type, S Mint	3,156					
1939, Arkansas Centennial (same as 1935)	2,104					
1939, Same type, D Mint	2,104					
1939, Same type, S Mint	2,105					
1936, Arkansas Centennial (Robinson)	25,265					
1935, Hudson, New York, Sesquicentennial	10,008					
1935S, California Pacific International Exposition	70,132					
1936D, California Pacific International Exposition	30,092					

Date	Distribution	AU-50	MS-60	MS-65		Notes
1935, Old Spanish Trail	10,008					
1936, Providence, Rhode Island, Tercentenary	20,013					
1936D, Same type, D Mint	15,010					
1936S, Same type, S Mint	15,011					
1936, Cleveland Centennial / Great Lakes Exposition	50,030					
1936, Wisconsin Territorial Centennial	25,015					
1936, Cincinnati Music Center	5,005					
1936D, Same type, D Mint	5,005					
1936S, Same type, S Mint	5,006					
1936, Long Island Tercentenary	81,826					
1936, York County, Maine, Tercentenary	25,015					
1936, Bridgeport, Connecticut, Centennial	25,015					
1936, Lynchburg, Virginia, Sesquicentennial	20,013					
1936, Elgin, Illinois, Centennial	20,015					
1936, Albany, New York, Charter	17,671					
1936S, San Francisco–Oakland Bay Bridge Opening	71,424					
1936, Columbia, South Carolina, Sesquicentennial	9,007					
1936D, Same type, D Mint	8,009					
1936S, Same type, S Mint	8,007					
1936, Delaware Tercentenary	20,993					
1936, Battle of Gettysburg Anniversary	26,928					
1936, Norfolk, Virginia, Bicentennial	16,936					
1937, Roanoke Island, North Carolina, 350th Anniversary	29,030					
1937, Battle of Antietam Anniversary	18,028					
1938, New Rochelle, New York, 250th Anniversary	15,266					
1946, Iowa Centennial	100,057					
1946, Booker T. Washington Memorial*	700,546					
1946D, Same type, D Mint	50,000					
1946S, Same type, S Mint	500,279					
1947, Same type as 1946	6,000					
1947D, Same type, D Mint	6,000					
1947S, Same type, S Mint	6,000					
1948, Same type as 1946	8,005					
1948D, Same type, D Mint	8,005					
1948S, Same type, S Mint	8,005					
1949, Same type as 1946	6,004					
1949D, Same type, D Mint	6,004					
1949S, Same type, S Mint	6,004					
1950, Same type as 1946	6,004					
1950D, Same type, D Mint	6,004					
1950S, Same type, S Mint	62,091					
1951, Same type as 1946	210,082					
1951D, Same type, D Mint	7,004					
1951S, Same type, S Mint	7,004					

* Minted; quantity melted unknown.

Date	Distribution	AU-50	MS-60	MS-65		Notes
1951, Carver/Washington	20,018					
1951D, Same type, D Mint	10,004					
1951S, Same type, S Mint	10,004					
1952, Same type as 1951	1,106,292					
1952D, Same type, D Mint	8,006					
1952S, Same type, S Mint	8,006					
1953, Same type as 1951	8,003					
1953D, Same type, D Mint	8,003					
1953S, Same type, S Mint	88,020					
1954, Same type as 1951	12,006					
1954D, Same type, D Mint	12,006					
1954S, Same type, S Mint	42,024					

Modern Commemoratives

Date		Distribution	MS-67	PF-67		Notes
1982D, George Washington, 250th Anniversary of Birth silver half dollar		2,210,458				
1982S, Same type, Proof	(4,894,044)					
1983P, Los Angeles Olympiad, Discus Thrower silver dollar		294,543				
1983D, Same type, D Mint		174,014				
1983S, Same type, S Mint	(1,577,025)	174,014				
1984P, Los Angeles Olympiad Olympic Coliseum silver dollar		217,954				
1984D, Same type, D Mint		116,675				
1984S, Same type, S Mint	(1,801,210)	116,675				

Date	Distribution		MS-67	PF-67			Notes
1984P, Los Angeles Olympiad, Olympic Torch Bearers gold $10	(33,309)						
1984D, Same type, D Mint	(34,533)						
1984S, Same type, S Mint	(48,551)						
1984W, Same type, W Mint	(381,085)	75,886					
1986D, Statue of Liberty Centennial clad half dollar		928,008					
1986S, Same type, S Mint, Proof	(6,925,627)						
1986P, Statue of Liberty Centennial silver dollar		723,635					
1986S, Same type, S Mint, Proof	(6,414,638)						
1986W, Statue of Liberty Centennial gold $5	(404,013)	95,248					
1987P, U.S. Constitution Bicentennial silver dollar		451,629					
1987S, Same type, S Mint, Proof	(2,747,116)						
1987W, U.S. Constitution Bicentennial gold $5	(651,659)	214,225					
1988D, Seoul Olympiad silver dollar		191,368					
1988S, Same type, S Mint, Proof	(1,359,366)						
1988W, Seoul Olympiad gold $5	(281,465)	62,913					
1989D, Congress Bicentennial clad half dollar		163,753					
1989S, Same type, S Mint, Proof	(767,897)						
1989D, Congress Bicentennial silver dollar		135,203					
1989D, Same type, inverted reverse							
1989S, Same type, S Mint, Proof	(762,198)						
1989W, Congress Bicentennial gold $5	(164,690)	46,899					
1990W, Eisenhower Centennial silver dollar		241,669					
1990P, Same type, P Mint, Proof	(1,144,461)						
1991D, Mount Rushmore Golden Anniversary clad half dollar		172,754					
1991S, Same type, S Mint, Proof	(753,257)						
1991P, Mount Rushmore Golden Anniversary silver dollar		133,139					
1991S, Same type, S Mint, Proof	(738,419)						
1991W, Mount Rushmore Golden Anniversary gold $5	(111,991)	31,959					
1991D, Korean War Memorial silver dollar		213,049					
1991P, Same type, P Mint, Proof	(618,488)						
1991D United Service Organizations silver dollar		124,958					
1991S, Same type, S Mint, Proof	(321,275)						

Date		Distribution	MS-67	PF-67				Notes
1992P, XXV Olympiad clad half dollar		161,607						
1992S, Same type, S Mint, Proof	(519,645)							
1992D, XXV Olympiad silver dollar		187,552						
1992S, Same type, S Mint, Proof	(504,505)							
1992W, XXV Olympiad gold $5	(77,313)	27,732						
1992D, White House 200th Anniversary silver dollar		123,803						
1992W, Same type, W Mint, Proof	(375,851)							
1992D, Columbus Quincentenary clad half dollar		135,702						
1992S, Same type, S Mint, Proof	(390,154)							
1992D, Columbus Quincentenary silver dollar		106,949						
1992P, Same type, P Mint, Proof	(385,241)							
1992W, Columbus Quincentenary gold $5	(79,730)	24,329						
1993W, Bill of Rights silver half dollar		193,346						
1993S, Same type, S Mint, Proof	(586,315)							
1993D, Bill of Rights silver dollar		98,383						
1993S, Same type, S Mint, Proof	(534,001)							
1993W, Bill of Rights gold $5	(78,651)	23,266						
(1993P) 1991–1995 World War II 50th Anniversary clad half dollar	(317,396)	197,072						
(1993D) 1991–1995 World War II 50th Anniversary silver dollar		107,240						
(1993W) Same type, W Mint, Proof	(342,041)							
(1993W) 1991–1995 World War II 50th Anniversary gold $5	(67,026)	23,672						
1994D, World Cup Tournament clad half dollar		168,208						
1994P, Same type, P Mint, Proof	(609,354)							
1994D, World Cup Tournament silver dollar		81,524						
1994S, Same type, S Mint, Proof	(577,090)							
1994W, World Cup Tournament gold $5	(89,614)	22,447						
1993 (1994) Thomas Jefferson silver dollar, P Mint		266,927						
1993 (1994) Same type, S Mint, Proof	(332,891)							
1994W, Vietnam Veterans Memorial silver dollar		57,290						
1994P, Same type, P Mint, Proof	(227,671)							
1994W, U.S. POW Museum silver dollar		54,893						
1994P, Same type, P Mint, Proof	(224,449)							
1994W, Women in Military Service Memorial silver dollar		69,860						
1994P, Same type, P Mint, Proof	(241,278)							

Date	Distribution		MS-67	PF-67			Notes
1994D, U.S. Capitol Bicentennial silver dollar	68,332						
1994S, Same type, S Mint, Proof		(279,579)					
1995S, Civil War Battlefield Preservation clad half dollar	119,520						
1995S, Same type, S Mint, Proof		(330,002)					
1995P, Civil War Battlefield Preservation silver dollar	45,866						
1995S, Same type, S Mint, Proof		(437,114)					
1995W, Civil War Battlefield Preservation gold $5	12,735						
1995W, Same type, W Mint, Proof		(55,246)					
1995S, XXVI Olympiad, Basketball clad half dollar	171,001						
1995S, Same type, S Mint, Proof		(169,655)					
1995S, XXVI Olympiad, Baseball clad half dollar	164,605						
1995S, Same type, S Mint, Proof		(118,087)					
1996S, XXVI Olympiad, Swimming clad half dollar	49,533						
1996S, Same type, S Mint, Proof		(114,315)					
1996S, XXVI Olympiad, Soccer clad half dollar	52,836						
1996S, Same type, S Mint, Proof		(112,412)					
1995D, XXVI Olympiad, Gymnastics silver dollar	42,497						
1995P, Same type, P Mint, Proof		(182,676)					
1995D, XXVI Olympiad, Paralympics silver dollar	28,649						
1995P, Same type, P Mint, Proof		(138,337)					
1995D, XXVI Olympiad, Track and Field silver dollar	24,976						
1995P, Same type, P Mint, Proof		(136,935)					
1995D, XXVI Olympiad, Cycling silver dollar	19,662						
1995P, Same type, P Mint, Proof		(118,795)					
1996D, XXVI Olympiad, Tennis silver $1	15,983						
1996P, Same type, P Mint, Proof		(92,016)					
1996D, XXVI Olympiad, Paralympics silver dollar	14,497						
1996P, Same type, P Mint, Proof		(84,280)					
1996D, XXVI Olympiad, Rowing silver $1	16,258						
1996P, Same type, P Mint, Proof		(151,890)					
1996D, XXVI Olympiad, High Jump silver dollar	15,697						
1996P, Same type, P Mint, Proof		(124,502)					

Date	Distribution	MS-67	PF-67				Notes
1995W, XXVI Olympiad, Torch Runner gold $5	14,675						
1995W, Same type, W Mint, Proof	(57,442)						
1995W, XXVI Olympiad, Stadium gold $5	10,579						
1995W, Same type, W Mint, Proof	(43,124)						
1996W, XXVI Olympiad, Flag Bearer gold $5	9,174						
1996W, Same type, W Mint, Proof	(32,886)						
1996W, XXVI Olympiad, Cauldron gold $5	9,210						
1996W, Same type, W Mint, Proof	(38,555)						
1995W, Special Olympics World Games silver dollar	89,301						
1995P, Same type, P Mint, Proof	(351,764)						
1996S, National Community Service silver dollar	23,500						
1996S, Same type, S Mint, Proof	(101,543)						
1996D, Smithsonian Institution 150th Anniversary silver dollar	31,320						
1996P, Same type, P Mint, Proof	(129,152)						
1996W, Smithsonian Institution 150th Anniversary gold $5	9,068						
1996W, Same type, W Mint, Proof	(21,772)						
1997P, U.S. Botanic Garden silver dollar	58,505						
1997P, Same type, P Mint, Proof	(189,671)						
1997S, Jackie Robinson silver dollar	30,180						
1997S, Same type, S Mint, Proof	(110,002)						
1997W, Jackie Robinson gold $5	5,174						
1997W, Same type, W Mint, Proof	(24,072)						
1997W, Franklin D. Roosevelt gold $5	11,894						
1997W, Same type, W Mint, Proof	(29,474)						
1997P, National Law Enforcement Memorial silver dollar	28,575						
1997P, Same type, P Mint, Proof	(110,428)						
1998S, Robert F. Kennedy silver dollar	106,422						
1998S, Same type, S Mint, Proof	(99,020)						
1998S, Black Revolutionary War Patriots silver dollar	37,210						
1998S, Same type, S Mint, Proof	(75,070)						
1999P, Dolley Madison silver dollar	89,104						
1999P, Same type, P Mint, Proof	(224,403)						
1999W, George Washington Death Bicentennial gold $5	22,511						
1999W, Same type, W Mint, Proof	(41,693)						
1999P, Yellowstone silver dollar	82,563						
1999P, Same type, S Mint, Proof	(187,595)						

Date	Distribution	MS-67	PF-67				Notes
2000P, Library of Congress silver dollar	53,264						
2000P, Same type, P Mint, Proof	(198,503)						
2000W, Library of Congress bimetallic (gold/platinum) $10	7,261						
2000W, Same type, W Mint, Proof	(27,445)						
2000P, Leif Ericson silver dollar	28,150						
2000P, Same type, P Mint, Proof	(144,748)						
2001D, American Buffalo silver dollar	227,131						
2001P, Same type, P Mint, Proof	(272,869)						
2001P, U.S. Capitol Visitor Center clad half dollar	99,157						
2001P, Same type, P Mint, Proof	(77,962)						
2001P, U.S. Capitol Visitor Center silver dollar	35,380						
2001P, Same type, P Mint, Proof	(143,793)						
2001W, U.S. Capitol Visitor Center gold $5	6,761						
2001W, Same type, W Mint, Proof	(27,652)						
2002D, Salt Lake City Olympics silver dollar	40,257						
2002P, Same type, P Mint, Proof	(166,864)						
2002W, Salt Lake City Olympics gold $5	10,585						
2002W, Same type, W Mint, Proof	(32,877)						
2002W, West Point Bicentennial silver dollar	103,201						
2002W, Same type, W Mint, Proof	(288,293)						
2003P, First Flight Centennial clad half dollar	57,122						
2003P, Same type, P Mint, Proof	(109,710)						
2003P, First Flight Centennial silver dollar	53,533						
2003P, Same type, P Mint, Proof	(190,240)						
2003W, First Flight Centennial gold $10	10,009						
2003W, Same type, W Mint, Proof	(21,676)						
2004P, Thomas Edison silver dollar	92,510						
2004P, Same type, P Mint, Proof	(211,055)						
2004P, Lewis and Clark silver dollar	142,015						
2004P, Same type, P Mint, Proof	(351,989)						
2005P, John Marshall silver dollar	67,096						
2005P, Same type, P Mint, Proof	(196,753)						
2005P, Marine Corps 230th Anniversary silver dollar	49,671						
2005P, Same type, P Mint, Proof	(548,810)						

Date	Distribution	MS-67	PF-67		Notes
2006P, Benjamin Franklin Tercentenary, "Scientist" silver dollar	58,000				
2006P, Same type, P Mint, Proof	(142,000)				
2006P, Benjamin Franklin Tercentenary, "Founding Father" silver dollar	58,000				
2006P, Same type, P Mint, Proof	(142,000)				
2006S, San Francisco Old Mint Centennial silver dollar	67,100				
2006S, Same type, S Mint, Proof	(160,870)				
2006S, San Francisco Old Mint Centennial gold $5	17,500				
2006S, Same type, S Mint, Proof	(44,174)				
2007P, Jamestown 400th Anniversary silver dollar	81,034				
2007P, Same type, P Mint, Proof	(260,363)				
2007W, Jamestown 400th Anniversary gold $5	81,623				
2007W, Same type, W Mint, Proof	(47,123)				
2007P, Little Rock Central High School Desegregation silver dollar	124,678				
2007S, Same type, P Mint, Proof	(66,093)				
2008S, Bald Eagle clad half dollar	120,180				
2008S, Same type, S Mint, Proof	(220,577)				
2008P, Bald Eagle silver dollar	119,204				
2008P, Same type, P Mint, Proof	(294,601)				
2008W, Bald Eagle gold $5	15,009				
2008W, Same type, W Mint, Proof	(59,269)				
2009P, Louis Braille Bicentennial silver dollar	82,639				
2009P, Same type, P Mint, Proof	(135,235)				
2009P, Abraham Lincoln Bicentennial silver dollar	125,000				
2009P, Same type, P Mint, Proof	(325,000)				
2010W, American Veterans Disabled for Life silver dollar	78,301				
2010W, Same type, W Mint, Proof	(202,770)				
2010P, Boy Scouts of America Centennial silver dollar	105,020				
2010P, Same type, P Mint, Proof	(244,963)				
2011S, Medal of Honor silver dollar	44,752				
2011P, Same type, P Mint, Proof	(112,833)				
2011P, Medal of Honor gold $5	8,233				
2011W, Same type, W Mint, Proof	(17,999)				
2011D, U.S. Army clad half dollar	39,442				
2011S, Same type, S Mint, Proof	(68,332)				
2011S, U.S. Army silver dollar	43,512				
2011P, Same type, P Mint, Proof	(119,829)				

Date	Distribution	MS-67	PF-67			Notes
2011P, U.S. Army gold $5	8,052					
2011W, Same type, W Mint, Proof	(17,148)					
2012W, Infantry Soldier silver dollar	44.348					
2012W, Same type, W Mint, Proof	(161,151)					
2012P, Star-Spangled Banner silver dollar	41,686					
2012P, Same type, P Mint, Proof	(169,065)					
2012W, Star-Spangled Banner gold $5	7,027					
2012W, Same type, W Mint, Proof	(18,313)					
2013W, Girl Scouts of the U.S.A. Centennial silver dollar	37,462					
2013W, Same type, W Mint, Proof	(86,355)					
2013D, 5-Star Generals clad half dollar	38,095					
2013S, Same type, S Mint, Proof	(47,326)					
2013W, 5-Star Generals silver dollar	34,638					
2013P, Same type, P Mint, Proof	(69,283)					
2013P, 5-Star Generals gold $5	5,667					
2013W, Same type, W Mint, Proof	(15,844)					
2014D, National Baseball Hall of Fame clad half dollar	142,405					
2014S, Same type, S Mint, Proof	(249,049)					
2014P, National Baseball Hall of Fame silver dollar	131,910					
2014P, Same type, P Mint, Proof	(267,847)					
2014W, National Baseball Hall of Fame gold $5	17,674					
2014W, Same type, W Mint, Proof	(32,428)					
2014P, Civil Rights Act of 1964 silver dollar	24,720					
2014P, Same type, P Mint, Proof	(61,992)					
2015D, U.S. Marshals Service 225th Anniversary clad half dollar	30,231					
2015S, Same type, S Mint, Proof	(76,549)					
2015P, U.S. Marshals Service 225th Anniversary silver dollar	38,149					
2015P, Same type, P Mint, Proof	(124,329)					
2015W, U.S. Marshals Service 225th Anniversary gold $5	6,743					
2015W, Same type, W Mint, Proof	(24,959)					
2015P, March of Dimes silver dollar	24,742					
2015W, Same type, W Mint, Proof	(32,030)					
2016P, Mark Twain silver dollar	26,291					
2016P, Same type, Proof	(78,549)					
2016W, Mark Twain gold $5	5,701					
2016W, Same type, Proof	(13,271)					
2016D, National Park Service 100th Anniversary clad half dollar	21,335					
2016S, Same type, S Mint, Proof	(54,962)					
2016P, National Park Service 100th Anniversary silver dollar	21,003					
2016P, Same type, Proof	(77,367)					

Date	Distribution	MS-67	PF-67			Notes
2016W, National Park Service 100th Anniversary gold $5	5,201					
2016W, Same type, Proof	(19,510)					
2017P, Lions Club International Century of Service silver dollar	17,247					
2017P, Same type, Proof	(68,519)					
2017S, Boys Town Centennial clad half dollar	15,525					
2017D, Same type, D Mint, Proof	(23,164)					
2017P, Boys Town Centennial silver dollar	12,234					
2017P, Same type, Proof	(31,610)					
2017W, Boys Town Centennial gold $5	2,947					
2017W, Same type, Proof	(7,347)					
2018P, World War I Centennial silver dollar	22,336					
2018P, Same type, Proof	(127,837)					
2018D, Breast Cancer Awareness clad half dollar	11,301					
2018S, Same type, S Mint, Proof	(22,392)					
2018P, Breast Cancer Awareness silver dollar	12,526					
2018P, Same type, Proof	(34,542)					
2018W, Breast Cancer Awareness gold $5	4,477					
2018W, Same type, Proof	(10,386)					
2019D, Apollo 11 50th Anniversary clad half dollar	41,738					
2019S, Same type, S Mint, Proof	(181,811)					
2019P, Apollo 11 50th Anniversary silver dollar	59,697					
2019P, Same type, Proof	(223,737)					
2019P, Apollo 11 50th Anniversary 5-oz. Proof silver dollar	(68,259)					
2019W, Apollo 11 50th Anniversary gold $5	12,035					
2019W, Same type, Proof	(34,037)					
2019D, American Legion 100th Anniversary clad half dollar	11,425					
2019S, Same type, S Mint, Proof	(27,300)					
2019P, American Legion 100th Anniversary silver dollar	13,788					
2019P, Same type, Proof	(63,144)					
2019W, American Legion 100th Anniversary gold $5	3,090					
2019W, Same type, Proof	(10,920)					
2020D, Naismith Memorial Basketball Hall of Fame 60th Anniversary clad half dollar	35,556					
2020S, Same type, S Mint, Proof	(26,119)					
2020S, Same type, Colorized	30,648					
2020P, Naismith Memorial Basketball Hall of Fame 60th Anniversary clad silver dollar	20,640					
2020P, Same type, Proof	(66,930)					
2020P, Same type, Colorized	24,523					
2020W, Naismith Memorial Basketball Hall of Fame 60th Anniversary gold $5	3,186					
2020W, Same type, Proof	(7,909)					

Date	Distribution	MS-67	PF-67			Notes
2020P, Women's Suffrage Centennial silver dollar	11,476					
2020P, Same type, Proof	(38,911)					
2021P, Christa McAuliffe silver dollar						
2021P, Same type, Proof						
2021D, National Law Enforcement Memorial and Museum clad half dollar						
2021S, Same type, S Mint, Proof						
2021P, National Law Enforcement Memorial and Museum silver dollar						
2021P, Same type, Proof						
2021W, National Law Enforcement Memorial and Museum gold $5						
2021W, Same type, Proof						
2022, Negro Leagues Baseball Centennial clad half dollar*						
2022, Same type, Proof						
2022, Negro Leagues Baseball Centennial silver dollar*						
2022, Same type, Proof						
2022, Negro Leagues Baseball Centennial gold $5*						
2022, Same type, Proof						

* The mintmarks of the planned 2022 Negro Leagues Baseball Centennial commemorative coins were unknown as of press time.

GOVERNMENT COMMEMORATIVE SETS

		Notes
(1983–1984) LOS ANGELES OLYMPIAD		
1983 and 1984 Proof dollars		
1983 and 1984 6-coin set. One each of 1983 and 1984 dollars, both Proof and Uncirculated gold $10		
1983 3-piece collector set. 1983 P, D, and S Uncirculated dollars		
1984 3-piece collector set. 1984 P, D, and S Uncirculated dollars		
1983 and 1984 gold and silver Uncirculated set. One each of 1983 and 1984 Uncirculated dollar and one 1984 Uncirculated gold $10		
1983 and 1984 gold and silver Proof set. One each of 1983 and 1984 Proof dollars and one 1984 Proof gold $10		
(1986) STATUE OF LIBERTY		
2-coin set. Proof silver dollar and clad half dollar		
3-coin set. Proof silver dollar, clad half dollar, and gold $5		
2-coin set. Uncirculated silver dollar and clad half dollar		
2-coin set. Uncirculated and Proof gold $5		
3-coin set. Uncirculated silver dollar, clad half dollar, and gold $5		
6-coin set. One each of Proof and Uncirculated half dollar, silver dollar, and gold $5		
(1987) CONSTITUTION		
2-coin set. Uncirculated silver dollar and gold $5		
2-coin set. Proof silver dollar and gold $5		
4-coin set. One each of Proof and Uncirculated silver dollar and gold $5		
(1988) SEOUL OLYMPIAD		
2-coin set. Uncirculated silver dollar and gold $5		
2-coin set. Proof silver dollar and gold $5		
4-coin set. One each of Proof and Uncirculated silver dollar and gold $5		
(1989) CONGRESS		
2-coin set. Proof clad half dollar and silver dollar		
3-coin set. Proof clad half dollar, silver dollar, and gold $5		
2-coin set. Uncirculated clad half dollar and silver dollar		
3-coin set. Uncirculated clad half dollar, silver dollar, and gold $5		
6-coin set. One each of Proof and Uncirculated clad half dollar, silver dollar, and gold $5		
(1991) MOUNT RUSHMORE		
2-coin set. Uncirculated clad half dollar and silver dollar		
2-coin set. Proof clad half dollar and silver dollar		
3-coin set. Uncirculated clad half dollar, silver dollar, and gold $5		
3 coin set. Proof half dollar, silver dollar, and gold $5		
6-coin set. One each of Proof and Uncirculated clad half dollar, silver dollar, and gold $5		
(1992) XXV OLYMPIAD		
2-coin set. Uncirculated clad half dollar and silver dollar		
2-coin set. Proof clad half dollar and silver dollar		
3-coin set. Uncirculated clad half dollar, silver dollar, and gold $5		
3-coin set. Proof half dollar, silver dollar, and gold $5		
6-coin set. One each of Proof and Uncirculated clad half dollar, silver dollar, and gold $5		

	Notes
(1992) CHRISTOPHER COLUMBUS	
2-coin set. Uncirculated clad half dollar and silver dollar	
2-coin set. Proof clad half dollar and silver dollar	
3-coin set. Uncirculated clad half dollar, silver dollar, and gold $5	
3-coin set. Proof silver half dollar, silver dollar, and gold $5	
6-coin set. One each of Proof and Uncirculated clad half dollar, silver dollar, and gold $5	
(1993) BILL OF RIGHTS	
2-coin set. Uncirculated silver half dollar and silver dollar	
2-coin set. Proof silver half dollar and silver dollar	
3-coin set. Uncirculated silver half dollar, silver dollar, and gold $5	
3-coin set. Proof silver half dollar, silver dollar, and gold $5	
6-coin set. One each of Proof and Uncirculated silver half dollar, silver dollar, and gold $5	
"Young Collector" set. Silver half dollar	
Educational set. Silver half dollar and James Madison medal	
Proof silver half dollar and 25-cent stamp	
(1993) WORLD WAR II	
2-coin set. Uncirculated clad half dollar and silver dollar	
2-coin set. Proof clad half dollar and silver dollar	
3-coin set. Uncirculated clad half dollar, silver dollar, and gold $5	
3-coin set. Proof clad half dollar, silver dollar, and gold $5	
6-coin set. One each of Proof and Uncirculated clad half dollar, silver dollar, and gold $5	
"Young Collector" set. Clad half dollar	
Victory Medal set. Uncirculated clad half dollar and reproduction medal	
(1993) THOMAS JEFFERSON	
"Coinage and Currency" set (issued in 1994). Silver dollar, Jefferson nickel, and $2 note	
(1994) WORLD CUP SOCCER	
2-coin set. Uncirculated clad half dollar and silver dollar	
2-coin set. Proof clad half dollar and silver dollar	
3-coin set. Uncirculated clad half dollar, silver dollar, and gold $5	
3-coin set. Proof clad half dollar, silver dollar, and gold $5	
6-coin set. One each of Proof and Uncirculated clad half dollar, silver dollar, and gold $5	
"Young Collector" set. Uncirculated clad half dollar	
"Special Edition" set. Proof clad half dollar and silver dollar	
(1994) U.S. VETERANS	
3-coin set. Uncirculated POW, Vietnam, and Women in Military Service silver dollars	
3-coin set. Proof POW, Vietnam, and Women in Military Service silver dollars	
(1995) SPECIAL OLYMPICS	
2-coin set. Proof Special Olympics silver dollar, 1995S Kennedy half dollar	
(1995) CIVIL WAR BATTLEFIELD PRESERVATION	
2-coin set. Uncirculated clad half dollar and silver dollar	
2-coin set. Proof clad half dollar and silver dollar	
3-coin set. Uncirculated clad half dollar, silver dollar, and gold $5	
3-coin set. Proof clad half dollar, silver dollar, and gold $5	
6-coin set. One each of Proof and Uncirculated clad half dollar, silver dollar, and gold $5	
"Young Collector" set. Uncirculated clad half dollar	

		Notes
2-coin "Union" set. Clad half dollar and silver dollar		
3-coin "Union" set. Clad half dollar, silver dollar, and gold $5		
(1995–1996) CENTENNIAL OLYMPIC GAMES		
4-coin set #1. Uncirculated half dollar (Basketball), dollars (Gymnastics, Paralympics), gold $5 (Torch Bearer)		
4-coin set #2. Proof half dollar (Basketball), dollars (Gymnastics, Paralympics), gold $5 (Torch Bearer)		
4-coin set #3. Proof half dollar (Baseball), dollars (Cyclist, Track Runner), gold $5 (Olympic Stadium)		
2-coin set #1: Proof silver dollars (Gymnastics, Paralympics)		
"Young Collector" set. Uncirculated Basketball half dollar		
"Young Collector" set. Uncirculated Baseball half dollar		
"Young Collector" set. Uncirculated Swimming half dollar		
"Young Collector" set. Uncirculated Soccer half dollar		
1995–1996 16-coin Uncirculated set. One each of all Uncirculated coins		
1995–1996 16-coin Proof set. One each of all Proof coins		
1995–1996 8-coin Proof silver dollars set		
1995–1996 32-coin set. One each of all Uncirculated and Proof coins		
(1996) NATIONAL COMMUNITY SERVICE		
Proof silver dollar and Saint-Gaudens stamp		
(1996) SMITHSONIAN INSTITUTION 150TH ANNIVERSARY		
2-coin set. Proof silver dollar and gold $5		
4-coin set. One each of Proof and Uncirculated silver dollar and gold $5		
"Young Collector" set. Proof silver dollar		
(1997) U.S. BOTANIC GARDEN		
"Coinage and Currency" set. Uncirculated silver dollar, Jefferson nickel, and $1 note		
(1997) JACKIE ROBINSON		
2-coin set. Proof silver dollar and gold $5		
4-coin set. One each of Proof and Uncirculated silver dollar and gold $5		
3-piece "Legacy" set. Baseball card, pin, and gold $5		
(1997) FRANKLIN D. ROOSEVELT		
2-coin set. One each of Proof and Uncirculated gold $5		
(1997) NATIONAL LAW ENFORCEMENT OFFICERS MEMORIAL		
Insignia set. Silver dollar, lapel pin, and patch		
(1998) ROBERT F. KENNEDY		
2-coin set. RFK silver dollar and JFK silver half dollar		
2-coin set. Proof and Uncirculated RFK silver dollars		
(1998) BLACK REVOLUTIONARY WAR PATRIOTS		
2-coin set. Proof and Uncirculated silver dollars		
"Young Collector" set. Uncirculated silver dollar		
Black Revolutionary War Patriots set. Silver dollar and four stamps		
(1999) DOLLEY MADISON COMMEMORATIVE		
2-coin set. Proof and Uncirculated silver dollars		
(1999) GEORGE WASHINGTON DEATH		
2-coin set. One each of Proof and Uncirculated gold $5		
(1999) YELLOWSTONE NATIONAL PARK		
2-coin set. One each of Proof and Uncirculated silver dollars		

	Notes

(2000) LEIF ERICSON MILLENNIUM
2-coin set. Proof silver dollar and Icelandic 1,000 kronur

(2000) MILLENNIUM COIN AND CURRENCY SET
3-piece set. Uncirculated 2000 Sacagawea dollar; Uncirculated 2000 Silver Eagle; George Washington $1 note, series 1999

(2001) AMERICAN BUFFALO
2-coin set. One each of Proof and Uncirculated silver dollar

"Coinage and Currency" set. Uncirculated American Buffalo silver dollar, face reprint of 1899 $5 Indian Chief Silver Certificate, 1987 Chief Red Cloud 10¢ stamp, 2001 Bison 21¢ stamp

(2001) U.S. CAPITOL VISITOR CENTER
3-coin set. Proof clad half dollar, silver dollar, and gold $5

(2002) SALT LAKE CITY OLYMPIC GAMES
2-coin set. Proof silver dollar and gold $5

4-coin set. One each of Proof and Uncirculated silver dollar and gold $5

(2003) FIRST FLIGHT CENTENNIAL
3 coin set. Proof clad half dollar, silver dollar, and gold $10

(2003) LEGACIES OF FREEDOM™
Uncirculated 2003 $1 American Eagle silver bullion coin and an Uncirculated 2002 £2 Silver Brittania coin

(2004) THOMAS A. EDISON
Edison set. Uncirculated silver dollar and light bulb

(2004) LEWIS AND CLARK
Coin and Pouch set. Proof silver dollar and beaded pouch

"Coinage and Currency" set. Uncirculated silver dollar, Sacagawea golden dollar, two 2005 nickels, replica 1901 $10 Bison note, silver-plated Peace Medal replica, three stamps, two booklets

(2004) WESTWARD JOURNEY NICKEL SERIES™
Westward Journey Nickel Series™ Coin and Medal set. Proof Sacagawea golden dollar, two 2004 Proof nickels, silver-plated Peace Medal replica

(2005) WESTWARD JOURNEY NICKEL SERIES™
Westward Journey Nickel Series™ Coin and Medal set. Proof Sacagawea golden dollar, two 2005 Proof nickels, silver-plated Peace Medal replica

(2005) CHIEF JUSTICE JOHN MARSHALL
"Coin and Chronicles" set. Uncirculated silver dollar, booklet, BEP intaglio portrait

(2005) AMERICAN LEGACY
American Legacy Collection. Proof Marine Corps silver dollar, Proof John Marshall silver dollar, 11-piece Proof set

(2005) MARINE CORPS 230TH ANNIVERSARY
Marine Corps Uncirculated silver dollar and stamp set

(2006) BENJAMIN FRANKLIN
"Coin and Chronicles" set. Uncirculated "Scientist" silver dollar, four stamps, *Poor Richard's Almanack* replica, intaglio print

(2006) AMERICAN LEGACY
American Legacy Collection. Proof 2006P Benjamin Franklin, Founding Father silver dollar; Proof 2006S San Francisco Old Mint silver dollar; Proof cent, nickel, dime, quarter, half dollar, and dollar

Notes

(2007) AMERICAN LEGACY

American Legacy Collection. 16 Proof coins for 2007: five state quarters; four Presidential dollars; Jamestown and Little Rock Central High School Desegregation silver dollars; Proof cent, nickel, dime, half dollar, and dollar

(2007) LITTLE ROCK CENTRAL HIGH SCHOOL DESEGREGATION

Little Rock Coin and Medal set. Proof 2007S silver dollar, bronze medal

(2008) BALD EAGLE

3-piece set. Proof clad half dollar, silver dollar, and gold $5

Bald Eagle Coin and Medal set. Uncirculated silver dollar, bronze medal

"Young Collector" set. Uncirculated clad half dollar

(2008) AMERICAN LEGACY

American Legacy Collection. 15 Proof coins for 2008: cent, nickel, dime, half dollar, and dollar; five state quarters; four Presidential dollars; Bald Eagle silver dollar

(2009) LOUIS BRAILLE

Uncirculated silver dollar in tri-folded package

(2009) ABRAHAM LINCOLN COIN AND CHRONICLES

Four Proof 2009S cents and Abraham Lincoln Proof silver dollar

(2012) STAR-SPANGLED BANNER

2 coin set. Proof silver dollar and gold $5

(2013) 5-STAR GENERALS

3-coin set. Proof clad half dollar, silver dollar, and gold $5

Profile Collection. Uncirculated half dollar and silver dollar, replica of 1962 General MacArthur Congressional Gold Medal

(2013) THEODORE ROOSEVELT COIN AND CHRONICLES

Theodore Roosevelt Presidential dollar; silver Presidential medal; National Wildlife Refuge System Centennial bronze medal; and Roosevelt print

(2013) GIRL SCOUTS OF THE U.S.A.

"Young Collector" set. Uncirculated silver dollar

(2014) NATIONAL BASEBALL HALL OF FAME

"Young Collector" set. Uncirculated half dollar

(2014) FRANKLIN D. ROOSEVELT COIN AND CHRONICLES

Franklin D. Roosevelt Proof dime and Presidential dollar; bronze Presidential medal; silver Presidential medal; four stamps; companion booklet

(2014) NATIONAL BASEBALL HALL OF FAME

"Young Collector" Set. Uncirculated half dollar

(2014) AMERICAN $1 COIN AND CURRENCY SET

2014D Native American – Native Hospitality Enhanced Uncirculated dollar and $1 Federal Reserve Note

(2015) HARRY S. TRUMAN COIN AND CHRONICLES

Harry S. Truman Reverse Proof Presidential dollar, silver Presidential medal, one stamp, information booklet

(2015) DWIGHT D. EISENHOWER COIN AND CHRONICLES

Dwight D. Eisenhower Reverse Proof Presidential dollar, silver Presidential medal, one stamp, information booklet

(2015) JOHN F. KENNEDY COIN AND CHRONICLES

John F. Kennedy Reverse Proof Presidential dollar, silver Presidential medal, one stamp, information booklet

(2015) LYNDON B. JOHNSON COIN AND CHRONICLES

Lyndon B. Johnson Reverse Proof Presidential dollar, silver Presidential medal, one stamp, information booklet

	Notes
(2015) MARCH OF DIMES SPECIAL SILVER SET	
Proof dime and March of Dimes silver dollar, Reverse Proof dime	
(2015) AMERICAN $1 COIN AND CURRENCY SET	
2015W Native American – Mohawk Ironworkers Enhanced Uncirculated dollar and $1 Federal Reserve Note	
(2015) U.S. MARSHALS	
3-coin Set. Proof clad half dollar, silver dollar, and gold $5	
(2016) NATIONAL PARK SERVICE 100TH ANNIVERSARY	
3-coin Set. Proof clad half dollar, silver dollar, and gold $5	
(2016) RONALD REAGAN COIN AND CHRONICLES	
Ronald Reagan Reverse Proof Presidential dollar, 2016W American Eagle silver Proof dollar, Ronald and Nancy Reagan bronze medal, engraved Ronald Reagan Presidential portrait, information booklet	
(2016) AMERICAN $1 COIN AND CURRENCY SET	
2016S Native American – Code Talkers Enhanced Uncirculated dollar and $1 Federal Reserve Note	
(2017) BOYS TOWN CENTENNIAL	
3-coin Set. Proof clad half dollar, silver dollar, and gold $5	
(2018) BREAST CANCER AWARENESS	
Coin and Stamp Set. Breast Cancer Awareness Proof half dollar and Breast Cancer Research stamp	
(2018) WORLD WAR I CENTENNIAL	
Silver Dollar and Air Service Medal Set. Proof World War I Centennial silver dollar and Proof silver Air Service medal	
Silver Dollar and Army Medal Set. Proof World War I Centennial silver dollar and Proof silver Army medal	
Silver Dollar and Coast Guard Medal Set. Proof World War I Centennial silver dollar and Proof silver Coast Guard medal	
Silver Dollar and Marine Corps Medal Set. Proof World War I Centennial silver dollar and Proof silver Marine Corps medal	
Silver Dollar and Navy Medal Set. Proof World War I Centennial silver dollar and Proof silver Navy medal	
(2019) APOLLO 11 50TH ANNIVERSARY	
2-coin Set. Uncirculated and Proof clad half dollars	
(2019) AMERICAN LEGION 100TH ANNIVERSARY	
3-coin Set. Proof clad half dollar, silver dollar, and gold $5	
Silver Dollar and Medal Set. American Legion 100th Anniversary Proof silver dollar and American Veterans medal	
(2019) AMERICAN $1 COIN AND CURRENCY SET	
2019P Native American – American Indians in Space Enhanced Uncirculated dollar and $1 Federal Reserve Note	
(2019) YOUTH COIN AND CURRENCY SET	
Five Proof clad America the Beautiful™ quarters and $2 Federal Reserve Note	
(2020) NAISMITH MEMORIAL BASKETBALL HALL OF FAME 60TH ANNIVERSARY	
"Kids Set." 2020S Proof clad half dollar	
(2021) NATIONAL LAW ENFORCEMENT MEMORIAL AND MUSEUM	
3-coin Set. Proof clad half dollar, silver dollar, and gold $5	

PROOF AND MINT SETS

Proof Sets

Date	Quantity Minted		Notes
1936	(3,837)		
1937	(5,542)		
1938	(8,045)		
1939	(8,795)		
1940	(11,246)		
1941	(15,287)		
1942, Both nickels	(21,120)		
1942, One nickel			
1950	(51,386)		
1951	(57,500)		
1952	(81,980)		
1953	(128,800)		
1954	(233,300)		
1955, Box pack	(378,200)		
1955, Flat pack			
1956	(669,384)		
1957	(1,247,952)		
1958	(875,652)		
1959	(1,149,291)		
1960, With Large Date cent	(1,691,602)		
1960, With Small Date cent			
1961	(3,028,244)		
1962	(3,218,019)		
1963	(3,075,645)		
1964	(3,950,762)		
1968S	(3,041,506)		
1968S, With No S dime			
1969S	(2,934,631)		
1970S	(2,632,810)		
1970S, With Small Date cent			
1970S, With No S dime (estimated mintage: 2,200)			
1971S	(3,220,733)		
1971S, With No S nickel (estimated mintage: 1,655)			
1972S	(3,260,996)		
1973S	(2,760,339)		
1974S	(2,612,568)		
1975S, With 1976 quarter, half, and dollar	(2,845,450)		
1975S, With No S dime			
1976S	(4,149,730)		
1976S, Silver-clad, 3-piece set	(3,998,621)		
1977S	(3,251,152)		
1978S	(3,127,781)		

Date	Quantity Minted		Notes
1979S, Type 1	(3,677,175)		
1979S, Type 2			
1980S	(3,554,806)		
1981S, Type 1	(4,063,083)		
1981S, Type 2 (all six coins in set)			
1982S	(3,857,479)		
1983S	(3,138,765)		
1983S, With No S dime			
1983S, Prestige set (Olympic dollar)	(140,361)		
1984S	(2,748,430)		
1984S, Prestige set (Olympic dollar)	(316,680)		
1985S	(3,362,821)		
1986S	(2,411,180)		
1986S, Prestige set (Statue of Liberty half, dollar)	(599,317)		
1987S	(3,792,233)		
1987S, Prestige set (Constitution dollar)	(435,495)		
1988S	(3,031,287)		
1988S, Prestige set (Olympic dollar)	(231,661)		
1989S	(3,009,107)		
1989S, Prestige set (Congressional half, dollar)	(211,807)		
1990S	(2,793,433)		
1990S, With No S cent	(3,555)		
1990S, With No S cent (Prestige set)			
1990S, Prestige set (Eisenhower dollar)	(506,126)		
1991S	(2,610,833)		
1991S, Prestige set (Mt. Rushmore half, dollar)	(256,954)		
1992S	(2,675,618)		
1992S, Prestige set (Olympic half, dollar)	(183,293)		
1992S, Silver	(1,009,586)		
1992S, Silver Premier set	(308,055)		
1993S	(2,409,394)		
1993S, Prestige set (Bill of Rights half, dollar)	(224,045)		
1993S, Silver	(570,213)		
1993S, Silver Premier set	(191,140)		
1994S	(2,308,701)		
1994S, Prestige set (World Cup half, dollar)	(175,893)		
1994S, Silver	(636,009)		
1994S Silver Premier set	(149,320)		
1995S	(2,010,384)		
1995S, Prestige set (Civil War half, dollar)	(107,112)		
1995S, Silver	(549,878)		
1995S, Silver Premier set	(130,107)		
1996S	(1,695,244)		
1996S, Prestige set (Olympic half, dollar)	(55,000)		
1996S, Silver	(623,655)		
1996S, Silver Premier set	(151,366)		
1997S	(1,975,000)		

Date	Quantity Minted		Notes
1997S, Prestige set (Botanic dollar)	(80,000)		
1997S, Silver	(605,473)		
1997S, Silver Premier set	(136,205)		
1998S	(2,086,507)		
1998S, Silver	(638,134)		
1998S, Silver Premier set	(240,658)		
1999S, 9-piece set	(2,543,401)		
1999S, 5-piece quarter set	(1,169,958)		
1999S, Silver 9-piece set	(804,565)		
2000S, 10-piece set	(3,082,572)		
2000S, 5-piece quarter set	(937,600)		
2000S, Silver 10-piece set	(965,421)		
2001S, 10-piece set	(2,294,909)		
2001S, 5-piece quarter set	(799,231)		
2001S, Silver 10-piece set	(889,697)		
2002S, 10-piece set	(2,319,766)		
2002S, 5-piece quarter set	(764,479)		
2002S, Silver 10-piece set	(892,229)		
2003S, 10-piece set	(2,172,684)		
2003S, 5-piece quarter set	(1,235,832)		
2003S, Silver 10-piece set	(1,125,755)		
2004S, 11-piece set	(1,789,488)		
2004S, 5-piece quarter set	(951,196)		
2004S, Silver 11-piece set	(1,175,934)		
2004S, Silver 5-piece quarter set	(593,852)		
2005S, 11-piece set	(2,275,000)		
2005S, 5-piece quarter set	(987,960)		
2005S, Silver 11-piece set	(1,069,679)		
2005S, Silver 5-piece quarter set	(608,970)		
2006S, 10-piece set	(2,000,428)		
2006S, 5-piece quarter set	(882,000)		
2006S, Silver 10-piece set	(1,054,008)		
2006S, Silver 5-piece quarter set	(531,000)		
2007S, 14-piece set	(1,702,116)		
2007S, 5-piece quarter set	(672,662)		
2007S, 4-piece Presidential set	(1,285,972)		
2007S, Silver 14-piece set	(875,050)		
2007S, Silver 5-piece quarter set	(672,662)		
2008S, 14-piece set	(1,382,017)		
2008S, 5-piece quarter set	(672,438)		
2008S, 4-piece Presidential set	(836,730)		
2008S, Silver 14-piece set	(763,887)		
2008S, Silver 5-piece quarter set	(429,021)		
2009S, 18-piece set	(1,482,502)		
2009S, 6-piece quarter set	(630,976)		
2009S, 4-piece Presidential set	(629,585)		
2009S, Silver 18-piece set	(697,365)		

Date	Quantity Minted		Notes
2009S, Silver 6-piece quarter set	(299,183)		
2009S, 4-piece Lincoln Bicentennial set	(201,107)		
2010S, 14-piece set	(1,103,815)		
2010S, 5-piece quarter set	(276,296)		
2010S, 4-piece Presidential set	(535,397)		
2010S, Silver 14-piece set	(585,401)		
2010S, Silver 5-piece quarter set	(274,034)		
2011S, 14-piece set	(1,098,835)		
2011S, 5-piece quarter set	(152,302)		
2011S, 4-piece Presidential set	(299,853)		
2011S, Silver 14-piece set	(574,175)		
2011S, Silver 5-piece quarter set	(147,901)		
2012S, 14-piece set	(794,002)		
2012S, 5-piece quarter set	(148,498)		
2012S, 4-piece Presidential set	(249,265)		
2012S, Silver 14-piece set	(395,443)		
2012S, Silver 8-piece Limited Edition set	(44,952)		
2012S, Silver 5-piece quarter set	(162,448)		
2013S, 14-piece set	(802,460)		
2013S, 5-piece quarter set	(128,377)		
2013S, 4-piece Presidential set	(266,677)		
2013S, Silver 14-piece set	(419,720)		
2013S, Silver 8-piece Limited Edition set	(47,971)		
2013S, Silver 5-piece quarter set	(138,451)		
2014S, 14-piece set	(802,460)		
2014S, 5-piece quarter set	(109,423)		
2014S, 4-piece Presidential set	(218,976)		
2014S, Silver 14-piece set	(404,665)		
2014S, Silver 8-piece Limited Edition set	(41,609)		
2014S, Silver 5-piece quarter set	(111,172)		
2015S, 14-piece set	(662,854)		
2015S, 5-piece quarter set	(99,466)		
2015S, 4-piece Presidential set	(222,068)		
2015S, Silver 14-piece set	(387,310)		
2015S, Silver 5-piece quarter set	(103,311)		
2016S, 13-piece set	(575,183)		
2016S, 5-piece quarter set	(91,674)		
2016S, 3-piece Presidential set	(231,549)		
2016S, Silver 13-piece set	(356,683)		
2016S, Silver 5-piece quarter set	(95,709)		
2016S, Silver 8-piece Limited Edition set	(49,647)		
2017S, 10-piece set	(568,678)		
2017S, 5-piece quarter set	(88,909)		
2017S, Silver 10-piece set	(358,085)		
2017S, Silver 5-piece quarter set	(89,632)		
2017S, Silver 8-piece Limited Edition set	(48,901)		
2018S, 10-piece set	(516,843)		

Date	Quantity Minted		Notes
2018S, 5-piece quarter set	(86,669)		
2018S, Silver 10-piece set	(331,883)		
2018S, Silver 5-piece quarter set	(79,259)		
2018S, 50th Anniversary silver 10-piece Reverse Proof set	(199,116)		
2018S, Silver 8-piece Limited Edition set	(49,473)		
2019S, 10-piece set, plus 2019W Proof cent	(593,978)		
2019S, 5-piece quarter set	(74,035)		
2019S, 4-piece American Innovation dollar set	(114,414)		
2019S, Silver 10-piece set, plus 2019W Reverse Proof cent	(412,609)		
2019S, Silver 5-piece quarter set	(78,559)		
2019S, Silver 8-piece Limited Edition set	(46,076)		
2020S, 10-piece set, plus 2020W Proof nickel			
2020S, 5-piece quarter set			
2020-S, 4-piece American Innovation dollar set			
2020S, Silver 10-piece set, plus 2020W Reverse Proof nickel			
2020S, Silver 5-piece quarter set			
2020S, Silver 8-piece Limited Edition set			
2021S, 7-piece set			
2021-S, 4-piece American Innovation dollar set			
2021S, Silver 7-piece set			
2021S, Silver 5-piece Limited Edition set			

Uncirculated Mint Sets

Date	Quantity Minted	Notes	Date	Quantity Minted	Notes
1947 P-D-S	5,000		1956 P-D	45,475	
1948 P-D-S	6,000		1957 P-D	34,324	
1949 P-D-S	5,000		1958 P-D	50,314	
1951 P-D-S	8,654		1959 P-D	187,000	
1952 P-D-S	11,499		1960 P-D	260,485	
1953 P-D-S	15,538		1961 P-D	223,704	
1954 P-D-S	25,599		1962 P-D	385,285	
1955 P-D-S	49,656		1963 P-D	606,612	

Date	Quantity Minted	Notes	Date	Quantity Minted	Notes
1964 P-D	1,008,108		1994 P-D	1,234,813	
1968 P-D-S	2,105,128		1995 P-D	1,038,787	
1969 P-D-S	1,817,392		1996 P-D, Plus 1996W dime	1,457,949	
1970 P-D-S, With Large Date cent	2,038,134		1997 P-D	950,473	
			1998 P-D	1,187,325	
1970 P-D-S, With Small Date cent			1999 P-D (18 pieces)	1,243,867	
			2000 P-D (20 pieces)	1,490,160	
1971 P-D-S (no Eisenhower dollar)	2,193,396		2001 P-D (20 pieces)	1,116,915	
			2002 P-D (20 pieces)	1,139,388	
1972 P-D-S (no Eisenhower dollar)	2,750,000		2003 P-D (20 pieces)	1,001,532	
			2004 P-D (22 pieces)	842,507	
1973 P-D-S	1,767,691		2005 P-D (22 pieces)	1,160,000	
1974 P-D-S	1,975,981		2006 P-D (20 pieces)	847,361	
1975 P-D, With 1976 quarter, half, dollar	1,921,488		2007 P-D (28 pieces)	895,628	
			2008 P-D (28 pieces)	745,464	
1776–1976, Siver clad, 3-piece set	4,908,319		2009 P-D (36 pieces)	784,614	
			2010 P-D (28 pieces)	583,897	
1976 P-D	1,892,513		2011 P-D (28 pieces)	533,529	
1977 P-D	2,006,869		2012 P-D (28 pieces)	392,224	
1978 P-D	2,162,609		2013 P-D (28 pieces)	376,844	
1979 P-D	2,526,000		2014 P-D (28 pieces)	327,969	
1980 P-D-S	2,815,066		2015 P-D (28 pieces)	*314,029*	
1981 P-D-S	2,908,145		2016 P-D (26 pieces)	296,582	
1984 P-D	1,832,857		2017 P-D (20 pieces)	*286,813*	
1985 P-D	1,710,571		2017S, 225th Anniversary Enhanced Uncirculated Set (10 pieces)	210,419	
1986 P-D	1,153,536				
1987 P-D	2,890,758				
1988 P-D	1,646,204		2018 P-D (20 pieces)	*257,424*	
1989 P-D	1,987,915		2019 P-D, plus 2019W cent (21 pieces)	*344,238*	
1990 P-D	1,809,184				
1991 P-D	1,352,101		2020 P-D (20 pieces)		
1992 P-D	1,500,143		2021 P-D (14 pieces)		
1993 P-D	1,297,431				

Special Mint Sets

Date	Quantity Minted	Notes
1965	2,360,000	
1966	2,261,583	
1967	1,863,344	

Souvenir Sets

Date	Quantity Minted	Notes	Date	Quantity Minted	Notes
1982P			1983P		
1982D			1983D		

SILVER BULLION

Actual size 3 inches.

America the Beautiful™ Silver Bullion

Date	Distribution	MS-67	PF-67		Notes
25¢ 2010(P), Hot Springs Nat'l Park (Arkansas)	33,000				
25¢ 2010P, Hot Springs Nat'l Park (Arkansas)	(26,788)				
25¢ 2010(P), Yellowstone Nat'l Park (Wyoming)	33,000				
25¢ 2010P, Yellowstone Nat'l Park (Wyoming)	(26,711)				
25¢ 2010(P), Yosemite Nat'l Park (California)	33,000				
25¢ 2010P, Yosemite Nat'l Park (California)	(26,716)				
25¢ 2010(P), Grand Canyon Nat'l Park (Arizona)	33,000				
25¢ 2010P, Grand Canyon Nat'l Park (Arizona)	(25,967)				
25¢ 2010(P), Mount Hood Nat'l Park (Oregon)	33,000				
25¢ 2010P, Mount Hood Nat'l Park (Oregon)	(26,637)				
25¢ 2011(P), Gettysburg Nat'l Military Park (Pennsylvania)	126,700				
25¢ 2011P, Gettysburg Nat'l Military Park (Pennsylvania)	(24,625)				
25¢ 2011(P), Glacier Nat'l Park (Montana)	126,700				
25¢ 2011P, Glacier Nat'l Park (Montana)	(20,805)				
25¢ 2011(P), Olympic Nat'l Park (Washington)	104,900				
25¢ 2011P, Olympic Nat'l Park (Washington)	(18,345)				
25¢ 2011(P), Vicksburg Nat'l Military Park (Mississippi)	58,100				
25¢ 2011P, Vicksburg Nat'l Military Park (Mississippi)	(18,528)				
25¢ 2011(P), Chickasaw Nat'l Recreation Area (Oklahoma)	48,700				
25¢ 2011P, Chickasaw Nat'l Recreation Area (Oklahoma)	(16,746)				
25¢ 2012(P), El Yunque Nat'l Forest (Puerto Rico)	24,000				
25¢ 2012P, El Yunque Nat'l Forest (Puerto Rico)	(17,314)				
25¢ 2012(P), Chaco Culture Nat'l Historical Park (NM)	24,400				
25¢ 2012P, Chaco Culture Nat'l Historical Park (NM)	(17,146)				
25¢ 2012(P), Acadia Nat'l Park (Maine)	25,400				
25¢ 2012P, Acadia Nat'l Park (Maine)	(14,978)				
25¢ 2012(P), Hawai'i Volcanoes Nat'l Park (Hawaii)	20,000				
25¢ 2012P, Hawai'i Volcanoes Nat'l Park (Hawaii)	(14,863)				
25¢ 2012(P), Denali Nat'l Park and Preserve (Alaska)	20,000				
25¢ 2012P, Denali Nat'l Park and Preserve (Alaska)	(15,225)				
25¢ 2013(P), White Mountain Nat'l Forest (New Hampshire)	35,000				

Date	Distribution	MS-67	PF-67			Notes
25¢ 2013P, White Mountain Nat'l Forest (New Hampshire)	(20,530)					
25¢ 2013(P), Perry's Victory and Int'l Peace Memorial (Ohio)	30,000					
25¢ 2013P, Perry's Victory and Int'l Peace Memorial (Ohio)	(17,707)					
25¢ 2013(P), Great Basin Nat'l Park (Nevada)	30,000					
25¢ 2013P, Great Basin Nat'l Park (Nevada)	(17,792)					
25¢ 2013(P), Ft McHenry Nat'l Monument and Historic Shrine (Maryland)	30,000					
25¢ 2013P, Ft McHenry Nat'l Monument and Historic Shrine (Maryland)	(19,802)					
25¢ 2013(P), Mount Rushmore Nat'l Memorial (South Dakota)	35,000					
25¢ 2013P, Mount Rushmore Nat'l Memorial (South Dakota)	(23,547)					
25¢ 2014(P), Great Smoky Mountains Nat'l Park (Tennessee)	33,000					
25¢ 2014P, Great Smoky Mountains Nat'l Park (Tennessee)	(24,710)					
25¢ 2014(P), Shenandoah Nat'l Park (Virginia)	24,400					
25¢ 2014P, Shenandoah Nat'l Park (Virginia)	(28,276)					
25¢ 2014(P), Arches Nat'l Park (Utah)	22,600					
25¢ 2014P, Arches Nat'l Park (Utah)	(22,262)					
25¢ 2014(P), Great Sand Dunes Nat'l Park (Colorado)	21,900					
25¢ 2014P, Great Sand Dunes Nat'l Park (Colorado)	(19,772)					
25¢ 2014(P), Everglades Nat'l Park (Florida)	34,000					
25¢ 2014P, Everglades Nat'l Park (Florida)	(28,183)					
25¢, 2015(P), Homestead Nat'l Monument of America (Nebraska)	35,000					
25¢, 2015P, Homestead Nat'l Monument of America (Nebraska)	(21,286)					
25¢, 2015(P), Kisatchie National Forest (Louisiana)	42,000					
25¢, 2015P, Kisatchie National Forest (Louisiana)	(19,449)					
25¢, 2015(P), Blue Ridge Parkway (North Carolina)	45,000					
25¢, 2015P, Blue Ridge Parkway (North Carolina)	(17,461)					
25¢, 2015(P), Bombay Hook National Wildlife Refuge (Delaware)	45,000					
25¢, 2015P, Bombay Hook National Wildlife Refuge (Delaware)	(17,309)					
25¢, 2015(P), Saratoga National Historical Park (New York)	45,000					
25¢, 2015P, Saratoga National Historical Park (New York)	(17,563)					
25¢, 2016(P), Shawnee National Forest (Illinois)	105,000					
25¢, 2016P, Shawnee National Forest (Illinois)	(18,781)					
25¢, 2016(P), Cumberland Gap National Historical Park (Kentucky)	75,000					
25¢, 2016P, Cumberland Gap National Historical Park (Kentucky)	(18,713)					
25¢, 2016(P), Harpers Ferry National Historical Park (West Virginia)	75,000					
25¢, 2016P, Harpers Ferry National Historical Park (West Virginia)	(18,743)					

Date	Distribution	MS-67	PF-67			Notes
25¢, 2016(P), Theodore Roosevelt National Park (North Dakota)	40,000					
25¢, 2016P, Theodore Roosevelt National Park (North Dakota)	(18,917)					
25¢, 2016(P), Fort Moultrie at Fort Sumter Nat'l Mon't (SC)	35,000					
25¢, 2016P, Fort Moultrie at Fort Sumter Nat'l Mon't (SC)	(17,882)					
25¢, 2017(P), Effigy Mounds National Monument (Iowa)	35,000					
25¢, 2017P, Effigy Mounds National Monument (Iowa)	(17,251)					
25¢, 2017(P), Frederick Douglass National Historic Site (DC)	20,000					
25¢, 2017P, Frederick Douglass National Historic Site (DC)	(17,678)					
25¢, 2017(P), Ozark National Scenic Riverways (Missouri)	20,000					
25¢, 2017P, Ozark National Scenic Riverways (Missouri)	(17,694)					
25¢, 2017(P), Ellis Island (Statue of Liberty National Monument) (NJ)	40,000					
25¢, 2017P, Ellis Island (Statue of Liberty National Monument) (NJ)	(17,670)					
25¢, 2017(P), George Rogers Clark National Historical Park (Indiana)	35,000					
25¢, 2017P, George Rogers Clark National Historical Park (Indiana)	(14,731)					
25¢, 2018(P), Pictured Rocks National Lakeshore (Michigan)	30,000					
25¢, 2018P, Pictured Rocks National Lakeshore (Michigan)	(17,773)					
25¢, 2018(P), Apostle Islands National Lakeshore (Wisconsin)	30,000					
25¢, 2018P, Apostle Islands National Lakeshore (Wisconsin)	(16,802)					
25¢, 2018(P), Voyageurs National Park (Minnesota)	30,000					
25¢, 2018P, Voyageurs National Park (Minnesota)	(16,839)					
25¢, 2018(P), Cumberland Island National Seashore (Georgia)	52,500					
25¢, 2018P, Cumberland Island National Seashore (Georgia)	(16,360)					
25¢, 2018(P), Block Island National Wildlife Refuge (Rhode Island)	80,000					
25¢, 2018P, Block Island National Wildlife Refuge (Rhode Island)	(15,902)					
25¢, 2019P, Lowell National Historical Park (Massachusetts)	80,000					
25¢, 2019(P), Lowell National Historical Park (Massachusetts)	(16,645)					
25¢, 2019(P), American Memorial Park (Northern Mariana Islands)	80,000					
25¢, 2019P, American Memorial Park (Northern Mariana Islands)	(16,283)					
25¢, 2019(P), War in the Pacific National Historical Park (Guam)	72,500					
25¢, 2019P, War in the Pacific National Historical Park (Guam)	(16,275)					
25¢, 2019(P), Frank Church River of No Return Wilderness (Idaho)	25,000					
25¢, 2019P, Frank Church River of No Return Wilderness (Idaho)	(16,417)					

Date	Distribution	MS-67	PF-67			Notes
25¢, 2019(P), San Antonio Missions National Historical Park (Texas)	55,200					
25¢, 2019P, San Antonio Missions National Historical Park (Texas)	(16,207)					
25¢, 2020(P), National Park of American Samoa (American Samoa)						
25¢, 2020P, National Park of American Samoa (American Samoa)						
25¢, 2020(P), Weir Farm National Historic Site (Connecticut)						
25¢, 2020P, Weir Farm National Historic Site (Connecticut)						
25¢, 2020(P), Salt River Bay National Hist'l Park and Ecological Preserve (USVI)						
25¢, 2020P, Salt River Bay National Hist'l Park and Ecological Preserve (USVI)						
25¢, 2020(P), Marsh-Billings-Rockefeller National Historical Park (Vermont)						
25¢, 2020P, Marsh-Billings-Rockefeller National Historical Park (Vermont)						
25¢, 2020(P), Tallgrass Prairie National Preserve (Kansas)						
25¢, 2020P, Tallgrass Prairie National Preserve (Kansas)						
25¢, 2021(P), Tuskegee Airmen National Historic Site (Alabama)						
25¢, 2021P, Tuskegee Airmen National Historic Site (Alabama)						

$1 Silver Eagles

Date	Distribution	MS-67	PF-67	Notes	Date	Distribution	MS-67	PF-67	Notes
$1 1986	5,393,005				$1 2006P, Rev Proof	(248,875)			
$1 1986S	(1,446,778)				$1 2007(W)	9,028,036			
$1 1987	11,442,335				$1 2007W, Burnished	621,333			
$1 1987S	(904,732)				$1 2007W	(821,759)			
$1 1988	5,004,646				$1 2008(W)	20,583,000			
$1 1988S	(557,370)				$1 2008W, Burnished	533,757			
$1 1989	5,203,327				$1 2008W, Burnished, Reverse of 2007	47,000			
$1 1989S	(617,694)								
$1 1990	5,840,210				$1 2008W	(700,979)			
$1 1990S	(695,510)				$1 2009(W)	30,459,000			
$1 1991	7,191,066				$1 2010	34,764,500			
$1 1991S	(511,925)				$1 2010W	(849,861)			
$1 1992	5,540,068				$1 2011	40,020,000			
$1 1992S	(498,654)				$1 2011W, Burnished	409,927			
$1 1993	6,763,762				$1 2011W	(947,355)			
$1 1993P	(405,913)				$1 2011P, Rev Proof	(99,882)			
$1 1994	4,227,319				$1 2011S, Burnished	99,882			
$1 1994P	(372,168)				$1 2012	33,121,500			
$1 1995	4,672,051				$1 2012W, Burnished	226,120			
$1 1995P	(438,511)				$1 2012W	(869,386)			
$1 1995W	(30,125)				$1 2012S	(285,184)			
$1 1996	3,603,386				$1 2012S, Rev Proof	(224,981)			
$1 1996P	(500,000)				$1 2013	42,675,000			
$1 1997	4,295,004				$1 2013W, Burnished	222,091			
$1 1997P	(435,368)				$1 2013W, Enhanced	235,689			
$1 1998	4,847,549				$1 2013W	(934,812)			
$1 1998P	(450,000)				$1 2013W, Rev Proof	(235,689)			
$1 1999	7,408,640				$1 2014	44,006,000			
$1 1999P	(549,769)				$1 2014W, Burnished	253,169			
$1 2000(W)	9,239,132				$1 2014W	(944,770)			
$1 2000P	(600,000)				$1 2015	47,000,000			
$1 2001(W)	9,001,711				$1 2015W, Burnished	201,188			
$1 2001W	(746,398)				$1 2015W	(707,518)			
$1 2002(W)	10,539,026				$1 2016	37,701,500			
$1 2002W	(647,342)				$1 2016W, Burnished	216,501			
$1 2003(W)	8,495,008				$1 2016W	(651,453)			
$1 2003W	(747,831)				$1 2017	18,065,500			
$1 2004(W)	8,882,754				$1 2017W, Burnished	176,739			
$1 2004W	(801,602)				$1 2017W	(440,586)			
$1 2005(W)	8,891,025				$1 2017S	(123,799)			
$1 2005W	(816,663)				$1 2018	15,700,000			
$1 2006(W)	10,676,522				$1 2018W, Burnished	138,947			
$1 2006W, Burnished	468,020				$1 2018W	(411,397)			
$1 2006W	(1,092,477)				$1 2018S	(208,258)			

Date	Distribution	MS-67	PF-67	Notes	Date	Distribution	MS-67	PF-67	Notes
$1 2019	14,863,500								
$1 2019W, Burnished	140,779								
$1 2019W	(372,118)								
$1 2019S	(192,811)								
$1 2019W, Enh. RevPf	(99,675)								
$1 2019S, Enh. RevPf	(29,909)								
$1 2020									
$1 2020W, Burnished									
$1 2020W, Enh. RevPf	7,500								
$1 2020W 75th Anniv. of the end of WWII (with privy mark)	75,000								
$1 2020S									
$1 2021									
$1 2021W, Burnished									
$1 2021W									
$1 2021S									
$1 2022									
$1 2022W, Burnished									
$1 2022W									
$1 2022S									

Silver Bullion Sets

Date			Notes
2006 20th Anniversary Silver Coin Set. Uncirculated, Proof, Reverse Proof			
2006W 20th Anniversary 1-oz. Gold- and Silver-Dollar Set. Uncirculated			
2011 25th Anniversary Five-Coin Set. 2011W Uncirculated, Proof; 2011P Reverse Proof; 2011S Uncirculated, 2011 Bullion (no mintmark)			
2012 75th Anniversary of San Francisco Mint Two-Piece Set. S-Mint Proof and Reverse Proof silver dollars			
2013 75th Anniversary of West Point Depository Two-Coin Set. W-Mint Enhanced Uncirculated and Reverse Proof silver dollars			

Note: See Gold Bullion Sets for 1997 Impressions of Liberty set.

GOLD BULLION

American Eagle $5 Tenth-Ounce Gold

Date	Distribution	MS-67	PF-67	Notes	Date	Distribution	MS-67	PF-67	Notes
$5 MCMLXXXVI (1986)	912,609				$5 2001	269,147			
$5 MCMLXXXVII (1987)	580,266				$5 2001W	(37,530)			
$5 MCMLXXXVIII (1988)	159,500				$5 2002	230,027			
$5 MCMLXXXVIII (1988)P	(143,881)				$5 2002W	(40,864)			
					$5 2003	245,029			
$5 MCMLXXXIX (1989)	264,790				$5 2003W	(40,027)			
$5 MCMLXXXIX (1989)P	(84,647)				$5 2004	250,016			
$5 MCMXC (1990)	210,210				$5 2004W	(35,131)			
$5 MCMXC (1990)P	(99,349)				$5 2005	300,043			
$5 MCMXCI (1991)	165,200				$5 2005W	(49,265)			
$5 MCMXCI (1991)P	(70,334)				$5 2006	285,006			
$5 1992	209,300				$5 2006W, Burnished	20,643			
$5 1992P	(64,874)				$5 2006W	(47,277)			
$5 1993	210,709				$5 2007	190,010			
$5 1993P	(58,649)				$5 2007W, Burnished	22,501			
$5 1994	206,380				$5 2007W	(58,553)			
$5 1994W	(62,849)				$5 2008	305,000			
$5 1995	223,025				$5 2008W, Burnished	12,657			
$5 1995W	(62,667)				$5 2008W	(28,116)			
$5 1996	401,964				$5 2009	270,000			
$5 1996W	(57,047)				$5 2010	435,000			
$5 1997	528,266				$5 2010W	(54,285)			
$5 1997W	(34,977)				$5 2011	350,000			
$5 1998	1,344,520				$5 2011W	(42,697)			
$5 1998W	(39,395)				$5 2012	290,000			
$5 1999	2,750,338				$5 2012W	(20,637)			
$5 1999W	(48,428)				$5 2013	555,000			
$5 1999W, Unc made from unpolished PF dies	14,500				$5 2013W	(21,738)			
					$5 2014	545,000			
$5 2000	569,153				$5 2014W	(22,725)			
$5 2000W	(49,971)				$5 2015	980,000			

Date	Distribution	MS-67	PF-67	Notes	Date	Distribution	MS-67	PF-67	Notes
$5 2015W	(26,769)				$5 2021W, Family of Eagles, Proof				
$5 2016	925,000								
$5 2016W	(37,312)				$5 2021W, Flying Eagle, Proof				
$5 2017	*395,000*				$5 2022				
$5 2017W	(20,969)				$5 2022W				
$5 2018	*230,000*								
$5 2018W	*(22,155)*								
$5 2019	*195,000*								
$5 2019W	*(17,504)*								
$5 2020									
$5 2020W									
$5 2021, Family of Eagles									
$5 2021, Flying Eagle									

American Eagle $10 Quarter-Ounce Gold

Date	Distribution	MS-67	PF-67	Notes	Date	Distribution	MS-67	PF-67	Notes
$10 MCMLXXXVI (1986)	726,031				$10 1999W, Unc from unpolished Proof dies	10,000			
$10 MCMLXXXVII (1987)	269,255								
$10 MCMLXXXVIII (1988)	49,000				$10 2000	128,964			
$10 MCMLXXXVIII (1988)P	(98,028)				$10 2000W	(36,036)			
					$10 2001	71,280			
$10 MCMLXXXIX (1989)	81,789				$10 2001W	(25,613)			
$10 MCMLXXXIX (1989)P	(54,170)				$10 2002	62,027			
					$10 2002W	(29,242)			
$10 MCMXC (1990)	41,000				$10 2003	74,029			
$10 MCMXC (1990)P	(62,674)				$10 2003W	(30,292)			
$10 MCMXCI (1991)	36,100				$10 2004	72,014			
$10 MCMXCI (1991)P	(50,839)				$10 2004W	(28,839)			
$10 1992	59,546				$10 2005	72,015			
$10 1992P	(46,269)				$10 2005W	(37,207)			
$10 1993	71,864				$10 2006	60,004			
$10 1993P	(46,464)				$10 2006W, Burnished	15,188			
$10 1994	72,650				$10 2006W	(36,127)			
$10 1994W	(48,172)				$10 2007	34,004			
$10 1995	83,752				$10 2007W, Burnished	12,766			
$10 1995W	(47,526)				$10 2007W	(46,189)			
$10 1996	60,318				$10 2008	70,000			
$10 1996W	(38,219)				$10 2008W, Burnished	8,883			
$10 1997	108,805				$10 2008W	(18,877)			
$10 1997W	(29,805)				$10 2009	110,000			
$10 1998	309,829				$10 2010	86,000			
$10 1998W	(29,503)				$10 2010W	(44,507)			
$10 1999	564,232				$10 2011	80,000			
$10 1999W	(34,417)				$10 2011W	(28,782)			

Date	Distribution	MS-67	PF-67	Notes	Date	Distribution	MS-67	PF-67	Notes
$10 2012	90,000				$10 2020				
$10 2012W	(13,926)				$10 2020W				
$10 2013	114,500				$5 2021, Family of Eagles				
$10 2013W	(12,782)				$5 2021, Flying Eagle				
$10 2014	90,000				$5 2021W, Family of Eagles, Proof				
$10 2014W	(14,790)								
$10 2015	158,000				$5 2021W, Flying Eagle, Proof				
$10 2015W	(15,775)				$10 2022				
$10 2016	152,000				$10 2022W				
$10 2016W	(22,828)								
$10 2017	64,000								
$10 2017W	(14,513)								
$10 2018	62,000								
$10 2018W	(12,769)								
$10 2019	38,000								
$10 2019W	(10,596)								

American Eagle $25 Half-Ounce Gold

Date	Distribution	MS-67	PF-67	Notes	Date	Distribution	MS-67	PF-67	Notes
$25 MCMLXXXVI (1986)	599,566				$25 1997W	(26,344)			
$25 MCMLXXXVII (1987)	131,255				$25 1998	169,029			
$25 MCMLXXXVII (1987)P	(143,398)				$25 1998W	(25,374)			
					$25 1999	263,013			
$25 MCMLXXXVIII (1988)	45,000				$25 1999W	(30,427)			
$25 MCMLXXXVIII (1988)P	(76,528)				$25 2000	79,287			
					$25 2000W	(32,028)			
$25 MCMLXXXIX (1989)	44,829				$25 2001	48,047			
$25 MCMLXXXIX (1989)P	(44,798)				$25 2001W	(23,240)			
					$25 2002	70,027			
$25 MCMXC (1990)	31,000				$25 2002W	(26,646)			
$25 MCMXC (1990)P	(51,636)				$25 2003	79,029			
$25 MCMXCI (1991)	24,100				$25 2003W	(28,270)			
$25 MCMXCI (1991)P	(53,125)				$25 2004	98,040			
$25 1992	54,404				$25 2004W	(27,330)			
$25 1992P	(40,976)				$25 2005	80,023			
$25 1993	73,324				$25 2005W	(34,311)			
$25 1993P	(43,819)				$25 2006	66,005			
$25 1994	62,400				$25 2006W, Burnished	15,164			
$25 1994W	(44,584)				$25 2006W	(34,322)			
$25 1995	53,474				$25 2007	47,002			
$25 1995W	(45,388)				$25 2007W, Burnished	11,455			
$25 1996	39,287				$25 2007W	(44,025)			
$25 1996W	(35,058)				$25 2008	61,000			
$25 1997	79,605				$25 2008W, Burnished	15,682			

Date	Distribution	MS-67	PF-67	Notes	Date	Distribution	MS-67	PF-67	Notes
$25 2008W	(22,602)				$25 2017W, Proof	(12,715)			
$25 2009	110,000				$25 2018	32,000			
$25 2010	81,000				$25 2018W, Proof	(9,961)			
$25 2010W, Proof	(44,527)				$25 2019	30,000			
$25 2011	70,000				$25 2019W, Proof	(9,479)			
$25 2011W, Proof	(26,781)				$25 2020				
$25 2012	43,000				$25 2020W, Proof				
$25 2012W, Proof	(12,919)				$25 2021, Family of Eagles				
$25 2013	57,000				$25 2021, Flying Eagle				
$25 2013W, Proof	(12,570)				$25 2021W, Family of Eagles, Proof				
$25 2014	35,000								
$25 2014W, Proof	(17,760)				$25 2021W, Flying Eagle, Proof				
$25 2015	78,000								
$25 2015W, Proof	(15,820)								
$25 2016	71,000								
$25 2016W, Proof	(22,001)								
$25 2017	37,000								

American Eagle $50 One-Ounce Gold

Date	Distribution	MS-67	PF-67	Notes	Date	Distribution	MS-67	PF-67	Notes
$50 MCMLXXXVI (1986)	1,362,650				$50 1994	221,633			
					$50 1994W	(46,674)			
$50 MCMLXXXVI (1986)W	(446,290)				$50 1995	200,636			
					$50 1995W	(46,368)			
$50 MCMLXXXVII (1987)	1,045,500				$50 1996	189,148			
					$50 1996W	(36,153)			
$50 MCMLXXXVII (1987)W	(147,498)				$50 1997	664,508			
					$50 1997W	(32,999)			
$50 MCMLXXXVIII (1988)	465,000				$50 1998	1,468,530			
					$50 1998W	(25,886)			
$50 MCMLXXXVIII (1988)W	(87,133)				$50 1999	1,505,026			
					$50 1999W	(31,427)			
$50 MCMLXXXIX (1989)	415,790				$50 2000	433,319			
					$50 2000W	(33,007)			
$50 MCMLXXXIX (1989)W	(54,570)				$50 2001	143,605			
					$50 2001W	(24,555)			
$50 MCMXC (1990)	373,210				$50 2002	222,029			
$50 MCMXC (1990)W	(62,401)				$50 2002W	(27,499)			
$50 MCMXCI (1991)	243,100				$50 2003	416,032			
$50 MCMXCI (1991)W	(50,411)				$50 2003W	(28,344)			
$50 1992	275,000				$50 2004	417,019			
$50 1992W	(44,826)				$50 2004W	(28,215)			
$50 1993	480,192				$50 2005	356,555			
$50 1993W	(34,369)				$50 2005W	(35,246)			

Date	Distribution	MS-67	PF-67	Notes	Date	Distribution	MS-67	PF-67	Notes
$50 2006	237,510				$50 2015	594,000			
$50 2006W, Burnished	45,053				$50 2015W, Burnished	6,533			
$50 2006W	(47,092)				$50 2015W, Proof	(32,652)			
$50 2006W, Rev Proof	(9,996)				$50 2016	817,500			
$50 2007	140,016				$50 2016W, Burnished	6,887			
$50 2007W, Burnished	18,066				$50 2016W, Proof	(40,044)			
$50 2007W	(51,810)				$50 2017	228,500			
$50 2008	710,000				$50 2017W, Burnished	5,800			
$50 2008W, Burnished	11,908				$50 2017W, Proof	(19,056)			
$50 2008W	(30,237)				$50 2018	191,000			
$50 2009	1,493,000				$50 2018W, Burnished	8,518			
$50 2010	1,125,000				$50 2018W, Proof	(15,570)			
$50 2010W, Proof	(59,480)				$50 2019	108,000			
$50 2011	857,000				$50 2019W, Burnished	5,741			
$50 2011W, Burnished	8,729				$50 2019W, Proof	(13,480)			
$50 2011W, Proof	(48,306)				$50 2020				
$50 2012	675,000				$50 2020W, Burnished	7,000			
$50 2012W, Burnished	6,118				$50 2020W, Proof				
$50 2012W, Proof	(23,630)				$50 2020W, 75th Anniv. of the End of WWII (with privy mark)	1,945			
$50 2013	758,500								
$50 2013W, Burnished	7,293								
$50 2013W, Proof	(24,710)				$50 2021, Family of Eagles				
$50 2014	425,000				$50 2021, Flying Eagle				
$50 2014W, Burnished	7,902				$50 2021W, Family of Eagles, Proof				
$50 2014W, Proof	(28,703)				$50 2021W, Flying Eagle, Proof				

American Eagle Gold Bullion Sets

GOLD BULLION SETS		Notes	1997 Impressions of Liberty Set. $100 platinum, $50 gold, $1 silver		Notes
1987 Gold Set. $50, $25					
1988 Gold Set. $50, $25, $10, $5			1998 Gold Set. $50, $25, $10, $5		
1989 Gold Set. $50, $25, $10, $5			1999 Gold Set. $50, $25, $10, $5		
1990 Gold Set. $50, $25, $10, $5			2000 Gold Set. $50, $25, $10, $5		
1991 Gold Set. $50, $25, $10, $5			2001 Gold Set. $50, $25, $10, $5		
1992 Gold Set. $50, $25, $10, $5			2002 Gold Set. $50, $25, $10, $5		
1993 Gold Set. $50, $25, $10, $5			2003 Gold Set. $50, $25, $10, $5		
1993 Bicentennial Gold Set. $25, $10, $5, $1 silver eagle, and medal			2004 Gold Set. $50, $25, $10, $5		
			2005 Gold Set. $50, $25, $10, $5		
1994 Gold Set. $50, $25, $10, $5			2006 Gold Set. $50, $25, $10, $5		
1995 Gold Set. $50, $25, $10, $5			2007 Gold Set. $50, $25, $10, $5		
1995 Anniversary Gold Set. $50, $25, $10, $5, and $1 silver eagle			2008 Gold Set. $50, $25, $10, $5		
			2010 Gold Set. $50, $25, $10, $5		
1996 Gold Set. $50, $25, $10, $5			2011 Gold Set. $50, $25, $10, $5		
1997 Gold Set. $50, $25, $10, $5			2012 Gold Set. $50, $25, $10, $5		

		Notes			Notes
2013 Gold Set. $50, $25, $10, $5					
2014 Gold Set. $50, $25, $10, $5					
2015 Gold Set. $50, $25, $10, $5					
2016 Gold Set. $50, $25, $10, $5					
2017 Gold Set. $50, $25, $10, $5					
2018 Gold Set. $50, $25, $10, $5					
2019 Gold Set. $50, $25, $10, $5					
2020 Gold Set. $50, $25, $10, $5					
2021 Gold Set. $50, $25, $10, $5					
2006 20TH ANNIVERSARY SETS					
2006W $50 Gold Set. Uncirculated, Proof, Reverse Proof					
2006W 1-oz. Gold- and Silver-Dollar Set. Uncirculated					
GOLD BULLION BURNISHED SETS 2006–2008					
2006W Burnished Gold Set. $50, $25, $10, $5					
2007W Burnished Gold Set. $50, $25, $10, $5					
2008W Burnished Gold Set. $50, $25, $10, $5					

American Buffalo .9999 Fine Bullion

Date	Distribution	MS-67	PF-67	Notes	Date	Distribution	MS-67	PF-67	Notes
$5 2008W, Burnished	17,429				$50 2019W	(14,836)			
$5 2008W	(18,884)				$50 2020				
$10 2008W, Burnished	9,949				$50 2020W				
$10 2008W	(13,125)				$50 2021				
$25 2008W, Burnished	16,908				$50 2021W				
$25 2008W	(12,169)				$50 2022				
$50 2006	337,012				$50 2022W				
$50 2006W	(246,267)								
$50 2007	136,503								
$50 2007W	(58,998)								
$50 2008	214,053*								
$50 2008W	(18,863)								
$50 2008W, Burnished	9,074								
$50 2009	200,000								
$50 2009W	(49,306)								
$50 2010	209,000								
$50 2010W	(49,263)								
$50 2011	250,000								
$50 2011W	(28,693)								
$50 2012	100,000								
$50 2012W	(19,765)								
$50 2013	198,500								
$50 2013W	(18,594)								
$50 2013W, Rev Proof	(47,836)								
$50 2014	180,500								
$50 2014W	(20,557)								
$50 2015	223,500								
$50 2015W	(16,591)								
$50 2016	219,500								
$50 2016W	(21,878)								
$50 2017	99,500								
$50 2017W	(15,810)								
$50 2018	121,500								
$50 2018W	(15,756)								
$50 2019	61,500								

* Includes 24,553 that were sold as Lunar New Year Celebration coins.

American Buffalo Gold Bullion Sets

Date		Notes
2008W Four-coin set ($5, $10, $25, $50)		
2008W Four-coin set ($5, $10, $25, $50), Burnished		
2008W Double Prosperity set. Uncirculated $25 Buffalo gold and $25 American Eagle coins		

First Spouse $10 Bullion

Date	Distribution	MS-67	PF-67	Notes	Date	Distribution	MS-67	PF-67	Notes
$10 2007W, M. Washington	(19,167) 17,661				$10 2012W, Caroline Harrison	(3,046) 2,436			
$10 2007W, Abigail Adams	(17,149) 17,142				$10 2012W, F. Cleveland, Type 2	(3,104) 2,425			
$10 2007W, T. Jefferson's Lib	(19,815) 19,823				$10 2013W, Ida McKinley	(1,769) 1,973			
$10 2007W, Dolley Madison	(17,943) 12,340				$10 2013W, Edith Roosevelt	(2,851) 1,913			
$10 2008W, Elizabeth Monroe	(7,800) 4,462				$10 2013W, Helen Taft	(2,579) 1,890			
$10 2008W, Louisa Adams	(6,581) 3,885				$10 2013W, Ellen Wilson	(2,551) 1,880			
$10 2008W, A. Jackson's Lib	(7,684) 4,609				$10 2013W, Edith Wilson	(2,452) 1,881			
$10 2008W, M. Van Buren's Lib	(6,807) 3,826				$10 2014W, F. Harding	(2,372) 1,944			
$10 2009W, Anna Harrison	(6,251) 3,645				$10 2014W, G. Coolidge	(2,315) 1,949			
$10 2009W, Letitia Tyler	(5,296) 3,240				$10 2014W, L. Hoover	(2,392) 1,936			
$10 2009W, Julia Tyler	(4,844) 3,143				$10 2014W, E. Roosevelt	(2,377) 1,886			
$10 2009W, Sarah Polk	(5,151) 3,489				$10 2015W, B. Truman	(2,747) 1,946			
$10 2009W, Margaret Taylor	(4,936) 3,627				$10 2015W, M. Eisenhower	(2,704) 2,102			
$10 2010W, Abigail Fillmore	(6,130) 3,482				$10 2015W, J. Kennedy	(11,222) 6,439			
$10 2010W, Jane Pierce	(4,775) 3,338				$10 2015W, Lady Bird Johnson	(2,611) 1,927			
$10 2010W, J. Buchanan's Lib	(7,110) 5,162				$10 2016W, P. Nixon	(2,645) 1,839			
$10 2010W, Mary Lincoln	(6,861) 3,695				$10 2016W, B. Ford	(2,471) 1,824			
$10 2011W, Eliza Johnson	(3,887) 2,905				$10 2016W, N. Reagan	(3,548) 2,009			
$10 2011W, Julia Grant	(3,943) 2,892				$10 2020W, Barbara Bush				
$10 2011W, Lucy Hayes	(3,868) 2,196								
$10 2011W, Lucretia Garfield	(3,653) 2,168								
$10 2012W, Alice Paul	(3,505) 2,798								
$10 2012W, F. Cleveland, Type 1	(3,158) 2,454								

MMIX Ultra High Relief Gold Coin

Date	Distribution	Unc.				Notes
MMIX (2009) Ultra High Relief $20 Gold Coin	114,427					

American Liberty Gold Coin

Date	Distribution	Unc.				Notes
$100 2015W, 1 oz.	49,325					
$100 1792–2017W, 1 oz.	32,612					
$10 2018W, 1/10 oz.	36,351					
$100 2019W, 1 oz.	10,421					

400th Anniversary of the Mayflower Gold Coins

Date	Distribution	Unc.				Notes
2020W	(4,842)					
2020W, Rev Proof	(4,991)					

75th Anniversary of the End of WWII Gold Coins

Date	Distribution	Unc.	Notes
2020W	(7,482)		

PLATINUM BULLION

American Eagle $10 Tenth-Ounce Platinum

Date	Distribution	MS-67	PF-67	Notes	Date	Distribution	MS-67	PF-67	Notes
$10 1997	70,250				$10 2004	15,010			
$10 1997W	(36,993)				$10 2004W	(7,161)			
$10 1998	39,525				$10 2005	14,013			
$10 1998W	(19,847)				$10 2005W	(8,104)			
$10 1999	55,955				$10 2006	11,001			
$10 1999W	(19,133)				$10 2006W, Burnished	3,544			
$10 2000	34,027				$10 2006W	(10,205)			
$10 2000W	(15,651)				$10 2007	13,003			
$10 2001	52,017				$10 2007W, Burnished	5,556			
$10 2001W	(12,174)				$10 2007W	(8,176)			
$10 2002	23,005				$10 2008	17,000			
$10 2002W	(12,365)				$10 2008W, Burnished	3,706			
$10 2003	22,007				$10 2008W	(5,138)			
$10 2003W	(9,534)								

American Eagle $25 Quarter-Ounce Platinum

Date	Distribution	MS-67	PF-67	Notes	Date	Distribution	MS-67	PF-67	Notes
$25 1997	27,100				$25 2006W, Burnished	2,676			
$25 1997W	(18,628)				$25 2006W	(7,813)			
$25 1998	38,887				$25 2007	8,402			
$25 1998W	(14,873)				$25 2007W, Burnished	3,690			
$25 1999	39,734				$25 2007W	(6,017)			
$25 1999W	(13,507)				$25 2007W, Frosted FREEDOM	(21)			
$25 2000	20,054								
$25 2000W	(11,995)				$25 2008	22,800			
$25 2001	21,815				$25 2008W, Burnished	2,481			
$25 2001W	(8,847)				$25 2008W	(4,153)			
$25 2002	27,405								
$25 2002W	(9,282)								
$25 2003	25,207								
$25 2003W	(7,044)								
$25 2004	18,010								
$25 2004W	(5,193)								
$25 2005	12,013								
$25 2005W	(6,592)								
$25 2006	12,001								

American Eagle $50 Half-Ounce Platinum

Date	Distribution	MS-67	PF-67	Notes	Date	Distribution	MS-67	PF-67	Notes
$50 1997	20,500				$50 2005W	(5,942)			
$50 1997W	(15,431)				$50 2006	9,602			
$50 1998	32,415				$50 2006W, Burnished	2,577			
$50 1998W	(13,836)				$50 2006W	(7,649)			
$50 1999	32,309				$50 2007	7,001			
$50 1999W	(11,103)				$50 2007W, Burnished	3,635			
$50 2000	18,892				$50 2007W	(25,519)			
$50 2000W	(11,049)				$50 2007W, Frosted FREEDOM	(21)			
$50 2001	12,815								
$50 2001W	(8,254)				$50 2008	14,000			
$50 2002	24,005				$50 2008W, Burnished	2,253			
$50 2002W	(8,772)				$50 2008W	(4,020)			
$50 2003	17,409								
$50 2003W	(7,131)								
$50 2004	13,236								
$50 2004W	(5,063)								
$50 2005	9,013								

American Eagle $100 One-Ounce Platinum

Date	Distribution	MS-67	PF-67	Notes	Date	Distribution	MS-67	PF-67	Notes
$100 1997	56,000				$100 2008	21,800			
$100 1997W	(20,851)				$100 2008W, Burnished	2,876			
$100 1998	133,002				$100 2008W	(4,769)			
$100 1998W	(14,912)				$100 2009W	(7,945)			
$100 1999	56,707				$100 2010W	(14,790)			
$100 1999W	(12,363)				$100 2011W	(14,835)			
$100 2000	10,003				$100 2012W	9,081			
$100 2000W	(12,453)				$100 2013W	5,763			
$100 2001	14,070				$100 2014	16,900			
$100 2001W	(8,969)				$100 2014W	(4,596)			
$100 2002	11,502				$100 2015	20,000			
$100 2002W	(9,834)				$100 2015W	(3,881)			
$100 2003	8,007				$100 2016	20,000			
$100 2003W	(8,246)				$100 2016W	(9,151)			
$100 2004	7,009				$100 2017	*20,000*			
$100 2004W	(6,007)				$100 2017W	(8,890)			
$100 2005	6,310				$100 2018	*30,000*			
$100 2005W	(6,602)				$100 2018W	*(14,499)*			
$100 2006	6,000				$100 2019	*40,000*			
$100 2006W, Burnished	3,068				$100 2019W	*(10,928)*			
$100 2006W	(9,152)				$100 2020				
$100 2007	7,202				$100 2020W				
$100 2007W, Burnished	4,177				$100 2021				
$100 2007W	(8,363)				$100 2021W				
$100 2007W, Frosted FREEDOM	(12)				$100 2022				
					$100 2022W				

Platinum Bullion Sets

	Notes			Notes
PLATINUM BULLION SETS		2007W. $100, $50, $25, $10		
1997. $100, $50, $25, $10		2007W, Burnished Set. $100, $50, $25, $10		
1998. $100, $50, $25, $10				
1999. $100, $50, $25, $10		2008W. $100, $50, $25, $10		
2000. $100, $50, $25, $10		2008W, Burnished Set. $100, $50, $25, $10		
2001. $100, $50, $25, $10				
2002. $100, $50, $25, $10		**2007 10TH ANNIVERSARY SET**		
2003. $100, $50, $25, $10		Two-coin set containing one Proof platinum half-ounce and one Enhanced Reverse Proof platinum half-ounce dated 2007W. Housed in hardwood box with mahogany finish		
2004. $100, $50, $25, $10				
2005. $100, $50, $25, $10				
2006W. $100, $50, $25, $10				
2006W, Burnished Set. $100, $50, $10				

American Palladium Eagles

American Eagle $25 One-Ounce Palladium

Date	Distribution	MS-67	PF-67	Notes	Date	Distribution	MS-67	PF-67	Notes
2017	15,000								
2018W	(14,986)								
2019W, Rev Proof	(18,115)								
2020W									
2021W									
2022W									

CIVIL WAR, HARD TIMES, AND OTHER TOKENS AND MEDALS

Notes

HAWAIIAN ISSUES

Kingdom of Hawaii

Date		Quantity Minted	VF-20	EF-40	AU-50	MS-60	MS-63	PF	Notes
1847 Cent		100,000							
1881 Five Cents									
1883 Ten Cents	(26)	250,000							
1883 Eighth Dollar	(20)								
1883 Quarter Dollar	(26)	500,000							
1883 Half Dollar	(26)	700,000							
1883 Dollar	(26)	500,000							

Plantation Tokens

Date	F-12	VF-20	EF-40	AU-50	Notes
Waterhouse / Kamehameha IV, ca. 1860					
Wailuku Plantation, 1 Real, 1880					
Wailuku Plantation, Half Real, 1880					
Thomas H. Hobron, 12-1/2 (cents), 1879					
Similar, two stars on both sides					
Thomas H. Hobron, 25 (cents), 1879 *(3 known)*					
Wailuku Plantation, 12-1/2 (cents), (1871), narrow starfish					
Similar, broad starfish					
Wailuku Plantation, VI (6-1/4 cents), (1871), narrow starfish					
Similar, broad starfish					

Date	F-12	VF-20	EF-40	AU-50			Notes
Haiku Plantation, 1 Rial, 1882							
Grove Ranch Plantation, 12-1/2 (cents), 1886							
Grove Ranch Plantation, 12-1/2 (cents), 1887							
Kahului Railroad, 10 cents, 1891							
Kahului Railroad, 15 cents, 1891							
Kahului Railroad, 20 cents, 1891							
Kahului Railroad, 25 cents, 1891							
Kahului Railroad, 35 cents, 1891							
Kahului Railroad, 75 cents, 1891							

PUERTO RICAN ISSUES

Date	Quantity Minted	F.	VF	EF	Unc.			Notes
1896 5 Centavos	600,000							
1896 10 Centavos	700,000							
1895 20 Centavos	3,350,000							
1896 40 Centavos	725,002							
1895 1 Peso	8,500,021							

THE PHILIPPINES (UNDER U.S. SOVEREIGNTY)

Half Centavo

Date		Quantity Minted	VF	EF	MS-60	MS-63	PF-63			Notes
1903	(2,558)	12,084,000								
1904	(1,355)	5,654,000								
1905, Proof only	(471)									
1906, Proof only	(500)									
1908, Proof only	(500)									

One Centavo

Date		Quantity Minted	VF	EF	MS-60	MS-63	PF-63			Notes
1903	(2,558)	10,790,000								
1904	(1,355)	17,040,400								
1905	(471)	10,000,000								
1906, Proof only	(500)									
1908, Proof only	(500)									
1908S		2,187,000								
1908S, S Over S										
1909S		1,737,612								
1910S		2,700,000								
1911S		4,803,000								
1912S		3,001,000								
1913S		5,000,000								
1914S		5,000,500								
1915S		2,500,000								
1916S		4,330,000								
1917S		7,070,000								
1917S, 7 Over 6										
1918S		11,660,000								
1918S, Large S										
1919S		4,540,000								
1920S		2,500,000								
1920		3,552,259								
1921		7,282,673								
1922		3,519,100								
1925M		9,325,000								
1926M		9,000,000								
1927M		9,279,000								
1928M		9,150,000								
1929M		5,657,161								
1930M		5,577,000								
1931M		5,659,355								
1932M		4,000,000								
1933M		8,392,692								
1934M		3,179,000								
1936M		17,455,463								

Five Centavos, Large Size (1903–1928)

Date		Quantity Minted	VF	EF	MS-60	MS-63	PF-63			Notes
1903	(2,558)	8,910,000								
1904	(1,355)	1,075,000								
1905, Proof only	(471)									
1906, Proof only	(500)									
1908, Proof only	(500)									
1916S		300,000								
1917S		2,300,000								
1918S										
1918S, Mule (Small-Date reverse of 20 centavos)		2,780,000								
1919S		1,220,000								
1920		1,421,078								
1921		2,131,529								
1925M		1,000,000								
1926M		1,200,000								
1927M		1,000,000								
1928M		1,000,000								

Five Centavos, Reduced Size (1930–1935)

Date	Quantity Minted	VF	EF	MS-60	MS-63			Notes
1930M	2,905,182							
1931M	3,476,790							
1932M	3,955,861							
1934M								
1934M, Recut 1	2,153,729							
1935M	2,754,000							

Ten Centavos, Large Size (1903–1906)

Date		Quantity Minted	VF	EF	MS-60	MS-63	PF-63			Notes
1903	(2,558)	5,102,658								
1903S		1,200,000								

Date		Quantity Minted	VF	EF	MS-60	MS-63	PF-63		Notes
1904	(1,355)	10,000							
1904S		5,040,000							
1905, Proof only	(471)								
1906, Proof only	(500)								

Ten Centavos, Reduced Size (1907–1935)

Date		Quantity Minted	VF	EF	MS-60	MS-63	PF-63		Notes
1907		1,500,781							
1907S		4,930,000							
1908, Proof only	(500)								
1908S		3,363,911							
1909S		312,199							
1911S		1,000,505							
1912S		1,010,000							
1912S, S Over S									
1913S		1,360,693							
1914S		1,180,000							
1915S		450,000							
1917S		5,991,148							
1918S		8,420,000							
1919S		1,630,000							
1920		520,000							
1921		3,863,038							
1929M		1,000,000							
1935M		1,280,000							

Twenty Centavos, Large Size (1903–1906)

Date		Quantity Minted	VF	EF	MS-60	MS-63	PF-63		Notes
1903	(2,558)	5,350,231							
1903S		150,080							
1904	(1,355)	10,000							
1904S		2,060,000							
1905, Proof only	(471)								
1905S		420,000							
1906, Proof only	(500)								

Twenty Centavos, Reduced Size (1907–1929)

Date	Quantity Minted	VF	EF	MS-60	MS-63	PF-63			Notes
1907	1,250,651								
1907S	3,165,000								
1908, Proof only	(500)								
1908S	1,535,000								
1909S	450,000								
1910S	500,259								
1911S	505,000								
1912S	750,000								
1913S	795,000								
1914S	795,000								
1915S	655,000								
1916S	1,435,000								
1917S	3,150,655								
1918S	5,560,000								
1919S	850,000								
1920	1,045,415								
1921	1,842,631								
1928M, Mule (reverse of 1903–1928 5 centavos)	100,000								
1929M	1,970,000								
1929M, 2 Over 2 Over 2									

Fifty Centavos, Large Size (1903–1906)

Date		Quantity Minted	VF	EF	MS-60	MS-63	PF-63			Notes
1903	(2,558)	3,099,061								
1903S *(2 known)*										
1904	(1,355)	10,000								
1904S		216,000								
1905, Proof only	(471)									
1905S		852,000								
1906, Proof only	(500)									

Fifty Centavos, Reduced Size (1907–1921)

Date	Quantity Minted	VF	EF	MS-60	MS-63	PF-63			Notes
1907	1,200,625								
1907S	2,112,000								
1908, Proof only	(500)								
1908S	1,601,000								
1909S	528,000								
1917S	674,369								
1918S	2,202,000								
1919S	1,200,000								
1920	420,000								
1921	2,316,763								

One Peso, Large Size (1903–1906)

Date		Quantity Minted	VF	EF	MS-60	MS-63	PF-63			Notes
1903	(2,558)	2,788,901								
1903S		11,361,000								
1904	(1,355)	11,355								
1904S		6,600,000								
1905, Proof only	(471)									
1905S, Curved Serif on "1"		6,056,000								
1905S, Straight Serif on "1"										
1906, Proof only	(500)									
1906S		201,000								

One Peso, Reduced Size (1907–1912)

Date	Quantity Minted	VF	EF	MS-60	MS-63	PF-63			Notes
1907, Proof only *(2 known)*									
1907S	10,278,000								
1908, Proof only	(500)								
1908S	20,954,944								
1909S	7,578,000								
1909S, S Over S									
1910S	3,153,559								
1911S	463,000								
1912S	680,000								

THE PHILIPPINES (COMMONWEALTH)

One Centavo

Date	Quantity Minted	VF	EF	MS-60	MS-63			Notes
1937M	15,790,492							
1938M	*10,000,000*							
1939M	*6,500,000*							
1940M	*4,000,000*							
1941M	*5,000,000*							
1944S	58,000,000							

Five Centavos, Copper-Nickel (1937–1941)

Date	Quantity Minted	VF	EF	MS-60	MS-63			Notes
1937M	2,493,872							
1938M	4,000,000							
1941M	2,750,000							

Five Centavos, Copper-Nickel-Zinc Alloy (1944–1945)

Date	Quantity Minted	VF	EF	MS-60	MS-63			Notes
1944	21,198,000							
1944S	14,040,000							
1945S	72,796,000							

Ten Centavos

Date	Quantity Minted	VF	EF	MS-60	MS-63			Notes
1937M	3,500,000							
1938M	3,750,000							
1941M	2,500,000							
1944D	31,592,000							
1945D	137,208,000							
1945D, D Over D								

Twenty Centavos

Date	Quantity Minted	VF	EF	MS-60	MS-63			Notes
1937M	2,665,000							
1938M	3,000,000							
1941M	1,500,000							
1944D	28,596,000							
1944D, D Over S								
1945D	82,804,000							

Fifty Centavos

Date	Quantity Minted	VF	EF	MS-60	MS-63			Notes
1944S	19,187,000							
1945S	18,120,000							
1945S, S Over S								

Commemorative Coinage

Date	Quantity Minted	VF	EF	MS-60	MS-63			Notes
1936M, Silver, fifty centavos	20,000							
1936M, Silver, one peso, busts of Murphy and Quezon	10,000							
1936M, Silver, one peso, busts of Roosevelt and Quezon	10,000							

MISSTRIKES AND ERRORS

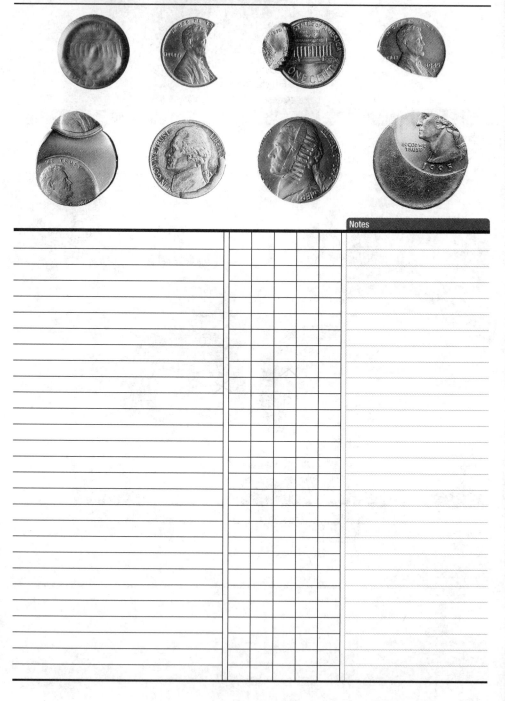

Notes

CANADIAN COINS

Note: Collector coins from the Royal Canadian Mint come in a variety of finishes, not limited to Proof. In the charts that follow, all of these different finishes (which include Specimen, Brilliant Uncirculated, Prooflike, and Bullion) are represented by the PF (Proof) column. Additionally, Canada has treated "commemorative" coins differently. Sometimes the event was marked on both the obverse and reverse; sometimes only one side varied from the standard issue. Some took the place of the standard circulation coinage of that year, while others circulated alongside the regular issue. Some were released like standard "circulating" coins; others came in special packaging and/or in special finishes. Some were released by both methods.

For the purposes of this check list, commemoratives that (a) replaced the standard circulating design for a given year or (b) were only released through standard "circulating" methods will be found within the regular chronological charts for the appropriate denomination. Commemoratives that did not replace the standard design, or which were channeled directly to collectors, are at the end of the listings, in a special "Commemoratives" section.

Note as well that "commemorative"-type packaging was used to mark some recent design changes. These items, like First-Strike Folders for the introduction of the Royal Canadian Mint mark on Queen Elizabeth Uncrowned Portrait coins, appear within the regular flow of the denomination-by-denomination charts.

Large Cents

Queen Victoria (1876–1901)

Date	Quantity Minted	G	VG	F	VF	EF	Unc.	Notes
1876H (01)	4,000,000				X			
1881H (01, 1a), Normal Legend					X			
1881H (01, 1a), Mixed Fonts	2,000,000							
1881H (01, 1a), Large Over Small D								
1882H (01, 1a, 2)	4,000,000				X			
1884 (01)	2,500,000							
1884 (02)								
1886 (01a, 2)	1,500,000							
1887 (02)	1,500,000							
1888 (02)	4,000,000			X				
1890H (03)	1,000,000							
1891 (02, 3), Large Leaves, Large Date								
1891 (02, 3), Large Leaves, Small Date	1,452,000							
1891 (02, 3), Small Leaves, Small Date								
1892 (02)								
1892 (03)	1,200,000							
1892, (04)								

Date	Quantity Minted	G	VG	F	VF	EF	Unc.	Notes
1893 (O4)	2,000,000							
1894 (O4), Fine 4	1,000,000							
1894 (O4), Crude 4								
1895 (O4)	1,200,000				X			
1896 (O4)	2,000,000				X			
1897 (O4)	1,500,000					X		
1898H (O4)	1,000,000							
1899 (O4)	2,400,000		X					
1900 (O4)	1,000,000				X			
1900H (O4)	2,600,000				X			
1901 (O4)	4,100,000		X					

King Edward VII (1902–1910)

Date	Quantity Minted	G	VG	F	VF	EF	Unc.	Notes
1902	3,000,000							
1903	4,000,000					X		
1904	2,500,000		X					
1905	2,000,000							
1906	4,100,000					X		
1907	2,400,000							
1907H	800,000							
1908	2,401,506					X		
1909	3,973,339				X			
1910	5,146,487				X			

King George V (1911–1920)

Without DEI GRA:
(1911)

With DEI GRA:
(1912–1920)

Date	Quantity Minted	G	VG	F	VF	EF	Unc.	Notes
1911, Without DEI GRA:	4,663,486					X		
1912, With DEI GRA:	5,107,642				X			

Date	Quantity Minted	G	VG	F	VF	EF	Unc.	Notes
1913	5,735,405					✗		
1914	3,405,958			✗				
1915	4,932,134				✗			
1916	11,022,367				✗			
1917	11,899,254			✗				
1918	12,970,798				✗			
1919	11,279,634				✗			
1920	6,762,247		✗					

Small Cents

King George V (1920–1936)

Date	Quantity Minted	G	VG	F	VF	EF	Unc.	Notes
1920	15,483,923			✗				
1921	7,601,627			✗				
1922	1,243,635							
1923	1,019,002							
1924	1,593,195							
1925	1,000,652							
1926	2,143,372							
1927	3,553,928							
1928	9,144,860				✗			
1929, Normal 9	12,159,840							
1929, High 9								
1930	2,538,613							
1931	3,842,776							
1932	21,316,190				✗			
1933	12,079,310				✗			
1934	7,042,358				✗			
1935	7,526,400				✗			
1936	8,768,769							
1936, Dot *(5 known)*	678,823							

King George VI (1937–1952)

With Et IND:IMP:
(1937–1947)

Without Et IND:IMP:
(1948–1952)

Date	Quantity Minted	G	VG	F	VF	EF	Unc.	Notes
1937					X			
1937, Matte Fields	10,040,231							
1937, Mirror Fields								
1938	18,365,608				X			
1939	21,600,319				X			
1940	85,740,532				X			
1941	56,336,011				X			
1942	76,113,708				X			
1943	89,111,969				X			
1944	44,131,216				X			
1945	77,268,591				X			
1946	56,662,071				X			
1947	31,093,901				X			
1947, Maple Leaf, Blunt 7	43,855,448							
1947, Maple Leaf, Pointed 7					X			
1948, "A" Points to Thin Denticle								
1948, "A" Points to Thick Denticle	25,767,779							
1948, "A" Points Between Denticles					X			
1949, "A" Points to Denticle	33,128,933							
1949, "A" Points Between Denticles					X			
1950	60,444,992				X			
1951	80,430,379				X			
1952	67,631,736				X			

Queen Elizabeth II, Laureate Portrait (1953–1964)

Date	Quantity Minted	VG	F	VF	EF	Unc.	PF	Notes
1953, No Shoulder Fold	67,806,016			X				
1953, With Shoulder Fold				X				
1954, With Shoulder Fold	22,181,760							
1954, No Fold (Prooflike only)								
1955, With Shoulder Fold	56,403,193							
1955, No Shoulder Fold								
1956	78,658,535	X						
1957	100,601,792	X						
1958	59,385,679	X						
1959	83,615,343	X						
1960	75,772,775	X						
1961	135,598,404				X			
1962	227,244,069		X		X			
1963	279,076,334		X					
1964	484,655,322			X				

Queen Elizabeth II, Tiara Portrait (1965–1989)
Round (1965–1981); 12-Sided (1982–1989)

| **Original Portrait (1965–1978)** | | **Confederation Centennial (dated 1867–1967)** | **Reduced Portrait (1979–1989)** |

Date	Quantity Minted	VG	F	VF	EF	Unc.	PF	Notes
1965, Small Beads, Pointed 5								
1965, Small Beads, Blunt 5	304,441,082							
1965, Large Beads, Blunt 5								
1965, Large Beads, Pointed 5				✕				
1966	184,151,087					✕		
1967, Confederation Cent'l	345,140,645					✕		
1968	329,695,772			✕				
1969	335,240,929					✕		
1970	311,145,010					✕		
1971	298,228,936					✕		
1972	451,304,591					✕		
1973	457,059,852					✕		
1974	692,058,489					✕		
1975	642,318,000					✕		
1976	701,122,890					✕		
1977	453,762,670					✕		
1978	911,170,647					✕		
1979, Reduced Portrait	754,394,064					✕		
1980	912,052,318					✕		
1981	(199,000) 1,209,468,500					✕		
1982, 12-Sided	(180,908) 911,001,000					✕		
1983, Near Beads	(166,779) 975,510,000					✕		
1983, Far Beads								
1984	(161,602) 838,225,000					✕		
1985, Blunt 5	(153,950) 771,772,500					✕		
1985, Pointed 5								
1986	(176,224) 740,335,000					✕		
1987	(175,686) 774,549,000					✕		
1988	(175,259) 482,676,752					✕		
1989	(154,693) 1,077,347,200					✕		

Queen Elizabeth II, Diadem Portrait (1990–2003)

| 12-Sided (1990–1996) | | Round (1997–2003) | 125th Anniv. of Confederation (dated 1867–1992) | Golden Jubilee (dated 1952–2002) |

Date	Quantity Minted		VG	F	VF	EF	Unc.	PF	Notes
1990	(158,068)	218,035,000							
1991	(131,888)	831,101,000			X				
1992, 125th Anniv of Confederation	(147,061)	673,512,000				X			
1993	(143,065)	808,585,000			X				
1994	(153,707)	639,516,000			X				
1995	(151,362)	624,983,000			X				
1996	(112,835)	445,746,000			X				
1997, Round		549,868,000			X				
1997, Bronze Proof	(113,647)								
1998		999,578,000			X				
1998W, Unc sets only	(—)								
1998, Bronze Proof	(93,362)								
1999		1,089,625,000			X				
1999, Bronze Proof	(95,113)								
1999P, Test only	(20,000+)								
2000		902,506,000							
2000W, Unc sets only	(—)								
2000, Bronze Proof	(90,921)								
2000P, Test only *(6 known)*									
2001		928,434,000							
2001, Bronze Proof	(74,194)								
2001P, BU, Specimen; Collector sets only	(—)								
2002, Golden Jubilee		830,040,000			X				
2002, Bronze Proof	(98,805)				X				
2002P		114,212,000							
2003, Diadem Portrait		748,123,000							
2003, Bronze Proof	(62,007)								
2003P		235,936,799							

Queen Elizabeth II, Uncrowned Portrait (2003–2012)

Date	Quantity Minted	VG	F	VF	EF	Unc.	PF	Notes
2003, Uncrowned Portrait	56,877,144				✗			
2003, Gold-Highlighted (from annual Mint report)	(10,000)							
2003P	354,994,666							
2003W, BU sets only	(71,142)			✗				
2004	653,317,000					✗		
2004P	134,906,000							
2004, Bronze Proof	(57,614)							
2005	759,658,000							
2005P	30,525,000							
2005P, First-Day Strike Folder	(1,919)							
2005, Bronze Proof	(62,286)							
2006, Zinc	886,275,000							
2006, Steel (error)								
2006P	233,000							
2006P/2006RCM, Last-Day/First-Day Strike Folder	(750)							
2006RCM, Zinc	176,000,000					✗		
2006RCM, Steel	137,733,000					✗		
2006, Bronze Proof	(57,885)							
2007, Zinc	9,625,999							
2007, Steel	938,270,000					✗		
2007, Bronze Proof	(37,373)							
2008, Steel	820,350,000					✗		
2008, Bronze Proof								
2009, Steel	419,105,000							
2009, Bronze Proof								
2010, Zinc								
2010, Steel								
2011, Zinc								
2011, Steel								
2012								

Five-Cent Pieces, Silver

Queen Victoria (1870–1901)

Date	Quantity Minted	G	VG	F	VF	EF	Unc.	Notes
1870, Wide Rim (O1)								
1870, Wide Rim, Plain Edge (Specimen only)	2,800,000							
1870, Narrow Rim (O2)								
1870, Narrow Rim, Plain Edge (Specimen only)								
1871 (O2)	1,400,000							
1872H (O2)	2,000,000							
1874H (O2), Plain 4	800,000							
1874H (O2), Crosslet 4								
1875H (O2), Small Date	1,000,000							
1875H (O2), Large Date								
1880H (O2, 3)	3,000,000							
1881H (O3)	1,500,000							
1882H (O4)	1,000,000							
1883H (O4) (2 known)	600,000							
1883H (O5)								
1884 (O5), Near 4	200,000							
1884 (O5), Far 4								
1885 (O5), Repunched Small 5								
1885 (O5), Small 5	1,000,000							
1885 (O5), Large 5								
1886 (O5), Small 6	1,700,000							
1886 (O5), Large 6								
1887 (O5)	500,000							
1888 (O5)	1,000,000							
1889 (O5)	1,200,000							
1890H (O5)	1,000,000							
1891 (O5, 2)	1,800,000							
1892 (O5, 2)	860,000							
1893 (O2)	1,700,000							
1894 (O2)	500,000							
1896 (O2)	1,500,000							
1897 (O2)	1,319,283							
1898 (O2)	580,717							
1899 (O2)	3,000,000							
1900 (O2), Round 0's (Large Date)	1,800,000							
1900 (O2), Oval 0's (Small Date)								
1901 (O2)	2,000,000							

King Edward VII (1902–1910)

Date	Quantity Minted	G	VG	F	VF	EF	Unc.	Notes
1902	2,120,000							
1902H, Large Broad H	2,200,000							
1902H, Small Narrow H								
1903H, Large H	2,640,000							
1903H, Small H								
1903	1,000,000							
1904	2,400,000							
1905	2,600,000							
1906	3,100,000							
1907	5,200,000							
1908, Small 8	1,220,524							
1908, Large 8								
1909, Round (Maple) Leaves	1,983,725							
1909, Pointed (Holly) Leaves								
1910, Round (Maple) Leaves	5,580,325							
1910, Pointed (Holly) Leaves								

King George V (1911–1921)

Without DEI GRA: (1911)   **With DEI GRA:** (1912–1921)

Date	Quantity Minted	G	VG	F	VF	EF	Unc.	Notes
1911, Without DEI GRA:	3,692,350							
1912, With DEI GRA:	5,863,170							
1913	5,488,048							
1914	4,202,179							
1915	1,172,258							
1916	2,481,675							
1917	5,521,373							
1918	6,052,298							
1919	7,835,400							
1920	10,649,851					✕		
1921 *(400–450 known)*	2,582,495							

Five-Cent Pieces, Nickel

King George V (1922–1936)

Date	Quantity Minted	G	VG	F	VF	EF	Unc.	Notes
1922	4,794,119							
1923	2,502,279							
1924	3,105,839							
1925	201,921							
1926, Near 6	938,162							
1926, Far 6								
1927	5,285,627							
1928	4,577,712							
1929	5,611,911							
1930	3,704,673							
1931	5,100,830							
1932	3,198,566							
1933	2,597,867							
1934	3,827,304							
1935	3,900,000							
1936	4,400,450							

King George VI (1937–1952)

Round
(1937–1942)

12-Sided, ET IND: IMP: on Obverse (1942–1947)

12-Sided, Beaver Reverse (1942; 1946–1950; 1951–1952)

12-Sided, DEI GRATIA on Obverse (1948–1952)

Victory Reverse
(1943–1945)

Isolation of Nickel Reverse (dated 1751–1951)

Date	Quantity Minted	G	VG	F	VF	EF	Unc.	Notes
1937	4,593,263							
1937, Matte Fields	(1,295)							
1937, Mirror Fields								

Date	Quantity Minted	G	VG	F	VF	EF	Unc.	Notes
1937	4,593,263							
1938	3,898,974			✕				
1939	5,661,123							
1940	13,920,197			✕				
1941	8,681,785							
1942, Nickel	6,847,544			✕				
1942, Tombac	3,396,234							
1943, Victory	24,760,256			✕				
1944, Tombac (1 known)	—							
1944, Steel	11,532,784			✕				
1944, No Chrome								
1945	18,893,216							
1945, No Chrome								
1946	6,952,684			✕				
1947, Normal	7,603,724			✕				
1947, Dot								
1947, Maple Leaf	9,595,124							
1948	1,810,789							
1949	13,037,090							
1950	11,970,521			✕				
1951, Isolation of Nickel Reverse	8,329,321			✕				
1951, High Relief (Second A in GRATIA Points to Denticle)	4,313,410							
1951, Low Relief (Second A in GRATIA Points Between Denticles)								
1952	10,891,148				✕			

Queen Elizabeth, Laurate Portrait (1953–1964)

12-Sided
(1953–1962)

Round
(1963–1964)

Date	Quantity Minted	VG	F	VF	EF	Unc.	PF	Notes
1953, No Shoulder Fold, Far Leaf	16,635,552							
1953, No Shoulder Fold, Near Leaf (Mule)				✕				
1953, With Shoulder Fold, Far Leaf (Mule)								
1953, With Shoulder Fold, Near Leaf								

Date	Quantity Minted	VG	F	VF	EF	Unc.	PF		Notes
1954					X				
1954, No Sholder Fold Mule *(2 known)*	6,998,662								
1955	5,355,028								
1956	9,399,854			X					
1957	7,387,703								
1957, Bugtail									
1958	7,607,521			X					
1959	11,552,523								
1960	37,157,433								
1961	47,889,051			X					
1962	46,307,305								
1962, Doubled Date									
1963, Round	43,970,320								
1964	78,075,068			X					
1964, Extra Water Line									

Queen Elizabeth, Tiara Portrait (1965–1989)

Original Portrait (1965–1978)	**Beaver Reverse (1965–1966; 1968–1989)**	**Confederation Centennial (dated 1867–1967)**	**Reduced Portrait (1979–1989)**

Date	Quantity Minted	VG	F	VF	EF	Unc.	PF		Notes
1965, Small Beads	84,876,018				X				
1965, Large Beads									
1966	27,976,648								
1967, Confederation Cent'l	36,876,574								
1968	99,253,330				X				
1969	27,830,229				X				
1970	5,726,010								
1971	27,312,609			X					
1972	62,417,387			X					
1973	53,507,435			X					
1974	94,704,645			X					
1975	138,882,000			X					
1976	55,140,213			X					
1977, High 7	89,120,791			X					
1977, Low 7									
1978	137,079,273			X					
1979, Reduced Portrait	186,295,825			X					
1980	134,878,000			X					

Date	Quantity Minted		VG	F	VF	EF	Unc.	PF	Notes
1981	(199,000)	99,107,900				✕			
1982	(180,908)	64,924,400			✕				
1983	(166,779)	72,596,000			✕				
1984	(161,602)	84,088,000			✕				
1985	(153,950)	126,618,000			✕				
1986	(176,224)	156,104,000			✕				
1987	(175,686)	106,299,000							
1988	(175,259)	75,025,000							
1989	(154,693)	141,570,538			✕				

Queen Elizabeth II, Diadem Portrait (1990–2003)

Beaver Reverse (1990–1992; 1993–2001; 2003)   **125th Anniv. of Confederation (dated 1867–1992)**   **Golden Jubilee (dated 1952–2002)**

Date	Quantity Minted		VG	F	VF	EF	Unc.	PF	Notes
1990	(158,068)	42,537,000							
1991	(131,888)	10,931,000							
1992, 125th Anniv of Confederation	(147,061)	53,732,000		✕					
1993	(143,065)	86,877,000							
1994	(153,707)	99,352,000							
1995	(151,362)	78,780,000							
1996, Far 6		36,686,000							
1996, Near 6									
1996, Near 6, Silver Proof	(112,835)								
1997		27,354,000							
1997, Silver Proof	(113,647)								
1998		156,873,000							
1998, Silver Proof	(93,632)								
1998W, Unc sets only		—							
1999		124,861,000					✕		
1999, Silver Proof	(95,113)								
1999P, Test only	(20,000+)								
2000		105,868,000				✕			
2000, Silver Proof	(90,921)								
2000W, Unc. sets only		—							
2000P, Multi-Ply Plated Steel		4,899,000							
2001		30,035,000							

Date	Quantity Minted	VG	F	VF	EF	Unc.	PF	Notes
2001P, Multi-Ply Plated Steel	136,656,000							
2001, Silver Proof	(74,194)							
2002P, Golden Jubilee	135,960,000					✕		
2002, Silver Proof	(98,805)							
2003P, Diadem Portrait	40,400,820							
2003, Silver Proof	(62,007)							

Queen Elizabeth II, Uncrowned Portrait (2003 to Date)

Beaver Reverse
(2003 to Date)

Living Traditions: Beaver
(2017)

Date	Quantity Minted	VG	F	VF	EF	Unc.	PF	Notes
2003P, Uncrowned Portrait	61,392,180					✕		
2003WP, BU sets only	—							
2004P	123,925,000							
2004, Silver Proof	(57,614)							
2005P	89,664,000			✕				
2005P, V-E Day	59,258,000							
2005, Silver Proof	(63,562)							
2006P	94,226,000							
2006, No P / No RCM	43,008,000							
2006, Silver Proof	(53,822)							
2006, RCM	45,082,000							
2007	221,472,000							
2008	278,530,000				✕			
2008, Silver Proof								
2009	266,448,000					✕		
2009, Silver Proof								
2010	126,800,000							
2010, Silver Proof								
2011	230,328,000					✕		
2011, Silver Proof								
2012	202,944,000							
2012, Silver Proof								
2013	78,120,000					✕		
2013, Silver Proof								
2014	66,364,000							
2014, Silver Proof								

Date	Quantity Minted	VG	F	VF	EF	Unc.	PF	Notes
2015	87,360,000					✕		
2015, Silver Proof								
2016	140,952,000							
2016, Silver Proof								
2017	106,680,000							
2017, Silver Proof								
2017, Living Traditions	20,000,000							
2018	87,528,000							
2018, Silver Proof								
2019	92,736,000							
2019, Silver Proof								
2020								
2020, Silver Proof								
2021								
2021, Silver Proof								
2022								
2022, Silver Proof								

Ten-Cent Pieces

Queen Victoria (1870–1901)

Date	Quantity Minted	VG	F	VF	EF	Unc.	PF	Notes
1870 (O1), Narrow 0								
1870 (O1), Plain Edge (Specimen only)	1,600,000							
1870 (O1), Wide 0								
1871 (O1)	800,000							
1871H (O1)	1,870,000							
1872H (O1)	1,000,000							
1874H (O1)	1,600,000							
1875H (O1)								
1880H (O1, 2)	1,500,000							
1881H (O1, 2)	950,000							
1882H (O3)	1,000,000							
1883H (O3)	300,000							
1884 (O4)	150,000							
1885 (O4)	400,000							
1885 (O5)								
1886, Small 6 (O4, 5)								
1886, Large Knobbed 6 (O4, 5)	800,000							
1886, Large Pointed 6 (O4, 5)								
1887 (O5)	350,000							
1888 (O5)	500,000							
1889 (O5)	600,000							
1890H (O5)	450,000							
1891 (O5), 21 Leaves	800,000							
1891 (O5), 22 Leaves								
1892 (O5, 6), Large 9, 2 Over 1	520,000							
1892 (O5, 6), Small 9								
1893 (O5, 6), Flat-Top 3	500,000							
1893 (O5, 6), Round-Top 3								
1894 (O5, 6)	500,000							
1896 (O5, 6)	650,000							
1898 (O5, 6)	720,000							
1899 (O6), Small 9's	1,200,000							
1899 (O6), Large 9's								
1900 (O6)	1,100,000							
1901 (O6)	1,200,000							

King Edward VII (1902–1910)

Date	Quantity Minted	VG	F	VF	EF	Unc.	PF		Notes
1902	720,000								
1902H	1,100,000								
1903	500,000								
1903H	1,320,000								
1904	1,000,000								
1905	1,000,000								
1906	1,700,000								
1907	2,620,000								
1908	776,666								
1909, Victorian Leaves	1,697,000								
1909, Broad Leaves									
1910	4,468,331								

King George V (1911–1936)

Without DEI GRA:
(1911)

With DEI GRA:
(1912–1936)

Date	Quantity Minted	VG	F	VF	EF	Unc.	PF		Notes
1911, Without DEI GRA:	2,737,584								
1912, With DEI GRA:, .925 Silver	3,235,557								
1913, Broad Leaves	3,613,937								
1913, Small Leaves									
1914	2,549,811								
1915	688,057								
1916	4,218,114								
1917	5,011,988								
1918	5,133,602								
1919	7,877,722								
1920, .800 Silver	6,305,345								
1921	2,469,562								
1928	2,458,602								
1929	3,253,888								
1930	1,831,043								
1931	2,067,421								
1932	1,154,317								

Date	Quantity Minted	VG	F	VF	EF	Unc.	PF	Notes
1932	1,154,317							
1933	673,368							
1934	409,067							
1935	384,056							
1936	2,460,871							
1936, Dot (Specimen only) *(5 known)*	191,237							

King George VI (1937–1952)

With Et IND: IMP:
(1937–1947)

With DEI GRATIA
(1948–1952)

Date	Quantity Minted	VG	F	VF	EF	Unc.	PF	Notes
1937	2,500,095							
1937, Matte Fields	(1,295)							
1937, Mirror Fields								
1938	4,197,323							
1939	5,501,748							
1940	16,526,470							
1941	8,716,386							
1942	10,214,011							
1943	21,143,229							
1944	9,383,582							
1945	10,979,570							
1946	6,300,066							
1947	4,431,926							
1947, Maple Leaf	9,638,793							
1948	422,741							
1949	11,336,172							
1950	17,823,075							
1951	15,079,265							
1951, Doubled-Die Reverse								
1952	10,474,455							

Queen Elizabeth II, Laureate Portrait (1953–1964)

Date	Quantity Minted	VG	F	VF	EF	Unc.	PF	Notes
1953, No Shoulder Fold	17,706,395							
1953, With Shoulder Fold								
1954	4,493,150							
1955	12,237,294	✕						
1956	16,732,844							
1956, Dot Below Date								
1957	16,110,229	✕						
1958	10,621,236							
1959	19,691,433							
1960	45,446,835			✕				
1961	26,850,859							
1962	41,864,335							
1963	41,916,208							
1964	49,518,549							

Queen Elizabeth, Tiara Portrait (1965–1989)

Original Portrait (1965–1978) — **Large Schooner Reverse (1965–1966; 1968–1969)** — **Confederation Centennial (dated 1867–1967)** — **Small Schooner Reverse (1969–1989)** — **Reduced Portrait (1979–1989)**

Date	Quantity Minted	VG	F	VF	EF	Unc.	PF	Notes
1965	56,965,392		✕					
1966	34,567,898							
1967, Confederation Cent'l, .800 Silver	32,309,135		✕					
1967, Confederation Cent'l, .500 Silver	30,689,080							
1968, .500 Silver	70,460,000		✕					
1968, Nickel, Ottawa Reeding	87,412,930		✕					
1968, Nickel, Philadelphia Reeding	85,170,000							
1969, Large Schooner Reverse *(15–20 known)*	—							
1969, Small Schooner Reverse	55,833,929			✕				

Date		Quantity Minted	VG	F	VF	EF	Unc.	PF	Notes
1970		5,249,296							
1971		41,016,968				X			
1972		60,169,387				X			
1973		167,715,435			X				
1974		201,566,565			X				
1975		207,680,000			X				
1976		95,018,533			X				
1977		128,452,206			X				
1978		170,366,431			X				
1979, Reduced Portrait		237,321,321			X				
1980		170,111,533			X				
1981	(199,000)	123,912,900			X				
1982	(180,908)	93,475,000			X				
1983	(166,779)	111,065,000			X				
1984	(161,602)	121,690,000			X				
1985	(153,950)	143,025,000			X				
1986	(176,224)	168,620,000			X				
1987	(175,686)	147,309,000							
1988	(175,259)	162,998,558					X		
1989	(154,693)	199,104,414					X		

Queen Elizabeth, Diadem Portrait (1990–2003)

| Schooner, Denticles on Reverse (1990–1991) | 125th Anniversary of Confederation (dated 1867–1992) | Schooner, Beads on Reverse (1993–2003) |

International Year of the Volunteer (2001)   **Golden Jubilee (dated 1952–2002)**

Date		Quantity Minted	VG	F	VF	EF	Unc.	PF	Notes
1990	(158,068)	65,023,000							
1991	(131,888)	50,397,000							
1992, 125th Anniv of Confederation	(147,061)	174,476,000				X			
1993, Beads	(143,065)	135,569,000							
1994	(153,707)	145,800,000							
1995	(151,362)	123,875,000					X		
1996		51,814,000					X		
1996, Silver Proof	(112,835)								

Date	Quantity Minted	VG	F	VF	EF	Unc.	PF	Notes
1997	43,126,000							
1997, Silver Proof	(113,647)							
1998	203,514,000							
1998, Silver Proof*	(93,632)							
1998W, Unc sets only	(—)							
1999	258,462,000				✕			
1999, Silver Proof	(95,113)							
1999P, Test only	(20,000+)							
2000	195,117,000							
2000, Silver Proof	(90,921)							
2000P (Test only)	200							
2001P	46,266,000							
2001P, International Year of the Volunteer	226,199,000			✕				
2001, International Year of the Volunteer, Silver Proof	(74,194)							
2002P, Golden Jubilee	252,563,000							
2002, Silver Proof	(98,805)							
2003P, Diadem Portrait	164,617,000							
2003, Diadem Portrait, Silver Proof	(62,007)							

* Includes Matte Finish and Mirror Finish Proofs.

Queen Elizabeth II, Uncrowned Portrait (2003 to Date)

Bluenose Reverse
(2003 to Date)

Wings of Peace
(2017)

Date	Quantity Minted	VG	F	VF	EF	Unc.	PF	Notes
2003P, Uncrowned Portrait	Incl. above							
2004P	213,025,000							
2004, Silver Proof	(57,614)							
2005P	211,350,000							
2005, Silver Proof	(62,286)							
2006P	331,647,000			✕				
2006, Silver Proof	(57,885)							
2006RCM	Incl. above							
2007, Straight 7	304,110,000			✕				
2007, Curved 7	Incl. above							
2007, Silver Proof	(37,373)							
2008	467,495,000							

Date	Quantity Minted	VG	F	VF	EF	Unc.	PF		Notes
2008, Silver Proof	(38,630)								
2009	370,700,000								
2009, Silver Proof	(27,550)								
2010	252,500,000				✗				
2010, Silver Proof	(32,350)								
2010, Silver Proof, George V	(5,000)								
2011	292,325,000				✗				
2011, Silver Proof	(32,900)								
2011, Silver Proof, George V	(6,000)								
2012	334,675,000								
2012, Proof	(27,250)								
2012, Silver Proof	(20,000)								
2013	104,775,000								
2013, Silver Proof	(20,000)								
2014	153,450,000								
2014, Proof	(11,250)								
2014, Silver Proof	(13,500)								
2015	112,475,000								
2015, Proof	(20,000)								
2015, Silver Proof	(20,000)								
2016	220,000,000				✗				
2016, Proof	(12,500)								
2016, Silver Proof	(20,000)								
2017	199,925,000								
2017, My Canada, My Inspiration: Wings of Peace	20,000,000								
2017, Proof, Wings of Peace	25,000								
2017, Silver Proof, Wings of Peace	20,000								
2018	118,525,000								
2018, Proof	25,000								
2018, Silver Proof	20,000								
2019									
2019, Proof	15,000								
2019, Silver Proof	15,000								
2020, Proof	20,000								
2020, Silver Proof	15,000								
2021									
2022									

Twenty-Five-Cent Pieces

Queen Victoria (1870–1901)

Date	Quantity Minted	VG	F	VF	EF	Unc.	PF	Notes
1870, Narrow 0 (O1)								
1870, Plain Edge (Specimen only)	900,000							
1870, Wide 0 (O2) *(4 known)*								
1871 (O1	400,000							
1871 (O2)								
1871H (O1	748,000							
1871H (O2)								
1872H (O2)	2,240,000							
1872H (O1) *(5 known)*								
1874H (O2)	2,600,000							
1875H (O2)								
1880H (O2), Wide 0								
1880H (O2), Narrow Over Wide 0	400,000							
1880H (O2), Narrow 0								
1881H (O2)	820,000							
1882H (O3)	600,000							
1883H (O4)	960,000							
1885 (O2)	192,000							
1886 (O2, 4, 5)								
1886, 6 Over 6 (O4, 5)	540,000							
1886, 6 Over 3 (O5)								
1887 (O5)	100,000							
1888 (O5), Narrow 8's	400,000							
1888 (O5), Broad 8's								
1889 (O5)	66,324							
1890H (O5)	200,000							
1891 (O5)	120,000							
1892 (O5)	510,000							
1893 (O5)	100,000							
1894 (O5)	220,000							
1899 (O5)	415,580							
1900 (O5)	1,320,000							
1901 (O5)	640,000							

King Edward VII (1902–1910)

Date	Quantity Minted	VG	F	VF	EF	Unc.	PF	Notes
1902	464,000							
1902H	800,000							
1903	846,150							
1904	400,000							
1905	800,000							
1906, Small Crown	1,237,843							
1906, Large Crown								
1907	2,088,000							
1908	495,016							
1909	1,335,929							
1910	3,577,569							

King George V (1911–1936)

Without DEI GRA:
(1911)

With DEI GRA:
(1912–1936)

Date	Quantity Minted	VG	F	VF	EF	Unc.	PF	Notes
1911, Without DEI GRA:	1,721,341							
1912, With DEI GRA:, .925 Silver	2,544,199							
1913	2,213,595							
1914	1,215,397							
1915	242,382							
1916	1,462,566							
1917	. 3,365,644							
1918	4,175,649							
1919	5,852,262							
1920, .800 Silver	1,975,278							
1921	597,337							
1927	468,096							
1928	2,114,178							
1929	2,690,562							
1930	968,748							

Date	Quantity Minted	VG	F	VF	EF	Unc.	PF	Notes
1931	537,815							
1932	537,994							
1933	421,282							
1934	384,350							
1935	537,772							
1936	972,094							
1936, Bar								
1936, Dot	153,322							

King George VI (1937–1952)

With Et IND: IMP:
(1937–1947)

With DEI GRATIA
(1948–1952)

Date	Quantity Minted	VG	F	VF	EF	Unc.	PF	Notes
1937	2,690,176							
1937, Doubled HP								
1937, Matte Fields	(1,295)							
1937, Mirror Fields								
1938	3,149,245							
1939	3,532,495							
1940	9,583,650							
1941	6,654,672							
1942	6,935,871							
1943	13,559,575							
1944	7,216,237							
1945	5,296,495							
1946	2,210,810							
1947	1,524,554							
1947, Dot								
1947, Maple Leaf	4,393,938							
1948	2,564,424							
1949	7,988,830							
1950	9,673,335							
1951, High Relief	8,290,719							
1951, Low Relief								
1952, Low Relief	8,859,642							
1952, High Relief								

Queen Elizabeth II, Laureate Portrait (1953–1964)

Date	Quantity Minted	VG	F	VF	EF	Unc.	PF		Notes
1953, No Shoulder Fold (Large Date)	10,546,769								
1953, With Shoulder Fold (Small Date)									
1954	2,318,891								
1955	9,552,505								
1956	11,269,353			✕					
1957	12,770,190								
1958	9,336,910								
1959	13,503,461								
1960	22,835,327				✕				
1961	18,164,368								
1962	29,559,266								
1963	21,180,652								
1964	36,479,343								

Queen Elizabeth, Tiara Portrait (1965–1989)

Original Portrait (1965–1978)	Caribou Reverse (1965–1966; 1968–1972; 1974–1989)	Confederation Centennial (dated 1867–1967)	RCMP Centennial Reverse (1973)	Reduced Portrait (1979–1989)

Date		Quantity Minted	VG	F	VF	EF	Unc.	PF	Notes
1965		44,708,869							
1966		25,626,315							
1967, Confederation Cent'l, .800 Silver		48,855,500							
1967, Confederation Cent'l, .500 Silver									
1968, .500 Silver		71,464,000							
1968, Nickel		88,686,931							
1969		133,037,929			✗				
1970		10,302,010			✗				
1971		48,170,428			✗				
1972		43,743,387			✗				
1973, RCMP, Small Bust, 120 Beads		134,958,587			✗				
1973, RCMP, Large Bust, 132 Beads									
1974		192,360,598			✗				
1975		141,148,000			✗				
1976		86,898,261			✗				
1977		99,634,555			✗				
1978, Small Denticles		176,475,408			✗				
1978, Large Denticles					✗				
1979, Reduced Portrait		131,042,905			✗				
1980		76,178,000			✗				
1981	(199,000)	131,580,272			✗				
1982	(180,908)	171,926,000			✗				
1983	(166,779)	13,162,000							
1984	(161,602)	119,084,307			✗				
1985	(153,950)	158,734,000			✗				
1986	(176,224)	132,220,000			✗				
1987	(175,686)	53,408,000							
1988	(175,259)	80,368,000							
1989	(154,693)	119,084,307			✗				

Queen Elizabeth, Diadem Portrait (1990–2003)

Caribou, Denticles on Reverse (1990–1991)	**125th Anniversary of Confederation (dated 1867–1992)**	**Caribou, Beads on Reverse (1993–2003)**

Date		Quantity Minted	VG	F	VF	EF	Unc.	PF	Notes
1990	(158,068)	31,258,000							
1991	(131,888)	459,000							
1992 **(a)**		153,000,000							
1992, 125th Anniv of Confederation, BU, Specimen sets	(442,986)								
1992, Proof	(147,061)								
1992, 125th Anniv of of Confederation, Silver Proof		—							
1993, Beads	(143,065)	73,758,000				✗			
1994	(153,707)	77,670,000							
1995	(151,362)	89,210,000							
1996		28,106,000							
1996, Silver Proof	(112,835)								
1997, BU, Specimen sets only	(314,015)								
1997, Silver Proof	(113,647)								
1998, BU, Specimen sets only	(234,288)								
1998, Silver Proof	(93,632)								
1998W, Unc sets only		—							
1999 **(b)**		262,781,500							
1999, BU, Specimen sets only	(342,587)								
1999P, Test only		20,000+							
1999, Silver Proof	(95,113)								
2000 **(c)**		439,986,730							
2000, BU, Specimen sets only	(377,833)								
2000, Silver Proof	(90,921)								
2000W, Unc sets only		—							
2001		8,409,000							
2001, Silver Proof	(74,194)								
2001P		52,153,000							
2002P		156,105,000				✗			
2002P, Canada Day		30,627,000							
2002P, Silver Proof	(98,805)								

Queen Elizabeth, Uncrowned Portrait (2003 to Date)

Caribou Reverse
(2003 to Date)

My Canada, My Inspiration:
Hope for a Green Future
(2017)

Date	Quantity Minted	VG	F	VF	EF	Unc.	PF	Notes
2003P, Diadem Portrait	15,905,090							
2003, Diadem Portrait, Silver Proof	(62,007)							
2003P, Uncrowned Portrait	66,861,633							
2003WP, BU sets only	71,142							
2004P	177,466,000				X			
2004P, Île Sainte-Croix	15,400,000							
2004P, Remembrance Day Poppy, Enameled	28,972,000				X			
2004, Silver Proof	(57,614)							
2005P	206,346,000				X			
2005P, Alberta Centennial	20,640,000				X			
2005P, Saskatchewan Centennial	19,290,000							
2005P, Year of the Veteran	29,390,000							
2005RCM, First-Day Strike Folder	(1,911)							
2005, Silver Proof	(62,286)							
2006P	423,189,000							
2006P, Breast Cancer Awareness, Enameled	29,798,000							
20006RCM	(d)				X			
2006RCM, Medal of Bravery	20,040,000							
2006P/2006RCM, Last-Day / First-Day Strike Folder	(742)							
2006, Silver Proof	(57,885)							
2007	274,763,000				X			
2007, Olympics (e)	112,000,000							
2007, Silver Proof	(40,218)							
2008	286,322,000				X			
2008, Olympics (f)	89,600,000							
2008, Armistice Poppy, Enameled	11,300,000							
2008, Silver Proof	286,322,000							
2009	20,446,000							
2009, Olympics (e)	112,000,000							
2009, Olympic Moments (g)	57,000,000							
2009, Silver Proof	(27,549)							

Date	Quantity Minted	VG	F	VF	EF	Unc.	PF	Notes
2010	167,500,000							
2010RCM, Remembrance Day Double Poppy	*							
2010, Silver Proof	(32,342)							
2011RCM	212,970,000					✕		
2011, Our Legendary Nature (h)	*							
2011, Silver Proof	(32,910)							
2012RCM	178,450,000							
2012, Heroes of 1812 (i)	(27,254) *							
2012, Silver Proof	(19,789)							
2013RCM	118,480,000							
2013, First Arctic Expedition (j)	*							
2013, Life in the North (k)	*							
2013, Silver Proof	(20,182)							
2014RCM	97,440,000							
2014, Proof	(11,251)							
2014, Silver Proof	(13,416)							
2015RCM	97,320,000							
2015, Flag (I)	(20,000) *							
2015, Poppy (I)	*							
2015, Flag, Silver Proof, Enameled	(20,000)							
2015, Proof								
2016RCM	106,880,000				✕			
2016, Proof	(12,500)							
2016, Silver Proof	(20,000)							
2017RCM	143,220,000							
2017, Stanley Cup	*							
2017, Hope for a Green Future (I)	*							
2017, Proof	(25,000)							
2017, Silver Proof	(20,000)							
2018	(25,000) 102,560,000							
2018, Silver Proof	(20,000)							
2019								
2019, Silver Proof								
2020								
2020, Silver Proof								
2021								
2021, Silver Proof								
2022								
2022, Silver Proof								

Date	Quantity Minted	VG	F	VF	EF	Unc.	PF	Notes

a. Twelve reverse designs commemorating the 125th anniversary of confederation.

b. Twelve 1999 reverse designs celebrating the new millennium.

c. Twelve 2000 reverse designs celebrating the new millennium.

d. Included in 2006P mintage.

e. Five designs celebrating the 2010 Olympics and Paralympics.

f. Four designs celebrating the 2010 Olympics.

g. Engraved and enameled versions of three designs celebrating three top Canadian Olympic performances.

h. Engraved and enameled versions of three designs commemorating species saved by Canadian conservation.

i. Engraved and enameled versions of four designs commemorating Canadian heroes of the War of 1812.

j. Two issues commemorating the centennial of the Canadian Artic Exposition: one design with crew's garments frosted, and one with the compass ring frosted.

k. Two issues symbolizing life in the Canadian north, one with frosted finish on the Bowhead whale, one with frosted finish on the Beluga whales.

l. Engraved and enameled versions.

Fifty-Cent Pieces

Queen Victoria (1870–1901)

Date	Quantity Minted	VG	F	VF	EF	Unc.	PF	Notes
1870, No LCW (O1)								
1870 (O1), No LCW, Plain Edge (Specimen only)	450,000							
1870, LCW (O2)								
1870, LCW (O2), Plain Edge (Specimen only)								
1871 (O2)	200,000							
1871H (O2)	45,000							
1872H (O2)	80,000							
1872H (O2), Inverted A Over V								
1881H (O3)	150,000							
1888 (O2, 3)	60,000							
1890H (O4)	20,000							
1892 (O3, 4)	151,000							
1894 (O4)	29,036							
1898 (O4)	100,000							
1899 (O4)	50,000							
1900 (O4)	118,000							
1901 (O4)	80,000							

King Edward VII (1902–1910)

Date	Quantity Minted	VG	F	VF	EF	Unc.	PF	Notes
1902	120,000							
1903H	140,000							
1904	60,000							
1905	40,000							

Date	Quantity Minted	VG	F	VF	EF	Unc.	PF	Notes
1906	350,000							
1907	300,000							
1908	128,119							
1909	302,118							
1910, Victorian Leaves	649,521							
1910, Edwardian Leaves								

King George V (1911–1936)

Without DEI GRA: (1911)   **With DEI GRA: (1912–1936)**

Date	Quantity Minted	VG	F	VF	EF	Unc.	PF	Notes
1911, Without DEI GRA:	209,972							
1912, With DEI GRA:	285,867							
1913	265,889							
1914	160,128							
1916	459,070							
1917	752,213							
1918	754,989							
1919	1,113,429							
1920, Narrow 0	584,691							
1920, Wide 0								
1921 *(fewer than 100 known)*	206,328							
1929	228,328							
1931	57,581							
1932	19,213							
1934	39,539							
1936	38,550							

King George VI (1937–1952)

With Et IND: IMP:
(1937–1947)

With DEI GRATIA
(1948–1952)

Date	Quantity Minted	VG	F	VF	EF	Unc.	PF	Notes
1937	192,016							
1937, Matte Fields	(1,295)							
1937, Mirror Fields								
1938	192,018							
1939	287,976							
1940	1,996,566							
1941	1,714,874							
1942	1,974,164							
1943	3,109,583							
1944	2,460,205			✕				
1945	1,959,528							
1946	950,235							
1946, Design in 6								
1947, Straight or Curved Left 7	424,885							
1947, Curved Right 7								
1947, Maple Leaf, Straight or Curved Left 7	38,433							
1947, Maple Leaf, Curved Right 7								
1948	37,784							
1949	858,991							
1949, Hoof Over 9								
1950, Lines in 0	2,384,179							
1950, No Lines								
1951	2,421,730							
1952	2,596,465							

Queen Elizabeth II, Laureate Portrait (1953–1964)

| **Coat of Arms Reverse (1953–1954)** | **Smaller Coat of Arms Reverse (1955–1958)** | **Modified Coat of Arms Reverse (1959–1964)** |

Date	Quantity Minted	VG	F	VF	EF	Unc.	PF	Notes
1953, Small Date, No Shoulder Fold								
1953, Large Date, No Shoulder Fold	1,630,429							
1953, Large Date, With Shoulder Fold								
1954	506,305							
1955, Smaller Coat of Arms	753,511							
1956	1,379,499							
1957	2,171,689			✕				
1958	2,957,266							
1958, Dot								
1959, Modified Coat of Arms	3,095,535							
1960	3,488,897							
1961	3,584,417							
1962	5,208,030							
1963	8,348,871							
1964	9,377,676							

Queen Elizabeth II, Tiara Portrait (1965–1989)

| **Original Portrait (1965–1967)** | **Coat of Arms Reverse (1965–1966)** | **Confederation Centennial (dated 1867–1967)** |

Reduced Diameter (1968–1976; 1978–1989 [with modifications])

Reduced Portrait, Lettering on Obverse; Beads on Reverse (1977; Obverse lettering used 1978–1989)

Date		Quantity Minted	VG	F	VF	EF	Unc.	PF	Notes
1965		12,629,974							
1966		7,920,496							
1967, Confederation Cent'l									
1967, Double Strike		4,211,392							
1967, Triple Strike									
1967, Flip Strike									
1968, Reduced Diameter		3,966,932					✕		
1969		7,113,929					✕		
1970		2,429,526					✕		
1971		2,166,444							
1972		2,515,632					✕		
1973		2,546,096							
1974		3,436,650					✕		
1975		3,710,000							
1976		2,940,719							
1977		709,839							
1978, Square Jewels		3,341,892							
1978, Round Jewels									
1979		3,425,000							
1980		1,574,000							
1981	(199,000)	2,690,272							
1982, Large Beads, High Relief	(180,908)	2,236,674							
1982, Small Beads, Low Relief									
1983	(166,779)	1,177,000							
1984	(161,602)	1,502,989							
1985	(153,950)	2,188,374				✕			
1986	(176,224)	781,400							
1987	(175,686)	373,000							
1988	(175,259)	220,000					✕		
1989	(154,693)	266,419							

Queen Elizabeth, Diadem Portrait (1990–2003)

125th Anniversary of Confederation (dated 1867–1992)

Coat of Arms, Denticles on Reverse (1990–1991)

Coat of Arms, Beads on Reverse (1993–1996)

Redesigned Coat of Arms, (1997–2003)

Date	Quantity Minted		VG	F	VF	EF	Unc.	PF	Notes
1990	(158,068)	207,000					✗		
1991	(131,888)	490,000							
1992, 125th Anniv of Confederation	(147,061)	248,000							
1993, Beads	(143,065)	393,000							
1994	(153,707)	987,000							
1995	(151,362)	626,000							
1996		458,000							
1996, Silver Proof	(112,835)								
1997, Redesigned Coat of Arms		387,000							
1997, Silver Proof	(113,647)								
1998		308,000							
1998, Silver Proof	(93,632)								
1998W, Unc sets only	(—)								
1999		496,000					✗		
1999, Silver Proof	(95,113)								
1999P, Test only		20,000+							
2000		559,000					✗		
2000, Silver Proof	(90,921)								
2000W, Unc sets only	(—)								
2000P, BU, in RCM Presentation Clocks only		50							
2001P		389,000							
2001P, Silver Proof	(86,194)								
2002, Silver Proof	(65,315)								
2002P, Unc, Specimen sets only	(67,672)								
2002P, Golden Jubilee		14,440,000				✗			
2003P, Unc, Specimen sets only	(—)								
2003, Silver Proof	(62,007)								
2003, Accession Set	(33,490)								

Queen Elizabeth II, Uncrowned Portrait (2003 to Date)

Date	Quantity Minted	VG	F	VF	EF	Unc.	PF	Notes
2003WP, BU sets only	(71,142)							
2004P, Unc, Specimen sets only	(—)							
2004, Silver Proof	(57,614)							
2005P	200,000							
2005P, First-Day Strike Folder	2,445							
2005, Silver Proof	(62,286)							
2006P	98,000							
2006RCM, BU sets only								
2006P/2006RCM, Last-Day/ First-Day Strike Folder	933							
2006, Silver Proof	(57,885)							
2006, Silver Proof, gold-plated	(4,162)							
2007RCM	250,000							
2007RCM, Silver Proof	(40,218)							
2008RCM, Unc, Specimen sets only	—							
2008RCM, Silver Proof	(40,306)							
2008RCM, Silver Proof (1908)	(3,248)							
2009RCM, Unc, Specimen sets only	120,000							
2009RCM, Silver Proof	(27,549)							
2010	150,000							
2010RCM, Silver Proof	(32,342)							
2011	175,000							
2011RCM, Silver Proof	(32,910)							
2011RCM, Silver Proof (1911–)	(5,952)							
2012	250,000							
2012RCM, Proof	(24,254)							
2012RCM, Silver Proof	(19,789)							
2013RCM	375,000							
2013RCM, Silver Proof	(20,182)							
2014RCM	500,000							
2014RCM, Proof	(11,251)							
2014RCM, Silver Proof	(13,416)							

Date	Quantity Minted	VG	F	VF	EF	Unc.	PF		Notes
2015RCM	625,000								
2015RCM, Proof	(20,000)								
2015RCM, Silver Proof	(20,000)								
2016RCM	625,000								
2016RCM, Proof	(20,000)								
2016RCM, Silver Proof	(20,000)								
2017RCM	75,000								
2017RCM, Canada 150	875,000								
2017RCM, Proof, Canada 150	(25,000)								
2017RCM, Silver Proof, Arms of Canada	(20,000)								
2017RCM, Silver Proof, Canada 150	(20,000)								
2017RCM, Silver Proof, 1967–2017	(20,000)								
2018RCM									
2018RCM, Proof	(25,000)								
2018RCM, Silver Proof	(20,000)								
2019RCM									
2019RCM, Proof	(20,000)								
2019RCM, Silver Proof	(15,000)								
2020RCM									
2020RCM, Proof	(20,000)								
2020RCM, Silver Proof	(15,000)								
2021RCM									
2021RCM, Proof									
2021RCM, Silver Proof									
2022RCM									
2022RCM, Proof									
2022RCM, Silver Proof									

One-Dollar Pieces

King George V (1935–1936)

Silver Jubilee Obverse (1935)

Standard Obverse (1936)

Date	Quantity Minted	VG	F	VF	EF	Unc.	PF	Notes
1935, Silver Jubilee	428,707							
1935, Matte Specimen								
1936	306,100							
1936, Matte Specimen								

King George VI (1937–1952)

With Et IND: IMP: (1937–1939; 1945–1947)

Voyageur Reverse (1937–1938; 1945–1948; 1950–1952)

With DEI GRATIA (1948–1952)

Royal Visit Reverse (1939)

Newfoundland Reverse (1949)

Date	Quantity Minted	VG	F	VF	EF	Unc.	PF	Notes
1937	241,002							
1937, Matte Fields	(1,295)							
1937, Mirror Fields								
1938	90,304							
1939, Royal Visit	1,363,816							
1945	38,391							
1946	93,055							
1947, Pointed 7	65,595							
1947, Pointed 7, Dot								
1947, Pointed 7, Doubled HP								
1947, Pointed 7, Doubled HP, Dot								
1947, Pointed 7, Tripled HP								
1947, Pointed 7, Tripled HP, Dot								
1947, Pointed 7, Quadrupled HP								
1947, Pointed 7, Quadrupled HP, Dot								
1947, Blunt 7								
1947, Matte Specimen								
1947, Matte Specimen, Doubled HP								
1947, Maple Leaf	21,135							
1947, Maple Leaf, Doubled HP								
1948	18,780							
1949, Newfoundland	672,218							
1950, Full Water Lines	261,002							
1950, Matte Specimen								
1950, 3–4 Short Water Lines								
1950, "Arnprior," 2-1/2 Water Lines								
1951, Full Water Lines	416,395							
1951, 3–4 Short Water Lines								
1951, "Arnprior," 2-1/2 Water Lines								
1952, Full Water Lines	406,148							
1952, 3–4 Short Water Lines								
1952, "Arnprior," 1-1/2 Short Water Lines								
1952, No Water Lines								

Queen Elizabeth II, Laureate Portrait (1953–1964)

**Voyageur Reverse
(1953–1957;
1959–1963)**

**British Columbia
Reverse (1958)**

**Confederation Meetings
Reverse (1964)**

Date	Quantity Minted	VG	F	VF	EF	Unc.	PF	Notes
1953, No Shoulder Fold, Narrow Rim								
1953, No Shoulder Fold, Narrow Rim, Short Water Lines	1,074,578							
1953, Shoulder Fold, Wide Rim								
1953, Shoulder Fold, Wide Rim, Short Water Lines								
1954, Full Water Lines	246,606							
1954, Short Water Lines								
1955, Full Water Lines	268,105							
1955, "Arnprior," 1-1/2 Water Lines								
1955, "Arnprior," Obv Die Breaks								
1956	209,092							
1957, Full Water Lines	496,389							
1957, One Water Line								
1958, British Columbia	3,039,630							
1959	1,443,502							
1960	1,420,486							
1961	1,262,231							
1962	1,884,789							
1963	4,179,981							
1964, Confederation Meetings	7,296,832							

Queen Elizabeth II, Tiara Portrait (1965–1989)

Round, Original Diameter (1965–1967)

Voyageur Reverse (1965–1966)

Confederation Centennial (dated 1867–1967)

Date	Quantity Minted	VG	F	VF	EF	Unc.	PF	Notes
1965, Sm Beads, Pointed 5, Type 1								
1965, Sm Beads, Blunt 5, Type 2								
1965, Lg Beads, Blunt 5, Type 3	10,768,569							
1965, Lg Beads, Pointed 5, Type 4								
1965, Med Beads, Ptd 5, Type 5								
1966, Large Beads	9,912,178							
1966, Small Beads								
1967, Confederation Cent'l, Large Beads Reverse, Flat Fields	6,767,496							
1967, Small Beads Reverse, Concave Fields								
1967, Diving Goose, 45 Degrees								

Reduced Diameter; Original Portrait (1968–1972)

Reduced Diameter, Reduced Portrait (1973–1977)

Reduced Diameter, Pre-1973 Portrait, Beaded (1978–1987)

Reduced Diameter; Voyageur Reverse (1968–1969; 1972; 1975–1976)

Reduced Diameter; Voyageur Reverse, First Modified (1977)

Reduced Diameter; Voyageur Reverse, Second Modified (1978–1987)

**Manitoba Reverse
(1970)**

**British Columbia Reverse
(1971)**

**Prince Edward Island
Reverse (1973)**

**Winnipeg Reverse
(1974)**

Date	Quantity Minted	VG	F	VF	EF	Unc.	PF	Notes
1968, Island					X			
1968, Small Island								
1968, No Island	5,579,714							
1968, Extra Water Lines								
1968, Doubled Horizon Lines								
1968, Doubled Top Horizon Line								
1969	4,809,313				X			
1970, Manitoba	4,140,058					X		
1970, Manitoba, Prooflike (cased)	(349,120)							
1970, Manitoba, Specimen	(1,000)							
1971, British Columbia	4,260,781					X		
1971, British Columbia, Prooflike (cased)	(181,091)							
1971, British Columbia, Silver	(585,217)							
1972	2,193,000					X		
1972, Silver	(341,581)							
1973, Prince Edward Island	3,196,452					X		
1973, Prince Edward Island, Prooflike (cased)	(466,881)							

Date		Quantity Minted	VG	F	VF	EF	Unc.	PF	Notes
1974, Winnipeg Centennial							✗		
1974, Winnipeg Centennial, Doubled Yoke, any variety		2,799,363							
1974, Winnipeg Cent'l, Prooflike (cased)									
1974, Winnipeg Cent'l, Prooflike (cased), Doubled Yoke	(363,786)								
1974, Winnipeg Centennial, Silver	(713,485)								
1975		3,256,000					✗		
1976		2,101,000					✗		
1977		1,393,745				✗			
1977, Short Water Lines									
1978		2,948,488				✗			
1979		2,954,842					✗		
1980		3,291,221					✗		
1981	(199,000)	2,788,900					✗		
1982	(180,908)	1,544,398				✗			
1982, Constitution		11,812,000							
1983	(166,779)	2,267,525				✗			
1984	(161,602)	1,223,486							
1984, Jacques Cartier		7,009,323					✗		
1985	(153,950)	3,104,092					✗		
Mule, 1985 New Zealand 50¢ Obverse, 1985 Canada Voyageur $1 Reverse		—							
1986	(176,224)	3,089,225					✗		
1987, Voyageur	(175,686)								

11-sided, Aureate Bronze Plated (1987–1989)

Loon Reverse (1987–1989)

Date		Quantity Minted	VG	F	VF	EF	Unc.	PF	Notes
1987, Loon	(178,120)	205,405,000					✗		
1988	(175,259)	138,893,539			✗				
1989	(154,693)	184,773,902			✗				

Queen Elizabeth II, Diadem Portrait (1990–2003)

Loon Reverse (1990–1991; 1993–2003)	125th Anniversary of Confederation (dated 1867–1992)	Golden Jubilee (dated 1952–2002; no date on reverse)

Date		Quantity Minted	VG	F	VF	EF	Unc.	PF	Notes
1990	(158,068)	68,402,000				X			
1991	(131,888)	23,156,000			X				
1992		4,242,085							
1992, 125th Anniv. of Confederation	(108,614)	23,010,915							
1993	(143,065)	33,662,000							
1994	(104,485)	16,232,530							
1995		27,492,630							
1995, Peacekeeping									
1995, Proof	(101,560)								
1996	(112,835)	17,101,000				X			
1997	(113,647)								
1998	(93,632)								
1998W	(—)								
1999	(95,113)								
2000	(90,921)								
2000W, BU and Specimen sets only									
2001, BU and Specimen sets only									
2001, Proof	(86,194)								
2002, Golden Jubilee	(98,805)	2,302,000							
2003, Diadem Portrait	(62,007)	5,101,000							

Queen Elizabeth II, Uncrowned Portrait (2003 to Date)

Loon Reverse (2003 to Date)	My Canada, My Inspiration: Connecting a Nation (2017)

Date	Quantity Minted	VG	F.	VF	EF	Unc.	PF		Notes
2003, Uncrowned Portrait	Inc. in 2003, Diadem								
2003W, BU and Proof sets only									
2004	(57,614) 3,408,000								
2004, Olympic Lucky Loon	6,526,000								
2004, Olympic Lucky Loon First-Day Strike Folder									
2005				✕					
2005, Marathon of Hope	(63,562) 32,336,000								
2005, First-Day Strike Folder	2,048								
2006	(54,022)								
2006RCM	37,085,000								
2006, Olympic Lucky Loon	10,495,000								
2006P/2006RCM Last-Day / First-Day Strike Folder	901								
2007RCM	(37,413) 38,045,000								
2008RCM	(38,630) 18,710,000								
2008RCM, Olympic Lucky Loon	10,851,000								
2009RCM	(27,549) 29,351,000								
2009RCM, Canadiens	10,250,000								
2010RCM	(32,300) 4,110,000								
2010, Olympic Lucky Loon	10,250,000								
2010, Navy Centennial	7,000,000								
2010, Saskatchewan Roughriders	3,000,000								
2011RCM	(32,910) 20,410,000								
2011RCM, Parks Canada	5,000,000								
2012RCM	(27,250) 2,414,000								
2012, Lucky Loonie	5,000,000								
2012, Lucky Loonie, Silver Proof	(19,775)								
2012, Security Stamp Added	107,105,000								
2012, Grey Cup	5,000,000								
2013	120,330,000								
2013, Silver Proof, Gold-Plated	(20,175)								
2014	(11,250) 20,945,000								
2014, Lucky Loonie	5,000,000								
2014, Lucky Loonie, Silver Proof	(13,400)								
2015	(20,000) 22,140,000			✕					
2015, Silver Proof, Gold-Plated	(14,000)								
2016	(12,500) 28,764,000								
2016, Lucky Loonie	5,000,000								
2016, Lucky Loonie, Silver Proof	(9,211)								
2016, Women's Right to Vote	5,000,000								

Date	Quantity Minted		VG	F	VF	EF	Unc.	PF		Notes
2017		15,750,000								
2017, Silver Proof	(8,000)									
2017, Connecting a Nation	(25,000)	10,000,000								
2017, Connecting a Nation, Silver Proof, Gold-Plated	(20,000)									
2017, Toronto Maple Leafs		5,150,000								
2018		33,930,000								
2018, Silver Proof, Gold-Plated	(20,000)									
2019										
2019, Silver Proof, Gold-Plated										
2019, Equality										
2020										
2020, Silver Proof, Gold-Plated										
2020, U.N. Charter (a)										
2021										
2022										

a. Engraved and enameled versions.

TWO-DOLLAR PIECES

Queen Elizabeth II, Diadem Portrait (1990–2003)

**Golden Jubilee
(dated 1952–2002)**

Date	Quantity Minted	VG	F	VF	EF	Unc.	PF	Notes
1996	375,483,000							
1996, Specimen (cased)	(66,843)							
1996, Proof (foldered)								
1996, Proof (cased)								
1996, Silver Ring, Gold-Plated Core Proof								
1996, White Gold Ring, Gold Core Proof	(5,000)							
1996, Silver Proof Piedfort	(11,526)							
1997	16,942,000							
1997, Silver Proof **(a)**	(113,647)							
1997W, Unc collector sets only	174,692							
1998	5,309,000							
1998, Silver Proof **(a)**	(93,632)							
1998, Specimen set	(67,697)							
1998W, Unc collector sets only	145,439							
1999, Polar Bear, Unc collector sets	117,318							
1999, Polar Bear, Specimen set	(46,785)							
1999, Nunavut	375,483,000							
1999, Nunavut, Mule	—							
1999, Nunavut, Unc collector set	74,821							
1999, Nunavut, BU set								
1999, Nunavut, Silver Proof **(a)**	(39,873)							
1999, Nunavut, Specimen set	(45,100)							
1999P, Test only	20,000							
2000, Polar Bear, Proof	(20,000)							
2000, Polar Bear, Silver Proof **(a)**	(90,921)							

a. Silver Proofs have a silver ring and core, with gold plating on the core. From 1996 through 2011 silver Proofs are .925 fine (i.e., sterling); from 2012 to date, silver Proofs are .9999 fine.

Date		Quantity Minted	VG	F	VF	EF	Unc.	PF	Notes
2000, Path to Knowledge	(1,500)	29,847,000							
2000, Path to Knowledge, Silver Proof (a)	(39,768)								
2000W, Polar Bear, Specimen set only	(186,985)								
2000W, Path to Knowledge, Specimen set only		*							
2001		11,910,000							
2001, Silver Proof (a)	(74,197)								
2001, Specimen set	(54,613)								
2001P, Unc collector sets only		115,897							
2002, Golden Jubilee	(98,805)	27,020,000			✘				
2002, Golden Jubilee, Silver Proof (a)	(65,315)								
2002, Golden Jubilee, Specimen set	(100,467)								
2003, Diadem Portrait		11,244,000							
2003, Diadem Portrait, Unc collector set		94,126							
2003, Diadem Portrait, Silver Proof (a)	(62,007)								

* Included in 2000, Path to Knowledge, mintage.

a. Silver Proofs have a silver ring and core, with gold plating on the core. From 1996 through 2011 silver Proofs are .925 fine (i.e., sterling); from 2012 to date, silver Proofs are .9999 fine.

Queen Elizabeth II, Uncrowned Portrait (2003 to Date)

**Polar Bear Reverse
(2003 to Date)**

**My Canada, My Inspiration:
Dance of the Spirits
(2017)**

Date		Quantity Minted	VG	F	VF	EF	Unc.	PF	Notes
2003, Uncrowned Portrait		4,120,104							
2003W, Uncrowned Portrait, Special Unc set		94,126							
2004		12,908,000							
2004, Unc collector set		96,847							
2004, Test		10,000							
2004, Silver Proof (a)	(57,614)								
2005		38,317,000							
2005, Unc collector set		112,878							

a. Silver Proofs have a silver ring and core, with gold plating on the core. From 1996 through 2011 silver Proofs are .925 fine (i.e., sterling); from 2012 to date, silver Proofs are .9999 fine.

Date	Quantity Minted	VG	F	VF	EF	Unc.	PF	Notes
2005, Special collector set	(40,000)							
2005, Silver Proof (a)	(63,560)							
2006, Polar Bear	(53,822)							
2006RCM, Polar Bear	35,319,000							
2006RCM, Polar Bear, BU								
2006, Test	unknown							
2006, Polar Bear, Last-Day / First-Day Strike folder	1,971							
2006, 10th Anniv, Polar Bear	5,005,000							
2006, 10th Anniv, Polar Bear, First-Day Strike folder	4,991							
2006, 10th Anniv, Polar Bear, BU / Specimen / PF set	(57,885)							
2006, 10th Anniv, Polar Bear, Gold Proof	(2,068)							
2006RCM, 10th Anniv, Churchill	25,274,000							
2006RCM, 10th Anniv, Churchill, BU	25,208							
2006RCM, Special Collector set	30,000							
2007RCM	38,957,000							
2007RCM, Silver Proof (a)	(37,373)							
2008RCM	12,390,000							
2008RCM, Silver Proof (a)	(38,630)							
2008RCM, Unc collector set	75,000							
2008, Quebec City	6,010,000							
2009RCM	38,430,000							
2009RCM, Silver Proof (a)	(27,550)							
2009RCM, Unc collector set	65,000							
2010RCM	8,220,000							
2010RCM, Silver Proof (a)	(32,340)							
2011RCM	27,488,000							
2011RCM, Silver Proof (a)	(32,910)							
2011, Boreal Forest	5,000,000							
2012RCM, Polar Bear (27,254)	1,531,000							
2012RCM, Polar Bear, Silver Proof (a)	(19,789)							
2012, Polar Bear, Security Features added	82,862,000							
2012, War of 1812, Security Features added	5,000,000							
2013	12,390,000							
2013, Unc collector set	75,000							
2013, Silver Proof (a)	(75,000)							

a. Silver Proofs have a silver ring and core, with gold plating on the core. From 1996 through 2011 silver Proofs are .925 fine (i.e., sterling); from 2012 to date, silver Proofs are .9999 fine.

Date		Quantity Minted	VG	F	VF	EF	Unc.	PF		Notes
2014	(11,250)	11,305,000								
2014, 100th Anniv of WWI		5,000,000								
2014, 100th Anniv of WWI, Silver Proof (a)	(13,416)									
2015	(20,000)	22,528,500								
2015, Silver Proof (a)	(20,000)									
2015, Sir John MacDonald		5,000,000								
2015, In Flanders Fields		12,500,000								
2016	(20,000)	20,669,000								
2016, Silver Proof (a)	(20,000)									
2016, Battle of the Atlantic		7,500,000								
2017		39,595,000								
2017, Silver Proof (a)	(20,000)									
2017, Dance of the Spirits (b)	(45,000)	*								
2017, Vimy Ridge (b)		*								
2018	(25,000)									
2018, Silver Proof (a)	(20,000)									
2018, Armistice (b)										
2019	(15,000)									
2019, Silver Proof (a)	(15,000)									
2019, D-Day (b)		2,500,000								
2020	(15,000)									
2020, Silver Proof (a)	(20,000)									
2020, Bill Reid / Haida Art (b)		875,000								
2020, End of WWII (b)		875,000								
2021										
2021, Silver Proof (a)										
2022										
2022, Silver Proof (a)										

* Included above.

a. Silver Proofs have a silver ring and core, with gold plating on the core. From 1996 through 2011 silver Proofs are .925 fine (i.e., sterling); from 2012 to date, silver Proofs are .9999 fine.
b. Engraved and enameled versions.

CANADIAN COMMEMORATIVE ISSUES

The Royal Canadian Mint is a prolific producer of fine collector coins, and an exhaustive list of all collector issues to date would be a book in itself. Commemorative issues are listed through 2010. Extra pages at the end of this section allow the reader to fill in items from their specialty.

Date	Distribution	Unc.	PF	Notes
ONE-CENT PIECES				
1998, Mint Anniversary, Matte Proof	(18,376)			
1998, Mint Anniversary, Mirror Proof	(24,893)			
2003, Queen Elizabeth II 50th Anniversary	(21,537)			
2003, RCM Annual Report	(7,746)			
2010, 75th Anniv of Voyageur Dollar	(4,996)			
THREE-CENT PIECES				
2001 First Canadian Postage Stamp Coin/ Medal/Stamp Set	(59,573)			
FIVE-CENT PIECES				
1998, Mint Anniversary, Matte Proof	(18,376)			
1998, Mint Anniversary, Mirror Proof	(24,893)			
2000, Les Voltigeurs de Québec	(34,024)			
2001, Royal Military College	(25,834)			
2002, Vimy Ridge	(22,646)			
2003, Coronation Aniversary, Silver Proof	(21,537)			
2004, 60th Anniversary D-Day	(20,019)			
2005, 60th Anniv VE Day	59,258,000			
2010, 75th Anniv of Voyageur Dollar	(4,996)			
TEN-CENT PIECES				
1997, J. Cabot Silv Pf	(49,848)			
1998, Mint Anniversary Matte Proof	(18,376)			
1998, Mint Anniversary, Mirror Proof	(24,893)			

Date	Distribution	Unc.	PF	Notes
2000, Credit Union, Silver Proof	(69,791)			
2003, Coronation Aniversary, Silver Proof	(21,537)			
2004P, Canadian Open Golf	39,486			
2004P, Canadian Open Golf Set: 10¢ (2), stamps, divot tool	20,736			
2010, 75th Anniv of Voyageur Dollar	(4,996)			
TWENTY-FIVE-CENT PIECES				
1992, New Brunswick*	(149,387) 2,174,000	X		
1992, New Brunswick, 180° Rotated Rev Die Incl. above		X		
1992, New Brunswick, 90° Rotated Rev Die Incl. above				
1992, N'west Terr.*	(149,387) 12,580,000	X		
1992, N'west Terr., 90° Rotated Rev Die Incl. above		X		
1992, Newfoundland*	(149,387) 11,405,000	X		
1992, Manitoba*	(149,387) 11,349,000	X		
1992, Yukon Territory*	(149,387) 10,388,000	X		
1992, Alberta*	(149,387) 12,133,300	X		
1992, PE Island*	(149,387) 13,001,000	X		
1992, Ontario*	(149,387) 14,263,000	X		
1992, Nova Scotia*	(149,387) 13,600,000	X		
1992, Quebec*	(149,387) 13,607,000	X		

Date	Distribution	Unc.	PF	Notes	Date	Distribution	Unc.	PF	Notes
TWENTY-FIVE-CENT PIECES					Mule, 1999 Non-Denominated Obverse, November Millennium Reverse	—			
1992, Saskatchewan* (149,387) 14,165,000		X							
1992, Saskatch., 180° Rotated Reverse Die Incl. above					1999, Millennium, December* (113,645) 43,339,200		X		
1992, British Columbia* (149,387) 14,001,000		X			2000, Canada Day 26,106				
1992/1993 Mule, 1867–1992 Obverse, 1993 Caribou Rev (1 known)	—				2000, Unc RCM Nickel Set (12)	876,041			
1998, Mint Anniversary, Matte Proof (18,376)					2000, Unc Nickel, RCM Medallion Set				
1998, Mint Anniversary, Mirror Proof (24,893)					2000, Unc Nickel, Nestlé Medallion Set				
1999, Unc RCM Nickel Set (12)	1,499,973				2000, Unc Nickel Deluxe Set				
1999, Unc Nickel, RCM Medallion Set Incl. above					2000, Proof Silver Set (12) (37,940)				
1999, Unc Nickel, Nestlé Medallion Set Incl. above					1999–2000, Proof Silver (24) Chinese Set				
1999, Proof Silver Set (60,245)					2000, Millennium, Pride (76,956) (January)* 50,666,800		X		
1999, Millennium, January* (113,645) 12,181,200		X			2000, Millen., Pride (Jan) 90° Rotated Rev Die Incl. above				
1999, Millennium, February* (113,645) 14,469,250		X			2000, Millennium, Pride (January) (Enameled)	49,399			
1999, Millennium, March* (113,645) 15,033,500		X			2000, Millennium, Ingenuity (February)* (76,956) 36,078,360		X		
1999, Millennium, April* (113,645) 15,446,000		X			Mule, Feb 25¢ Obverse, RCM Medallion Obverse	—			
1999, Millennium, May* (113,645) 15,566,100		X			2000, Millenium, Achievm't (March)* (76,956) 35,312,750		X		
1999, Millennium, June* (113,645) 20,432,750		X			2000, Millenium, Health (April)* (76,956) 35,470,900		X		
1999, Millennium, July* (113,645) 17,321,000		X			2000, Millenium, Natural Legacy (May)* (76,956) 36,236,900		X		
1999, Millennium, August* (113,645) 18,153,700		X			2000, Millenium, Harmony (June)* (76,956) 35,184,200		X		
1999, Millennium, September* (113,645) 31,539,350		X			2000, Millen., Harmony (June) 90° Rotated Reverse Die Incl. above				
Mule, 1999 Non-Denom Obv, Sept Millennium Rev	—				2000, Millenium, Celebration (July)* (76,956) 35,144,100		X		
1999, Millennium, October* (113,645) 32,136,650		X			2000, Millenium, Family (August)* (76,956) 35,107,700		X		
1999, Millennium, November* (113,645) 27,162,800		X							

* Proof coins are silver.

Date	Distribution	Unc.	PF	Notes	Date	Distribution	Unc.	PF	Notes
TWENTY-FIVE-CENT PIECES					2006P, Breast Cancer	29,798,000			
2000, Millenium, Wisdom (Sept)*	(76,956) 35,123,950	X			2006P, Breast Cancer, First-Day Strike	7,348			
2000, Millenium, Creativity (October)*	(76,956) 35,316,770	X			2006P, Mont. Canadiens				
2000, Millenium, Freedom (Nov)*	(76,956) 35,188,900	X			2006P, Ottawa Senators	11,765			
					2006P, Tor. Maple Leafs				
2000, Millenium, Community (Dec)*	(76,956) 35,155,400	X			2006P, Quebec Winter Carnival	8,200			
2001P, Canada Day	96,352				2006, QEII's 80th Birthday	24,977			
2002P, Canada Day (Enameled)	49,901				2006, Medal of Bravery	20,040,000			
2002P, Canada Day (Non-enameled)	30,627,000				2006, Medal of Bravery, First-Day Strike	4,906			
2003P, Canada Day	63,511				2006P, Santa/Rudolph	99,258			
2003, Coronation Anniv, Silver Proof	(21,537)				2007RCM, Canada Day	27,743			
2004P, Canada Day, Maple Leaves	44,752				2007, Maple Leaf (Enameled; Oh! Canada! sets only	23,582			
2004P, Canada Day, Moose	16,028				2007, Hummingbird	25,000			
2004P, Poppy (Enameled)	28,972,000				2007, Nuthatch	25,000			
2004, Poppy (Gold-Highlighted Silver, from annual Mint Report)	(12,677)				2007, Baby Rattle	29,964			
					2007, Balloons	24,531			
					2007, Fireworks	8,910			
2004, Poppy, First-Day Strike	9,824				2007, Bouquet	10,318			
2004P, Île St. Croix	15,400,000				2007, Calgary Flames	832			
2004P, Santa Claus	62,777				2007, Edmonton Oilers	2,2123			
2005P, Canada Day	58,370				2007, Montreal Canadiens	2,952			
2005P, Alberta Cent'l	20,640,000				2007, Ottawa Senators	1,634			
2005P, Alberta Cent'l, First-Day Strike	9,108				2007, Toronto Maple Leafs	3,527			
2005P, Saskatch. Centennial	19,290,000				2007, Vancouver Canucks	1,264			
					2007, Curling	22,400,000			
2005P, Saskatch. Cent'l, First-Day Strike	6,980				2007, Curling, First-Day Strike Folder	10,000			
2005P, Year of Vet	29,390,000				2007, Ice Hockey	22,400,000			
2005P, Year of Vet, First-Day Strike	8,361				2007, Ice Hockey, First-Day Strike Folder	10,000			
2005P, Netherlands Liberation*	(3,500) 17,500				2007, Wheelchair Curling	22,400,000			
2005P, Stocking	72,831				2007, Wheelchair Curling, First-Day Strike Folder	10,000			
2006P, Canada Day	30,328				2007, Biathlon	22,400,000			

* Proof coins are silver.

Date	Distribution	Unc.	PF	Notes	Date	Distribution	Unc.	PF	Notes
TWENTY-FIVE-CENT PIECES					2009, Women's Ice Hockey (Non-enameled)	19,000,000			
2007, Biathlon, First-Day Strike Folder	10,000				2009, Women's Ice Hockey (Enameled)				
2007, Alpine Skiing	22,400,000				2009, Cindy Klassen (Non-enameled)	19,000,000			
2007, Alpine Skiing, First-Day Strike Folder	10,000				2009, Cindy Klassen (Enameled)				
2007, Christmas Tree	8,910				2009, Notre-Dame-du-Saguenay				
2008, Canada Day					2009, Speed Skating	22,400,000			
2008, Snowboarding	22,400,000				2009, Speed Skating, First-Day Strike Folder	10,000			
2008, Snowboarding, First-Day Strike Folder	10,000				2009, Cross-Country Skiing	22,400,000			
2008, Freestyle Skiing	22,400,000				2009, Cross-Country Skiing, First-Day Strike Folder	10,000			
2008, Freestyle Skiing, First-Day Strike Folder	10,000				2009, Ice Sledge Hockey	22,400,000			
2008, Figure Skating	22,400,000				2009, Ice Sledge Hockey, First-Day Strike Folder	10,000			
2008, Figure Skating, First-Day Strike Folder	10,000				2009, Santa/Maple Leaves				
2008, Bobsleigh	22,400,000				2010, Goldfinch	14,000			
2008, Bobsleigh, First-Day Strike Folder	10,000				2010, 75th Anniv of Voyageur Dollar	(4,996)			
2008, Woodpecker	25,000				**FIFTY-CENT PIECES**				
2008, Cardinal	25,000				1995, Silver Proof, Atlantic Puffins				
2008, Teddy Bear					1995, Silver Proof, Whooping Crane				
2008, Party Hat					1995, Silver Proof, Gray Jays	(172,377)			
2008, Trophy					1995, Silver Proof, Ptarmigans				
2008, Flag					1995, Puffins-Crane 2-Coin Set				
2008, Wedding Cake					1995, Jays-Ptarmigan 2-Coin Set				
2008, Miga					1996, Little Wild Ones Silver Proof Set	(206,552)			
2008, Quatchi									
2008, Sumi									
2008, Santa									
2009, Oh! Canada									
2009, Balloons									
2009, Baby									
2009, Fireworks									
2009, Flower									
2009, Wedding Doves									
2009, Men's Ice Hockey (Non-enameled)	19,000,000								
2009, Men's Ice Hockey (Enameled)									

Date	Distribution	Unc.	PF	Notes	Date	Distribution	Unc.	PF	Notes
FIFTY-CENT PIECES					1998, Silver Proof, 1888 Figure Skating				
1996, Silver Proof, Moose Calf					1998, Silver Proof, 1898 Ski Racing				
1996, Silver Proof, Wood Ducklings	*				1998, Silver Proof, 1888 Soccer Tour	*			
1996, Silver Proof, Cougar Kittens					1998, Silver Proof, 1978 Grand Prix				
1996, Silver Proof, Black Bear Cubs					1999, Cats of Canada Silver Proof Set				
1996, Moose–Ducklings 2-Coin Set	(184,536)				1999, Silver Proof, Tonkinese	(83,423)			
1996, Cougars–Bears 2-Coin Set					1999, Silv Pf, Lynx				
1997, Best Friends Silver Proof Set					**FIFTY-CENT PIECES**				
1997, Silver Proof, Newfoundland					1999, Silv Pf, Cymric	*			
1997, Silver Proof, Duck Tolling Retriever					1999, Silv Pf, Cougar				
1997, Silver Proof, Labrador Retriever	*				1999, Firsts in Sports Silver Proof Set				
1997, Silver Proof, Eskimo Dog					1999, Silver Proof, 1904 Canadian Open				
1997, Newfoundland–Duck Tolling 2-Coin Set					1999, Silver Proof, 1874 Int'l Yacht Race	(52,115)			
1997, Labrador–Eskimo Dog 2-Coin Set					1999, Silver Proof, 1909 Grey Cup				
1998, Ocean Giants Silver Proof Set					1999, Silver Proof, 1939 Basketball				
1998, Silver Proof, Killer Whales					2000, Birds of Prey Silver Proof Set				
1998, Silver Proof, Humpback Whale	(133,310)				2000, Silver Proof, Bald Eagle				
1998, Silver Proof, Beluga Whales					2000, Silv Pf, Osprey	(123,628)			
1998, Silver Proof, Blue Whale					2000, Silv Pf, Great Horned Owl				
1998, Mint Anniversary, Matte Proof	(18,376)				2000, Silver Proof Red-Tailed Hawk				
1998, Mint Anniversary, Mirror Proof	(24,893)				2000, Firsts in Sports Silver Proof Set				
1998, Firsts in Sports Silver Proof Set	(56,428)				2000, Silver Proof, 1875 Hockey				
					2000, Silver Proof, 1760 Curling	(50,091)			
					2000, Silver Proof, 1840 Steeplechase				
					2000, Silver Proof, 1910 5-Pin Bowling				

* Included in previous.

Date	Distribution	Unc.	PF	Notes	Date	Distribution	Unc.	PF	Notes
FIFTY-CENT PIECES					2002, Silver Proof, Le Vaisseau Fantome	*			
2001, Canadian Festivals Silver Proof Set					2002, Tulips (Gold-Highlighted)	(19,986)			
2001, Silv Pf, Quebec					2003, Canadian Festivals Silver Proof Set				
2001, Silver Proof, Nunavut	(58,123)				2003, Silver Proof, Yukon				
2001, Silver Proof, Newfoundland					2003, Silver Proof, Saskatchewan	(26,451)			
2001, Silver Proof, Prince Edward Island					2003, Silver Proof, Northwest Territories				
2001, Folklore/ Legends Silver Proof Set					2003, Silver Proof, New Brunswick				
2001, Silver Proof, The Sled	(28,979)				2003, Daffodils (Gold-Highlighted)	(36,293)			
2001, Silver Proof, The Maiden's Cave					2003, Coronation Anniversary, Silv Pf	(21,537)			
2001, Silver Proof, Les Petits Sauteux					2004, Easter Lily (Gold-Highlighted)	(24,495)			
2002, Golden Jubilee					2004, QEII 4-Effigies Silver Proof Set	(12,230)			
2002, Golden Jubilee 5-Piece Gift Set	14,440,000				2004, Silv Pf, Laureate	(12,230)			
2002, Golden Jubilee 10-Piece Gift Set					2004, Silv Pf, Diademed	(12,230)			
					2004, Silv Pf, Crowned	(12,230)			
2002, Golden Jubilee, Gold Plated, Accession set only	(33,490)				2004, Silver Proof, Uncrowned	(12,230)			
2002, Canadian Fests Silver Proof Set					2004, Tiger Swallowtail (Hologram)	(20,462)			
2002, Silver Proof, Nova Scotia					2004, Clouded Sulphur (Gold-Highlighted)	(15,281)			
2002, Silver Proof, Ontario					2005, Spangled Fritillary (Hologram)	(35,950)			
2002, Silver Proof, Manitoba	(61,900)				2005, Monarch (Enameled)				
2002, Silver Proof, Alberta					2005, Battles of WWII Specimen Set	20,000			
2002, Silver Proof, British Columbia					2005, Battle of Britain	20,000			
2002, Folklore/Legends Silver Proof Set					2005, Liberation of the Netherlands	20,000			
2002, Silver Pf, The Pig	(19,789)				2005, Conquest of Sicily	20,000			
2002, Silver Proof, The Shoemaker					2005, Battle of the Scheldt	20,000			
					2005, Raid on Dieppe	20,000			

* Included in previous.

Date	Distribution	Unc.	PF	Notes	Date	Distribution	Unc.	PF	Notes
FIFTY-CENT PIECES					2009–2010, Edmonton Oilers				
2005, Battle of the Atlantic	20,000				2009–2010, Montreal Canadiens				
2005, Montreal Canadiens Legends Set					2009–2010, Ottawa Senators				
2005, Jean Beliveau	25,000				2009–2010, Toronto Maple Leafs				
2005, Guy LaFleur					2009–2010, Vancouver Canucks				
2005, Jacques Plante									
2005, Maurice Richard					2010, Miga Ice Hockey				
2005, Toronto Maple Leafs Legends Set					2010, Quatchi Ice Hockey				
2005, Johnny Bower	25,000				2010, Sumi Ice Sledge Hockey				
2005, Tim Horton					2010, Quatchi Miga Skating				
2005, Dave Keon					2010, Quatchi Miga Bobsleigh				
2005, Daryl Sittler									
2005, Rose (Gold-Highlighted)	(17,418)				2010, Miga Ariels				
2006, Daisies (Gold-Highlighted)	(18,190)				2010, Miga Skeleton				
2006, Silvery Blue (Hologram)	(24,016)				2010, Quatchi Snowboard				
2006, Short-Tailed Swallowtail (Enameled)					2010, Miga Alpine Skiing				
2006, RCM Annual Report	(4,162)				2010, Sumi Paralympic Skiing				
2007, Forget-Me-Not (Gold-Highlighted)	(22,882)				2010, Quatchi Slalom				
2007, Holiday Ornaments	(16,989)				2010, Miga Speed Skating				
2008, Holiday Snowman					2010, Vancouver and Inukshuk (Lenticular)				
2008, Mint Anniversary	(16,000)								
2008, Milk Delivery	(25,000)				2010, Albertosaurus	(14,500)			
2009, Six-String Nation Guitar	30,000				2010, Daspletosaurus Torosus	(11,500)			
2009, Holiday Toy Train					2010, Sinosauropteryx	(20,000)			
2009, Calgary Flames					2010RCM, Santa Claus	(21,400)			
2009, Edmonton Oilers					**ONE-DOLLAR PIECES**				
2009, Montreal Canadiens					1973, RCMP	1,031,271			
2009, Ottawa Senators					1975, Calgary	833,095			
2009, Toronto Maple Leafs					1976, Library of Parliament	483,722			
2009, Vancouver Canucks					1977, Silver Jubilee	744,848			
2009–2010, Calgary Flames									

Date	Distribution	Unc.	PF	Notes
ONE-DOLLAR PIECES				
1978, Commonwealth Games	640,000			
1979, Griffon Tercentennial	688,671			
1980, Arctic Territories	389,564			
1981, Trans-Canada Railway	(353,742) 148,647			
1982, Regina Centennial	(577,959) 144,989			
1982, Constitution	(107,353) 11,812,000			
1982, Constitution, Coin Alignment	Incl. above			
1982, Constitution, Thin Planchet (3 known)	Incl. above			
1983, University Games	(340,068) 159,450			
1984, Toronto Sesquicentennial	(571,563) 133,563			
1984, Jacques Cartier	(87,776) 7,009,323			
1985, National Parks	(537,297) 162,813			
1986, Vancouver	(496,418) 127,574			
1987, John Davis Expeditions	(405,688) 118,722	X		
1988, Saint-Maurice Ironworks	(259,230) 106,702			
1989, MacKenzie River	(272,319) 110,650			
1990, Henry Kelsey	(222,983) 85,763			
1991, SS *Frontenac*	(222,892) 82,642			
1992, Kingston-York Stage	(187,612) 78,160			
1992, Confederation 125th Anniversary	(108,614) 23,915,000			
1993, Stanley Cup	(294,314) 88,150			
1994, RCMP Dog Sled	(178,485) 62,295			

Date	Distribution	Unc.	PF	Notes
1994, War Memorial	(103,746) 20,004,830			
1995, Peacekeeping Monument	(93,095) 18,502,750			
1995, Hudson's Bay Co.	(166,259) 61,819			
1996, McIntosh Apple	(133,779) 58,834			
1997, Flying Loon 10th Anniversary, Specimen and BU sets only	97,595			
1997, Flying Loon 10th Anniversary, Silver Proof	(24,995)			
1997, Canada-USSR Hockey	(184,965) 155,252			
1998, RCMP 125th Anniversary	(130,795) 81,376			
1999, Juan Perez Voyage	(126,435) 67,655			
1999, International Year of Older Persons	(24,976)			
2000, Voyage of Discovery	(121,575) 62,975			
2001, National Ballet	(89,390) 53,668			
2001, Pattern Dollar of 1911	(24,996)			
2002, Accession Golden Jubilee, Silver	(29,688) 65,410			
2002, Accession Golden Jubilee (Gold-Highlighted)	(65,315)			
2002, Queen Mother Elizabeth	(9,994)			
2002, Family of Loons (150th Anniversary), Specimen sets only	67,672			
2002, Centre Ice Loon (Gold-Plated), Souvenir Album only	(25,000)			
2003, Cobalt Silver Discovery	(88,536) 51,130			
2003, Coronation Golden Jubilee	(21,537)			

Date	Distribution	Unc.	PF	Notes
ONE-DOLLAR PIECES				
Accession / Coronation Golden Jubilee	(unique)			
2004, Olympic Lucky Loonie	6,526,000			
2004, Olympic Lucky Loonie, First Strike	34,488			
2004, Lucky Loonie (Enameled Silver)	(19,994)			
2004, Jack Miner Sanctuary / Goose, Specimen sets only	46,493			
2004, Elusive Loon, Coin/Stamps sets only	(25,105)			
2004, Île Sainte-Croix	(106,974) 42,582			
2004, Île Sainte-Croix, Fleur-de-lis Privy Mark	8,315			
2004, The Poppy	(24,547)			
2005, Terry Fox	12,909,000			
2005, Terry Fox, First-Day Strike	19,933			
2005, National Flag	(95,431) 50,948			
2005, National Flag (Gold-Highlighted)	(62,483)			
2005, National Flag (Enameled)	(4,898)			
2005, Tufted Puffin, Specimen sets only	40,000			
2006, Olympic Lucky Loonie	10,495,000			
2006RCM, Olympic Lucky Loonie				
2006RCM, Olympic Lucky Loonie, First-Day Strike	20,010			
2006RCM, Olym Lucky Loonie, Pf (Bookmark)	(104,432)			
2006, Lucky Loonie (Enameled Silver)	(19,973)			
2006, Lullaby Loonie, Baby Gift sets only	(18,225)			
2006, Snowy Owl, Specimen sets only	40,000			

Date	Distribution	Unc.	PF	Notes
2006, Victoria Cross	(59,599) 27,254			
2006, Victoria Cross (Gold-Highlighted)	Incl. above			
2006, Medal of Bravery	(8,343)			
2006, Medal of Bravery (Enameled)	(4,999)			
2006, .9999 Gold Louis d'Or	(5,648)			
2007, Trumpeter Swans, Specimen sets only	40,000			
2007, Thayendanegea	(32,224) 16,378			
2007, Thayendanegea (Gold-Highlighted)	(60,000)			
2007, Thayendanegea (Enameled)	(4,760)			
2007, Rattle				
2007, Rattle (Gold-Highlighted), Baby Gift Proof sets only				
2007, Child's Blocks, Baby Keepsake Tins sets only				
2007, Celebration of Arts	(6,466)			
2007, .9999 Gold Louis d'Or	(3,457)			
2008, Luckie Loonie (first issued in 2007 Collection)				
2008, Lucky Loonie	(30,000)			
2008, Quebec City	(65,000) 35,000			
2008, Quebec City (Gold-Highlighted)	(60,000)			
2008, RCM Centennial	(25,000)			
2008, "The Poppy" Armistice	(5,000)			
2008, Olympic Lucky Loon	10,851,000			
2008, Olympic Lucky Loon, First-Day Strike	4,297			
2008, Olympic Lucky Loon, Key Chain	591			
2008, Olympic Lucky Loon (Enameled Silver)	(30,000)			

Date	Distribution	Unc.	PF	Notes	Date	Distribution	Unc.	PF	Notes
ONE-DOLLAR PIECES					2009, Toronto Maple Leafs, Road Jersey				
2008, Common Eider	40,000				2009, Vancouver Canucks, Road Jersey				
2008, .9999 Louis d'Or	(10,000)				2009, Calgary Flames				
2008, Calgary Flames, Road Jersey					2009, Edmonton Oilers				
2008, Calgary Flames, Home Jersey					2009, Montreal Canadiens				
2008, Edmonton Oilers, Road Jersey					2009, Ottawa Senators				
2008, Edmonton Oilers, Home Jersey					2009, Toronto Maple Leafs				
2008, Montreal Canadiens, Road Jersey					2009, Vancouver Canucks				
2008, Montreal Canadiens, Home Jersey					2010, The Sun	(5,000)			
2008, Ottawa Senators, Road Jersey					2010, Vancouver Lucky Loonie	10,250,000			
2008, Ottawa Senators, Home Jersey					2010, Vancouver Lucky Loonie (First-Day Folder)	12,000			
2008, Toronto Maple Leafs, Road Jersey					2010, Vancouver Lucky Loonie (Enameled; With Puck)				
2008, Toronto Maple Leafs, Home Jersey					2010, Vancouver Lucky Loonie (Enameled; With Bag)	2,140			
2008, Vancouver Canucks, Road Jersey					2010, Vancouver Lucky Loonie (Enameled; With lanyard)	7,062			
2008, Vancouver Canucks, Home Jersey					2010, Vancouver Lucky Loonie (Enameled Silver)	(40,000)			
2009, Great Blue Heron	40,000				2010, Navy Centennial	7,000,000			
2009, Montreal Canadiens Centennial	9,500				2010, Saskatchewan Roughriders	3,100,000			
2009, Montreal Canadiens Cent'l (Gold-Highlighted)	9,500				2010, Anticipating the Games	40,000			
2009, Centennial of Flight	(50,000) 30,000				2010, Ilanaaq (first issued in 2007 Collection)				
2009, Centennial of Flight (Gold-Highlighted)	(50,000)				2010, 75th Anniv of Voyageur Dollar	(7,500)			
2009, Calgary Flames, Road Jersey					2010, Anticipating the Games, Silver, Enameled	(13,250)			
2009, Edmonton Oilers, Road Jersey					2010, Navy Centennial, Gold-Plated Bronze	10,000			
2009, Montreal Canadiens, Road Jersey					2010, Northern Harrier	(21,000)			
					2010, Poppy, Enameled	(5,000)			
2009, Ottawa Senators, Road Jersey					2010, Saskatchewan Roughriders, Gold-Plated Bronze	32,750			

Date	Distribution	Unc.	PF	Notes	Date	Distribution	Unc.	PF	Notes
TWO-DOLLAR PIECES					2009, Hanging Stockings	(15,000)			
1999, Nunavut	375,483,000				2010, Dromaeosaurus	(20,000)			
1999, Nunavut, Specimen	20,000				2010, Euoplocephalus Tutus	(13,000)			
1999, Nunavut, Silver/Gilt	(39,873)				**FIVE-DOLLAR PIECES**				
TWO-DOLLAR PIECES					1973, Map of North America	537,898			
1999, Nunavut, White Gold / Gold	(4,298)				1973, Kingston and Sailboats				
1999, Nunavut, Mule					1974, Athlete w. Torch	1,990,570			
2000, Path of Knowledge	29,880,000				1974, Olympic Rings and Wreath				
2000, Path of Knowledge, Nickel/Bronze	1,500				1974, Canoeing	1,990,570			
2000, Path of Knowledge, Silver/Gilt	(39,768)				1974, Rowing				
2000, Path of Knowledge, White Gold / Gold	(5,881)				1975, Marathon	1,985,000			
2002, Golden Jubilee	(98,805) 27,008,000				1975, Women's Javelin				
					1975, Diving	1,985,000			
2006, Churchill	25,274,000				1975, Swimming				
2006, Churchill, Brilliant Uncirculated Strike	25,208				1976, Fencing	1,887,630			
2006, 10th Anniversary Polar Bear	(57,885) 5,005,000				1976, Boxing				
					1976, Olympic Village	1,887,629			
2006, 10th Anniversary Polar Bear, First-Day Strike	4,991				1976, Olympic Flame				
2006, 10th Anniversary Polar Bear, Gold Proof	(2,068)				1998, Norman Bethune	(65,831)			
					1999, Viking Settlement	(28,450)			
2008, Quebec 400th Anniversary	6,010,000				2001, Wireless Transmission (in Set With British £2 Coin)	(15,011)			
2010, Lynx Kittens	(14,750)				2003, FIFA World Cup	(21,542)			
THREE-DOLLAR PIECES					2004, Canadian Open	(18,750)			
2006, The Beaver	20,000				2004, Majestic Moose	(12,822)			
2010, Return of the Tyee	(15,000)				2005, White-Tailed Deer	(6,439)			
					2005, Atlantic Walrus	(5,519)			
2010, Barn Owl, Gold-Plated	(10,500)				2005, Peregrine Falcon	(7,226)			
2010, Polar Bear, Gold-Plated	(8,500)				2005, 60th Anniversary of WWII	(10,000) 25,000			
FOUR-DOLLAR PIECES					2005, Alberta Centennial	(20,000)			
2007, Parasaurolophus	(13,010)				2005, Saskatchewan Centennial	(20,000)			
2008, Triceratops	(20,000)				2006, Sable Island Horse	(10,108)			
2009, T. Rex	(20,000)				2006, Breast Cancer Awareness	(11,048)			

Date	Distribution	Unc.	PF	Notes	Date	Distribution	Unc.	PF	Notes
FIVE-DOLLAR PIECES					**FIFTEEN-DOLLAR PIECES**				
2006, Snowbirds	(10,034)				1992, Speed Skater				
2009, Canada in Japan, Silver	(40,000)				1992, Speed Skater, No Edge Lettering				
EIGHT-DOLLAR PIECES					1992, Spirit of the Generations	(105,645)			
2004, Great Grizzly	(12,942)								
2005, Railway Bridge	(9,892)				1992, Spirit of the Generations, No Edge Lettering				
2005, Chinese Memorial (Packaged With Above)	(9,892)								
2007, Ancient China	(19,954)				1998, Year of the Tiger	(68,888)			
2007, Maple of Long Life	(11,624)				1999, Year of the Rabbit	(77,791)			
2009, Maple of Wisdom	(14,888)				2000, Year of the Dragon	(88,634)			
2009, Maple of Wisdom	(7,500)				2001, Year of the Snake	(60,754)			
2010, Maple of Strength	(5,000)				2002, Year of the Horse	(59,395)			
TEN-DOLLAR PIECES					2003, Year of the Ram	(53,714)			
1973, Map of World	543,098				2004, Year of the Monkey	(46,175)			
1973, Montreal Skyline									
1974, Head of Zeus	1,974,939				2005, Year of the Rooster	(44,690)			
1974, Temple of Zeus									
1974, Lacrosse	1,974,939				2006, Year of the Dog	(41,617)			
1974, Cycling					2007, Year of the Pig	(48,888)			
1975, Men's Hurdles	2,476,217				2008, Year of the Rat	(48,888)			
1975, Women's Shot Put					2009, Year of the Ox	(48,888)			
1975, Paddling	2,476,216				2008, Victoria	10,000			
1975, Sailing					2008, Edward VII	10,000			
1976, Field Hockey	1,985,257				2008, George V	10,000			
1976, Soccer					2008, George VI	10,000			
1976, Olym Stadium	1,985,257				2008, Elizabeth II	10,000			
1976, Olym Velodrome					2008, Jack of Hearts	(25,000)			
2005, Year of the Veteran	(6,549)				2008, Queen of Spades	(25,000)			
2005, Pope John Paul II	(24,716)				2009, King of Hearts	(25,000)			
2006, Fortress of Louisbourg	(5,544)				2009, Ten of Spades	(25,000)			
2005, Year of the Veteran	(6,500)				2010, Year of the Tiger, Scalloped	(19,888)			
2005, Pope John Paul II	(25,000)								
2006, Fortress of Louisburg	(5,500)				2010, Year of the Tiger, Round	(9,999)			
2010, Blue Whale	(10,000)				**TWENTY-DOLLAR PIECES**				
2010, First Notes from Bank of Canada	(7,000)				1967, Centennial of Confederation, Gold	334,288			
					1985, Downhill Skiing	(406,360)			
					1985, Speed Skating	(354,222)			
					1985, Speed Skating, No Edge Lettering				

Date	Distribution	Unc.	PF	Notes	Date	Distribution	Unc.	PF	Notes
TWENTY-DOLLAR PIECES					2001, The Russell "Light Four"	(41,828)			
1986, Hockey	(396,602)				2001, The Marco Polo				
1986, Hockey, No Edge Lettering					2001, The Scotia				
1986, Biathlon	(308,086)				2002, The Gray-Dort	(35,944)			
1986, Biathlon, No Edge Lettering					2002, The William Lawrence	*			
1986, Cross-Country Skiing	(303,199)				2002, D-10 Locomotive				
1986, Free-Style Skiing	(294,322)				2003, HMCS Bras d'Or	(31,997)			
1986, Free-Style Skiing, No Edge Lettering					2003, C.N.R. FA-1 Diesel Electric Locomotive				
1987, Figure Skating	(334,875)				2003, Bricklin SV-1				
1987, Curling	(286,457)				2003, Niagara Falls	(29,967)			
1987, Ski-Jumping	(290,954)				2003, Rocky Mountains	(28,793)			
1987, Bobsleigh	(274,326)				2004, Icebergs, Holog	(24,879)			
1990, Avro Anson / N.A. Harvard	(41,844)				2004, Northern Lights, Hologram	(34,135)			
1990, Avro Lancasater	(43,596)				2004, Hopewell Rocks	(16,918)			
1991, A.E.A. Silver Dart	(35,202)				2005, Diamonds	(35,000)			
1991, de Havilland Beaver	(36,197)				2005, Three-Masted Ship	(18,276)			
1992, Curtiss JN-4	(33,105)				2005, North Pacific Rim	(21,695)			
1992, de Havilland Gipsy Moth	(32,537)				2005, Mingan Archip				
1993, Fairchild 71c	(32,199)				2006, Ketch	(10,299)			
1993, Lockheed 14 Super Electra	(32,550)				2006, Georgian Bay Islands	(20,218)			
1994, Curtiss HS-2L	(31,242)				2006, Nahanni National Park				
1994, Canadian Vickers Vedette	(30,880)				2006, Jasper National Park				
1995, Fleet 80 Canuck	(17,438)				2006, Notre Dame Basilica				
1995, DHC-1 Chipmunk	(17,722)				2006, CN Tower	(30,353)			
1996, CF-100 Canuck	(18,508)				2006, Pengrowth Saddledome				
1996, CF-105 Arrow	(27,163)				2007, Brigantine	(7,490)			
1997, F86 Sabre	(16,440)				2007, First International Polar Year, Silver	(8,352)			
1997, Tutor Jet	(18,414)				2007, First International Polar Year (Blue Plasma)	(3,005)			
1998, Argus	(14,711)				2007, Crystal Snowflake (Aquamarine)	(1,433)			
1998, Waterbomber	(15,237)				2007, Crystal Snowflake (Iridescent)	(1,404)			
1999, Twin Otter	(14,173)				2007, Holiday Sleigh Ride	(6,041)			
1999, Dash 8	(14,138)								
2000, Taylor Steam Buggy	(44,367)								
2000, The Bluenose									
2000, The Toronto									

Date	Distribution	Unc.	PF	Notes	Date	Distribution	Unc.	PF	Notes
TWENTY-DOLLAR PIECES					**TWENTY-FIVE-DOLLAR PIECES**				
2008, Crystal Snowflake (Amethyst)	(15,000)				2007, Curling	(45,000)			
					2007, Ice Hockey	(45,000)			
2008, Crystal Snowflake (Sapphire)	(15,000)				2007, Athletes' Pride	(45,000)			
					2007, Biathlon	(45,000)			
2008, Holiday Carols	(10,000)				2007, Alpine Skiing	(45,000)			
2008, Crystal Raindrop (Enameled, With Crystal)	(15,000)				2008, Snowboarding	(45,000)			
					2008, Freestyle Skiing	(45,000)			
2008, The Royal Hudson	(10,000)				2008, Home of Winter Games	(45,000)			
2008, Agriculture	(10,000)				2008, Figure Skating	(45,000)			
2009, Coal Mining	(10,000)				2008, Bobsleigh	(45,000)			
2009, The Jubilee	(10,000)				2009, Speed Skating	(45,000)			
2009, Autumn Showers Raindrop (Enameled, With Crystal)	(10,000)				2009, Cross Country Skiing	(45,000)			
					2009, Olympic Spirit	(45,000)			
2009, Crystal Snowflake (Blue)	(15,000)				2009, Skeleton	(45,000)			
2009, Crystal Snowflake (Pink)	(15,000)				2009, Ski Jumping	(45,000)			
2009, Calgary Flames	(10,000)				**THIRTY-DOLLAR PIECES**				
2009, Edmonton Oilers	(10,000)				2005, Welcome Figure Totem Pole	(9,904)			
2009, Montreal Canadiens	(10,000)				2006, Dog Sled Team	(7,384)			
2009, Ottawa Senators	(10,000)				2006, National War Memorial	(8,876)			
2009, Toronto Maple Leafs	(10,000)				2006, Beaumont-Hamel Memorial	(15,325)			
2009, Vancouver Canucks	(10,000)				2006, 5th Anniversary of Canadarm	(9,357)			
2009, Summer Moon Mask	(10,000)				2007, Vimy Memorial	(5,190)			
2009, Jacques Cartier at Gaspé	(1,534)				2007, Panoramic Niagara Falls	(5,181)			
2010, Crystal Snowflake (Blue)	(7,500)				2008, IMAX	(15,000)			
2010, First Notes from Bank of Canada	(6,750)				2009, International Year of Astronomy	(10,000)			
2010, Holiday Pine Cones, Moonlight	(5,000)				**FIFTY-DOLLAR PIECES**				
2010, Holiday Pine Cones, Ruby	(5,000)				2005, 60th Anniversary End of WWII	4,000			
					2006, The Four Seasons	(1,999)			
2010, Maple Leaf	(10,000)				2006, Spring	300			
2010, The Selkirk	(6,000)				2006, Summer	300			
2010, Water Lily	(10,000)				2006, Autumn	300			
					2006, Winter	300			
					2007, 60th Wedding Anniversary Queen Elizabeth and Prince Philip	(1,945)			

Date	Distribution	Unc.	PF	Notes	Date	Distribution	Unc.	PF	Notes
FIFTY-DOLLAR PIECES					1993, Featherstonhaugh (25,971)				
2008, 100th Anniv RCM	(4,000)				1994, The Home Front	(16,201)			
2009, 150th Anniversary Parliament	(2,000)				1995, Louisbourg	(16,916)			
SEVENTY-FIVE-DOLLAR PIECES					1996, Klondike	(17,973)			
2005, Pope John Paul II	(1,870)				1997, Alexander Graham Bell	(14,775)			
2007, RCMP	(8,000)				1998, Insulin	(11,220)			
2007, Athletes' Pride	(8,000)				1999, Newfoundland	(10,242)			
2007, Canada Geese	(8,000)				2000, Northwest Passage	(9,767)			
2008, Four Host First Nations	(8,000)				2001, Library of Parliament	(8,080)			
2008, Home of the Winter Games	(8,000)				2002, Oil Industry (Enameled)	(9,994)			
2008, Inukshuk	(8,000)				2003, Marquis Wheat	(9,993)			
2009, Wolf	(8,000)				2004, St. Lawrence Seaway	(7,454)			
2009, Olympic Spirit	(8,000)				2005, Supreme Court	(5,092)			
2009, Moose	(8,000)				2006, Military Academy Hockey Series	(5,402)			
$100 PIECES					2007, Dominion 140th Anniversary	(5,000)			
1976, 14-kt Montreal Olympics	650,000				2008, Fleuve Fraser River	(5,000)			
1976, 22-kt Montreal Olympics	(337,342)				2009, 10th Anniversary of Nunavut	(5,000)			
1977, Silver Jubilee	(180,396)				**$150 PIECES**				
1978, Canadian Unity	(200,000)				1995, Canada Lynx	(908)			
1979, Year of the Child	(250,000)				1996, Peregrine Falcon	(871)			
1980, Arctic Territories	(130,000)				1997, Wood Bison	(529)			
1981, "O Canada"	(100,950)				1998, Grey Wolf	(855)			
1982, Constitution	(121,708)				2000, Year of the Dragon	(8,874)			
1983, St. John's Newfoundland	(83,128)				2001, Year of the Snake	(6,571)			
1984, Jacques Cartier	(67,662)				2002, Year of the Horse	(6,843)			
1985, National Parks	(61,332)				2003, Year of the Sheep	(3,927)			
1986, Year of Peace	(76,409)				2004, Year of the Monkey	(3,392)			
1987, XV Winter Olym, Lettered Edge	(142,750)				2005, Year of the Rooster	(3,731)			
1987, XV Winter Olym, Plain Edge					2006, Year of the Dog	(2,604)			
1988, Bowhead Whale	(52,594)				2007, Year of the Pig	(4,888)			
$100 PIECES					2008, Year of the Rat	(4,888)			
1989, Sainte-Marie	(59,657)				2009, Year of the Ox	(4,888)			
1990, International Literacy Year	(49,940)				2009, Blessings of Wealth	(5,000)			
1991, Empress of India	(33,966)				2010, Year of the Tiger	(4,888)			
1992, Montreal	(28,162)				2010, Year of the Tiger, Round	(2,500)			
					2011, Year of the Rabbit	(4,888)			

Date	Distribution	Unc.	PF	Notes	Date	Distribution	Unc.	PF	Notes
$175 PIECES					2005, Britannia 1870 25¢ Note	(994)			
1992, Olympics Cent'l	(22,092)				2005, Pacific Time 4:00				
$200 PIECES					2005, Mountain Time 5:00				
1992, Olympics Cent'l	(22,092)				2005, Central Time 6:00				
1990, Flag's Silver Jubilee	(20,980)				2005, Eastern Time 7:00	(1,199)			
1991, Hockey	(10,215)				2005, Atlantic Time 8:00				
1992, Niagara Falls	(9,465)				2005, Newfoundland Time 8:30				
1993, RCMP	(10,807)								
1994, Anne of Green Gables	(10,655)				2005, "Welcome" Totem Pole	(948)			
1995, The Sugar Bush	(9,579)				2006, Britannia 1900 25¢ Note	(940)			
1996, Canadian Pacific Railway	(8,047)				2006, Canadarm2	(565)			
1997, Haida Raven Legend	(11,610)				2006, Crystal Snowflake (Embedments)	(861)			
1998, Legend of the White Buffalo	(7,149)				2006, Queen's 80th Birthday (Enameled)	(996)			
1999, Mi'kmaq Butterfly	(6,510)				2007, Britannia 1923 25¢ Note	(1,250)			
2000, Inuit Mother and Child	(6,284)				2007, Olympic Ideals	2,500			
2001, Cornelius Krieghoff	(5,406)				2007, Panoramic Camera, Rockies	(1,000)			
2002, Tom Thompson	(5,264)				2007, Woolly Mammoth	(400)			
2003, Lionel LeMoine FitzGerald	(4,118)				2008, Scimitar Cat	(200)			
2004, Alfred Pellan	(3,917)				2008, Competition	(2,500)			
2005, Fur Traders	(3,699)				2008, Newfoundland and Labrador	(1,000)			
2006, Lumbering	(3,185)				2008, Alberta	(1,000)			
2007, Cod Fishing	(4,000)				2008, Four Seasons Moon Mask	(1,200)			
2008, Agriculture	(4,000)				2008, IMAX	(1,000)			
2009, Coal Mining	(4,000)				2009, Steppe Bison	(200)			
2010, First Canadian Olympic Gold	(2,010)				2009, Yukon Territory	(1,000)			
$250 PIECES					2009, PE Island	(1,000)			
2006, Dog Sled Team	(953)				2009, Summer Moon Mask	(1,200)			
2007, Early Canada	(2,500)				2009, Friendship	(2,500)			
$300 PIECES					**$350 PIECES**				
2002, Queen Elizabeth II Triple Cameos	(999)				1998, Flowers of the Coat of Arms (Canada)	(1,999)			
$300 PIECES					1999, Golden Slipper (Prince Edward Island)	(1,990)			
2003, Great Seal of Canada	(998)				2000, Pacific Dogwood (British Columbia)	(1,971)			
2004, QEII Quadruple Cameos	(998)								

Date	Distribution	Unc.	PF	Notes	Date	Distribution	Unc.	PF	Notes
$350 PIECES									
2001, Mayflower (Nova Scotia)	(1,988)								
2002, Wild Rose (Alberta)	(2,001)								
2003, White Trillium (Ontario)	(1,865)								
2004, Fireweed (Yukon Territory)	(1,836)								
2005, Western Red Lilly (Saskatchewan)	(1,845)								
2006, Iris Versicolor (Quebec)	(1,624)								
2007, Purple Violet (New Brunswick)	(1,400)								
2008, Purple Saxifrage (Nunavut)	(1,400)								
2009, Pitcher Plant, Newfoundland/Labrador	(1,400)								
$500 PIECES									
2007, Queen's 60th Wedding Anniversary	(200)								
2008, 100th Anniversary RCM	(250)								
2009, 150th Anniversary Parliament	(200)								
$2,500 PIECES									
2007, Early Canada	(20)								
2009, Canada of Today	(50)								
2009, Surviving the Flood	(40)								
2010, The Eagle	(20)								
2010, The Eagle (Enameled)	(20)								
2010, The Eagle (Antique)	(20)								

			Notes

Notes

Notes

Notes

Notes